WHAT
ROOSEVELT
THOUGHT

Today we are faced with the pre-eminent fact that, if civilization is to survive, we must cultivate the science of human relationships—the ability of all peoples, of all kinds, to live together and work together, in the same world, at peace.

FRANKLIN D. ROOSEVELT

(Undelivered Address for Jefferson Day, 1945)

WHAT ROOSEVELT THOUGHT

THE SOCIAL AND POLITICAL IDEAS OF FRANKLIN D. ROOSEVELT

THOMAS H. GREER

Michigan State University Press
2000

∞ The paper used in this publication meets the minimum requirements of ANSI/NISO
Z39.48–1992 (R 1997) (Permanence of Paper).

Michigan State University Press
East Lansing, Michigan 48823-5202

Printed and bound in the United States of America.

07 06 05 04 03 02 01 00   1 2 3 4 5 6 7 8 9 10

LIBRARY OF CONGRESS CATALOGING-IN-PUBLICATION DATA

Greer, Thomas H.
What Roosevelt thought: the social and political ideas of Franklin D. Roosevelt / by
Thomas H. Greer.
    p.   cm.—(Red Cedar Classics)
    Includes bibliographical references (p.) and index.
    ISBN 0-87013-565-1 (alk. paper)
    1. Roosevelt, Franklin D. (Franklin Delano), 1882–1945—Political and social views.
2. United States—Politics and government—1933–1945—Philosophy. 3. Social values—
United States. I. Title II. Series.

E807.G7 2000
973.917'092—dc21   00–033249

A RED CEDAR CLASSIC

Cover design by Michael J. Brooks
Cover photo by Diane Smook© is of the statue of Franklin Delano Roosevelt, sculpted by
Kelli Paduzzi, that is located in the Memorial Park, Washington, D.C. Used by permission.

Visit Michigan State University Press on the World Wide Web at:
        www.msu.edu/unit/msupress

Dedicated to Tommy and Beth
and Their Generation Everywhere

Acknowledgments

I WISH TO MAKE GRATEFUL ACKNOWLEDGMENT to all those who helped make my book possible. I am indebted to the staff of the Roosevelt Library, and especially to Herman Kahn, William Nichols, George Roach, Jerome Deyo, Raymond Corey, Gloria Golden, and Louise Evans.

Also, I wish to thank my colleague, Karl Thompson, who read and criticized the manuscript. Portions were also read by Harry Kimber, Edward Blackman, Walter Adams, and Werner Bohnstedt, all of whom gave helpful comments. I appreciate, too, the substantial aid of research grants by Michigan State University. Finally, I am grateful to my wife, Margarette M. Greer, for her steady encouragement and advice.

Herman Kahn, Director of the Roosevelt Library, has extended me permission to quote from the Roosevelt manuscripts there. All materials cited, unless otherwise indicated, are at Hyde Park. Roosevelt's speeches may be found there in typescript form, as well as in the published collections listed in my "Bibliographical Note." For permission to quote certain passages from their publications, I express appreciation to Harper & Brothers, The Macmillan Company, and Random House.

Preface to the 2000 Edition

THE ORIGINAL EDITION OF THIS BOOK was published in clothbound form in 1958. It is now being reissued as a part of the Michigan State University Press's series, the "Red Cedar Classics." The text remains the same as the original issue; and its printing now, in the year 2000, is even more timely than before. As we finish one century and face a new millenium, Franklin Roosevelt and his ideas can be seen in a still fuller perspective. This is especially true for the hundreds of thousands of persons, since 1997, who have witnessed the record of his deeds and words at the splendid F. D. R. Memorial Park in the nation's Capitol. And, at this special moment in history, numerous social observers have nominated Roosevelt as the outstanding "Leader of the Twentieth Century."

Preface to the 1958 Edition

SOME WILL OBJECT to using the word philosophy in connection with Franklin D. Roosevelt's thought. Indeed, he was not a philosopher in the academic sense and had only a slight interest in philosophic literature. Paradoxical though it may seem, this indifference stemmed from the breadth of his views and interests. He was concerned with human life, with the world, and with power. Philosophy, on the other hand, has become a highly specialized subject—given more to ingrown puzzles than to the current of life about us. In his thought and action Roosevelt reflected a national characteristic. As De Tocqueville observed more than a century ago, Americans pay slight attention to philosophy, yet practice a common philosophical method without troubling to define its rules.

Roosevelt's education at Groton and Harvard, his travels abroad, and his wide range of reading gave him superior grounding in Western cultural traditions. He had an absorbing interest in history and, though lacking a scholar's command, understood its importance and usefulness more than some historians. But most extraordinary in his intellectual growth was his capacity for learning by direct experience and through personal associations. He has been pictured as an extreme extrovert—

giving out and impressing. But he could listen, too, and in his close relationships he learned more from others than they learned from him. He liked to charm, to provoke; he also liked to be challenged and to receive fresh ideas. These he received during his lifetime, orally (as he liked best) and in letters from men and women of every walk of life, every corner of the world, and every philosophical complexion. He had a remarkable memory, too, which enabled him to accumulate and retain ideas far beyond the ability of most persons. This faculty was a source of continual astonishment to reporters at his biweekly press conferences.

There have been men, and there are men today, with better educations than he had, with equal or superior powers of absorption, with keener memories, and with greater imaginations. Why, then, should attention be paid to his thought or philosophy? The answer is patent and simple: Roosevelt had the greatest political experience of any American of our time. His ideas were developed during a life of continuing interest and participation in politics and government. And his was a career that reached the top in national and world influence, that carried highest responsibility during economic storm, recovery, war, and the planning for international organization.

As a practical philosopher, he was typically American. His "worldview" has been mentioned so often that his American orientation is sometimes forgotten. His main ideas can be understood correctly only if the American point of view, or frame of reference, is kept in mind. This is not to say that he lacked sympathy for the peoples of other lands. But his point of departure was naturally his own country, and very often his native Dutchess County. He had a deep and abiding love for America. This feeling was the driving force toward the two chief goals of his career—conservation of America's resources and security for America's people. The institutions and programs he supported were those he thought best for the United States in the twentieth century; he believed that they could be applied to other lands only where conditions approximated those at home.

The fact that Roosevelt was an experienced practitioner of politics has been offered as the compelling reason why his views on public affairs should receive consideration. His involvement in politics, at the same time, created a serious obstacle to contemporary understanding of his ideas. He believed, as most Americans believe, in the party system, and he chose to work in the Democratic Party. While this aroused automatic support for his ideas among "regular" Democrats, it had the opposite effect upon "regular" Republicans and other political opponents. In consequence, it remains difficult, to this day, for many persons to consider Roosevelt's views dispassionately. They feel that his ideas, as well as his record, must be categorically defended (in the case of Democrats) or categorically attacked (in the case of Republicans). Time has not yet dissolved stubborn partisan prejudices, which were magnified by his long stay in the White House.

My aim in writing this book has been to find and set forth precisely what Roosevelt thought on vital social and political questions. His ideas are presented here as objectively as possible for the sake of the record, the use of the present and future, and without regard to party or faction. Rather than the particular measures that he supported, I have been concerned primarily with the *thinking* which underlay them. I have not, of course, tried to deal with his political or administrative behavior—except in so far as it may have illuminated his ideas.

The sources for identification of these ideas are bountiful and open. I have drawn directly from the public speeches and writings, and from the vast collection of private and official correspondence in the Library at Hyde Park. The "Bibliographical Note" at the back of this book explains the uses which I have made of these materials and lists the memoirs and general works which are essential to a rounded picture. In view of this, I have thought it possible to reduce to a minimum the supporting documentary notes. In general, they have been restricted to important quotations, the sources of which are not fully indicated in the text.

The question of authorship has frequently been raised in connection with Roosevelt's speeches and writings. Notes and letters dictated or written by him may be readily identified by the trained historian. However, much of his public expression represented in some degree a collaboration with secretaries, agency heads, and speech drafters—a common practice among top executives in modern government and business. But those of his literary aides who have written on the subject—notably Samuel Rosenman, Robert Sherwood, Raymond Moley, Rexford Tugwell, and Grace Tully—have affirmed that the important statements uttered by Roosevelt were in the last analysis his own and bore his peculiar stamp. I have taken the position that where a certain view is consistently repeated in his papers it may reasonably be regarded as Roosevelt's.

And I am more interested in these views for themselves than I am in another intriguing question: how did they come into Roosevelt's mind? While I have tried, wherever possible, to outline the context in which his thoughts developed, I have not attempted to define their ultimate origin or the exact processes of his mind. This, I am sure, goes beyond available data and our understanding of human intelligence.

T. H. G.

East Lansing, Michigan
March, 1958

Contents

The Social

and Political Ideas

of

Franklin D. Roosevelt

What
Roosevelt
Thought

1

Vision of the Abundant Life

"THE GREAT TEACHER SAID 'I come that ye may have life and that ye may have it more abundantly.' The object of all our striving should be to realize that 'abundant life.'" [1] In these words, written during the first year of the New Deal, Roosevelt expressed his underlying social view. The laws that he sponsored, the agencies that he established, the political maneuvers that he devised—these were but means to the end: a more abundant life for every man, woman, and child.

Roosevelt, of course, had no patent on the phrase, "more abundant life," and he was by no means unique among politicians in favoring the idea. Calvin Coolidge, who went on the record against sin, no doubt believed in abundant living, too. It is in the specifications of the good society that Roosevelt set forth a distinctive point of view.

Religious Conviction

Of the many precedents which Roosevelt established as president, one has received less notice than it deserved. On the morning of his first inauguration, March 4, 1933, he attended special church services at St. John's with members of his family and Cabinet. He did this on successive inaugurations, as well as on special occasions—each time asking for divine guidance in the tasks ahead. The precedent had

3

genuine significance. It was symbolic of the religious faith which lay
at the center of his outlook on life.

While he could be facetious or irreverent about almost anything in
the world of men, he held religion—his own and that of others—to be a
highly personal and sacred matter. People around him of all faiths (and
of none) were impressed by his religious sincerity and simplicity.

He accepted Christian truths as naturally as his birthright. His beliefs, taught to him at an early age by his mother, were strengthened
during his schooling at Groton. The Reverend Endicott Peabody,
Headmaster of Groton, had substantial influence in shaping the peculiar quality of young Roosevelt's conviction. Peabody, following the
tradition of the English public schools, emphasized the making of
Christian gentlemen as Groton's aim. He was imbued with deep religious feeling, unimpeded by concern for theological subtleties.
Through his daily chapel talks, instruction in "Sacred Science," and
fatherly relation to Groton boys, "The Rector" communicated much of
this spirit to the student body. Young Roosevelt's mind seemed particularly open to this influence, and Peabody, throughout his lifetime,
remained a source of idealistic inspiration.

There was a militant strain in the Reverend Peabody's religion,
mixed with a gladness in fighting for the right. One of his favorite
prayers, reflecting his spirit of enthusiasm, duty, and uplift, might have
been a favorite of Roosevelt's, too: "O God, author of the world's joy,
bearer of the world's pain, make us glad that we have inherited the
world's burden; deliver us from the luxury of cheap melancholy; and
at the heart of all our trouble and sorrow, let unconquerable gladness
dwell." [2]

Roosevelt talked little about religion. His wife once asked him, early
in their married life, what his beliefs were. His reply was that there
were some questions which were better not explored too far. He believed in a beneficent God, the Ten Commandments, the Sermon on
the Mount, and the direct teachings of the Bible. He was not disturbed
by doubts and was repelled by doctrinal arguments. The simplicity of
his beliefs was thoroughly satisfying to him, and he was a little puzzled
by the wonderment it caused in others.

While he showed slight interest in theology, Roosevelt had great
reverence for the Bible. The old Dutch family Bible, used in each of
his inaugural ceremonies, was a treasured possession, and not entirely
because of filial sentiment. He regarded the Scriptures as an incom-
parable source of wisdom and frequently turned to them in his writing
and speaking. He saw that in the Bible the people of America and the

Western world had the broadest single basis for religious unity, a goal that was close to his heart.

He viewed the Bible and religion chiefly in ethical terms. Thus, he usually referred to the Sermon on the Mount as the heart of Christian teaching. His concern for the common man and his passion for social betterment may well have grown out of his religious convictions; in any event, they were mutually reinforcing. From the beginning of his political career, he looked upon social and governmental problems as basically moral in nature, and he came to identify his conception of "social justice" with Christianity itself. With his ethical approach to both religion and government, he saw no real conflict between Church and State. The higher aims of both coincided, and the two, "while wholly separate in their functioning, can work hand in hand."[3] He hoped for a spiritual revival which would support and supplement the efforts of the secular arm toward a better society.

Roosevelt, like his old Headmaster at Groton, had no use for "gloomy" religion. He was not perturbed by the trend away from orthodoxy and ritual, but welcomed "modern" religion. "The churches today," he wrote, "are beginning to go along with the new scientific growth and are opening the way to a simpler faith, a deeper faith, a happier faith, than ever our forefathers had."[4] He wanted, too, the greatest possible freedom of belief. He often quoted George Mason's statement in the Virginia Declaration of Rights: "That religion, or the duty which we owe to our Creator, and the manner of discharging it, can be directed only by reason and conviction, not by force or violence. . . ."

Being tolerant of all faiths, he urged greater collaboration among them. Sectarian disputes pained him, and he pleaded that they be put aside. "We who have faith cannot afford to fall out among ourselves. . . . For as I see it, the chief religious issue is not between our various beliefs. It is between belief and unbelief."[5] He himself wore his church affiliation lightly. Harold Ickes once asked him how he happened to become an Episcopalian. He explained that his father, James, had been a member of the Dutch Reform faith when he first settled in Hyde Park. But the nearest church of that denomination was five miles away, and James did not think much of its minister. So he fell into the habit of attending near-by St. James, and eventually became senior warden. Franklin's mother, Sara, was originally a Unitarian, but she followed her husband to the Episcopal pew. Roosevelt told Ickes that his family was "very Low Church" and that he personally preferred a Presbyterian, Methodist, or Baptist sermon. Nevertheless, son, like father, became senior warden of St. James, and Roosevelt took pride in the tradition.[6]

Divine Purpose, Free Will, and Progress

"There is a mysterious cycle in human events. To some generations much is given. Of other generations much is expected. This generation of Americans has a rendezvous with destiny." Thus, on a warm June evening in the convention hall at Philadelphia, the Democratic standard-bearer struck the climax of his speech accepting renomination for a second term. His voice, high-pitched and tense, carried beyond the convention walls to the outermost corners of the land. His prophetic phrase was to live in the hearts and minds of the generation which heard it. For that generation, indeed, was destined to defend a faith and a way of life. "That prophecy comes true," the President declared in 1939. "To us much is given; more is expected." [7]

Roosevelt, plainly, saw patterns in history. To him the universe was no chaotic swirl, devoid of meaning. At the same time, he rejected any notion of mechanical determinism. There was a divine purpose, according to which human wills co-operated with God in the making of a better world. He believed that men (and generations) were given tasks to perform, and with those tasks the strength and ability to carry them through. As president, he felt he had a particular duty in the divine scheme of things, as had every other human soul. He believed that God was directly interested in and active in the world of men, and that God responded to prayer.

He proclaimed Sunday, September 8, 1940, as a day of national prayer. In times of sorrow and disaster, he observed, "we are especially conscious of the Divine Power and our dependence upon God's merciful guidance." And when the Normandy invasion of World War II was launched, on June 6, 1944, he instinctively turned to prayer. In announcing that crucial operation to the people by radio, the Commander-in-chief indulged in no militant rhetoric, but reflecting his true impulse "in this poignant hour," he asked the nation to join him in beseeching God. His "D-Day Prayer," quietly read to millions of his countrymen, is a model of simple and reverent prose. It starts out:

Almighty God; our sons, pride of our nation, this day have set upon a mighty endeavor, a struggle to preserve our Republic, our religion, our civilization, and to set free a suffering humanity.
Lead them straight and true; give strength to their arms, stoutness to their hearts, steadfastness in their faith.
They will need thy blessing. Their road will be long and hard. For the

enemy is strong. He may hurl back our forces. Success may not come with rushing speed, but we shall return again and again; and we know that by thy grace, and by the righteousness of our cause, our sons will triumph.

Roosevelt had profound trust in his judgment after prayer. This explained in large measure his serenity after a decision had been made. His White House associates wondered how a man could rest at night with the burdens he carried. But Roosevelt enjoyed the sleep of the confident; divine guidance was to him an intimate reality and comforter.

While he believed in a divine plan and in the controlling hand of a beneficent God, he nevertheless gave important place to man's freedom of will. Individual freedom was circumscribed by God's command, but Roosevelt conceived that it was the Lord's purpose to give humanity a large measure of freedom in the working out of its own destiny. He rejected the notion that men should sit back and let God and nature "take their course." He thought that human beings were endowed with splendid power to solve their own problems, and that they were morally bound to make use of it. The tough problems might take a long time in being solved. There would be many trials and many errors. But he was convinced that, with God's help, the answers could be found if only the will to find them were strong enough. "The future," he stated simply, "rests . . . on the affirmative action which we take in America." [8]

He denied every form of determinism—economic, geographic, racial, or historical. Nations, as well as individuals, were free. He gave particular emphasis to this idea when Hitler threatened to drag all Europe into war. He sought to check the widespread feeling that conflict was inevitable, that nations and their leaders were being driven to destruction by mysterious, irresistible pressures. "There is no fatality which forces the old world towards new catastrophe," he declared. "Men are not prisoners of fate, but only prisoners of their own minds. They have within themselves the power to become free at any moment." [9] The wary reader may find inconsistency here. For Roosevelt, who had previously spoken of a "mysterious cycle in human events," was now rejecting the notion of "fate." The crux of the matter is this: he *did* believe in a divine destiny, but he could not accept the thought that Hitler's New Order was a part of God's plan. In other words, there could be no fate, no "wave of the future," outside of God's testament.

And in Roosevelt's view, the divine plan, with its allowance for personal freedom, was a plan for human progress. This was not just wishful thinking; it rested upon faith in Providence, supported by reason and history. He conceded that there were ups and downs in the rugged path of humanity, but insisted that the general movement was upward —spiritually as well as materially. Even the reverses, the pitfalls and mistakes, contributed to ultimate progress. As he once put it, "Out of every crisis, every tribulation, every disaster, mankind rises with some share of greater knowledge of higher decency, of purer purpose." [10]

To Roosevelt, the general improvement of human life, whether seen in the view of centuries or of decades, was too obvious to be doubted. At the peak of the prosperity boom of the twenties, he, like everyone else, was apt to speak of progress in terms of the material standard of living. When he delivered the Phi Beta Kappa address at Harvard in June, 1929, he hailed the breaking down of the remnants of caste and privilege and the placing of men and women on a more comparable and competitive basis. "The Kansas farmer and the New York mechanic send their sons and daughters to college. . . ." Then he pointed to the advances in sanitation, transportation, and electric lights; "there is a motor car for one out of every four inhabitants of the United States." In creature comforts, he went on, "we have gained more in fifty years than in the previous five centuries." Working conditions, education, and recreation were better, too. "The point to emphasize is that in all this what used to be the privilege of the few has come to be the accepted heritage of the many." [11]

As governor, and later as president, he continued to see progress ahead as well as behind. This philosophic view, combined with a naturally sanguine disposition, made him a supreme optimist. And optimism, thought Roosevelt, was more than a happy mood. It was a significant historical force, essential to the forging of American unity. Since the nation was compounded of people of diverse origins, worship of traditions would have divided Americans into distinct cultural groups. As he expressed it on the occasion of the fiftieth anniversary of the Statue of Liberty, "The realization that we are all bound together by hope of a common future rather than by reverence for a common past has helped us to build upon this continent a unity unapproached in any similar area or population in the whole world." [12]

The truly subversive person in the American saga was the cynic, the pessimist, the man of little faith: "the only thing we have to fear is fear itself." Years after that ringing assurance, given on the panicky Fourth of March, 1933, he held as strongly to his conviction. "It is unintelligent to be defeatist," he told his countrymen in 1940, while Nazi triumphs threatened all he was sworn to defend. And at the war's bitter close, when many despaired of building a peaceful world, he remained unshaken. For these were the last words he wrote: "The only limit to our realization of tomorrow will be our doubts of today. Let us move forward with strong and active faith." [13]

Because he believed in the future, he had a special feeling for young people, who would be the inheritors and makers of better days. He encouraged them to dream and act, even though they might at times be led astray. "I am unwilling to sneer at the vision of youth merely because vision is sometimes mistaken." [14] For he knew that the spirit of youth could perform mighty deeds. Our Lord, he reminded Young Democrats in 1936, was only thirty years of age when he began his ministry. The War of Independence was a "young man's crusade," and the Constitution likewise was the creation of youthful minds. In an era of rapid change, he declared later at Chapel Hill, young people had a larger role than ever to play, and must assume it more quickly. They were the immediate heirs of progress: "That is why I myself associate myself so enthusiastically with the younger generation."

The Nature of Man

Roosevelt could not embrace one church dogma—the doctrine of original sin and consequent depraved nature of man. He gave formal assent to it, but his heart and mind protested. Here may be found a vulnerable point in the structure of his thought: he accepted as a premise the essential goodness of most human beings.

He did not take the extreme eighteenth century view that *all* men were inherently good, but he believed in the decency of the great majority. As a matter of fact, he usually expressed this mathematically as a ninety to ten ratio. "If you treat people right, they will treat you right— ninety percent of the time," he told Frances Perkins. There will always be a minority, in every walk of life, who will be selfish and take unfair advantage. But "ninety percent" or more will want to do right, just as ninety percent of the world's population want peace, rather than aggrandizement. He suggested, further, that even the "bad" people were victims of an evil environment; and he hoped, through social reform, to remove the conditions which bred crime and indecency.

In his estimate of human goodness, Roosevelt probably overweighed the noble impulses in most of mankind. The theologian who holds that there is a sinful tendency in every heart will declare his belief false; the man of letters will call it shallow; the practical man of affairs will say it is unrealistic. But the judgment of all men is fallible when it probes the human heart. Roosevelt's view was at bottom a mystical one, and is not susceptible to rational proof or disproof.

Man is good, Roosevelt thought, and the uppermost element in his nature is spirit. His emphasis upon spiritual values has sometimes been overlooked, because when he became president, his immediate problems were largely material ones. The New Deal legislation, which came to be identified with his ideas, dealt with tangibles like food, homes, railroads, money, trees, and jobs. But to Roosevelt, such physical things were only means to higher ends; he was simply doing "first things first." For, unlike Adam Smith or Karl Marx, he rejected as unreal the concept of the "economic man." He believed that man was a harmony of elements, each of which was essential for the support of the others. Man must eat, but "man does not live by bread alone." He saw economic reforms as necessary for the succor of the spirit; they were therefore, in a deeper sense, *moral* propositions. In discussing farm and tariff problems in 1932, Roosevelt made explicit this relationship: "It is a moral as well as an economic question that we face. . . . We want the opportunity to live in comfort, reasonable comfort, out of which we may build spiritual values." [15]

He was scornful of the acquisitive values that accompanied the race for economic gain. In dedicating the birthplace of Woodrow Wilson at Staunton, Virginia, he remarked with feeling, "I like the old phrase that this was a home of plain living and high thinking and wherever the family moved . . . they carried with them ideals which put faith in spiritual values above every material consideration." [16] By "spiritual values" he meant the broadest human aspirations, both natural and divine. The general quality of his conception is suggested in the contrast he once drew between materialistic and humanistic criteria for evaluating a civilization. "The success of democratic institutions is measured," he judged, "not by extent of territory, financial power, machines or armaments, but by the desires, the hopes, and the deep-lying satisfactions of the individual men, women and children who make up its citizenship." [17]

If there was a focus in Roosevelt's concept of spiritual striving, it was the idea of love. While governor he made a commencement address at Fordham University, and on that occasion he gave a characteristic expression of his view. Discounting the importance of material accomplishments and limiting the role of human laws, he stated that the supreme rule was the divine command: "Thou shalt love the Lord thy God with all thy heart, and with all thy soul, and with all thy mind," and, "Thou shalt love thy neighbor as thyself." [18]

He regarded man's reason as next in importance to the power of love. Time and again he called for study and analysis of facts, development of the arts of persuasion, "application of the rule of reason in the affairs of men." And he held that this capacity was not restricted to the fortunate few. He had faith in the ability of the people as a whole to learn from the past and so to create their own future.

He himself was no "intellectual." He did not enjoy thinking for the sake of cerebral exercise and had an aversion for sheer abstraction. His mind was razor sharp, but he "thought" only in relation to some concrete human problem or activity. And when he did think, he used not only logic, but *all* his faculties. Roosevelt was conscious of his method and was satisfied with it, believing that a person who judged and acted on the basis of intellect alone was often untrue to his nature. As Frances Perkins wrote, "His emotions, his intuitive understanding, his imagination, his moral and traditional bias, his sense of right and wrong—all entered into his thinking. . . ." Reasoning meant, to him, the harmonious functioning of man's nature.

Basic Human Rights

When Roosevelt served as governor, one of the major issues between him and the legislature was the question of support for the aged. He deplored the traditional "poorhouses" and sought, and successfully, to replace them with a system of state pensions. He contended that the cost of pensions would actually be less to taxpayers than the maintenance of adequate institutions, but his principal argument rested upon respect for human dignity. In a message to the lawmakers he declared, "We can no longer be satisfied with the old method of putting them away in dismal institutions with the accompanying loss of self-respect, personality, and interest in life." [19] Old people should be helped to maintain themselves in their own homes, where they could hold up their heads as citizens. He did not have extravagance in mind; he told his press conference in 1935 that the New York pension averaged only about $250 per year. "Oh, it is not a very good living, no, but it gets most of the old people by." The important thing was the principle of personal worth which the pension upheld.

As individuals of worth, all men had certain "unalienable rights." Roosevelt did not invent this idea, but he "discovered" or made explicit rights that had not been generally recognized before. His best-known pronouncement was the "Four Freedoms," a lucid condensation of the paramount rights of man. He set forth the new charter of freedom in the course of his Annual Message to Congress, in January, 1941—at a moment when human rights were being ground down in Europe and Asia. After speaking of national defense and his proposal of "Lend-Lease" aid to the democracies, the President looked ahead to the ultimate objectives of American policy:

> In the future days, which we seek to make secure, we look forward to a world founded upon four essential freedoms.
> The first is freedom of speech and expression—everywhere in the world.
> The second is freedom of every person to worship God in his own way—everywhere in the world.
> The third is freedom from want—which, translated into world terms, means economic understandings which will secure to every nation a healthy peacetime life for its inhabitants—everywhere in the world.
> The fourth is freedom from fear—which, translated into world terms, means a world-wide reduction of armaments to such a point and in such a thorough fashion that no nation will be in a position to commit an act of physical aggression against any neighbor—anywhere in the world.

While cynics mocked, Roosevelt insisted that his was not a vision of a distant millenium. "It is a definite basis for a kind of world attainable in our own time and generation." This latter phrase was no doubt a rhetorical indulgence, justified in his mind as a timely booster of national and world morale. Accomplishment of such a Utopian goal was possible, but not likely in his own day. Apparently he himself recognized this in afterthought, for he never again referred to a specific time. Two months later he hedged in this fashion while addressing White House correspondents: "They [the Four Freedoms] may not be immediately attainable throughout the world but humanity does move toward those glorious ideals through democratic processes." In 1943 he placed his ideals in deeper perspective and made his position unmistakably clear:

> I am everlastingly angry only at those who assert vociferously that the four freedoms . . . are nonsense because they are unattainable. If those people had lived a century and a half ago they would have sneered and said that the Declaration of Independence was utter piffle. If they had lived nearly a thousand years ago they would have laughed uproariously at the ideals of Magna Charta. And if they had lived several thousand years ago they would have derided Moses when he came from the mountain with the Ten Commandments.
> We concede that these great teachings are not perfectly lived up to today, but I would rather be a builder than a wrecker, hoping always that the structure of life is growing, not dying.[20]

The idea of the Four Freedoms did not come as a sudden revelation to Roosevelt, but was a lifetime in gestation. Forethoughts may be found in his early writings, and his presidential papers make frequent reference to one or more of the fundamental rights. The one most often emphasized during his first two terms in the White House was freedom of religion, linked with freedom of education. The first explicit statement of his rounded view, however, came in a press conference of July 5, 1940, some six months before his official enunciation of the Four Freedoms. In replying informally to a query by a reporter regarding his long-range peace objectives, he outlined *five* "freedoms." They were, in this order: freedom of information, religion, expression; freedom from fear and freedom from want. The only change he made from this in the historic declaration of January, 1941, was to reverse the order of "fear" and "want," and to reduce the total to *four* by combining "expression" and "information" into one freedom.

In the Four Freedoms, he simplified and generalized the paramount rights of men, "everywhere in the world." For his own country, he did not enlarge upon the immortal generalization of Jefferson: "life, liberty, and the pursuit of happiness." The task at home was not more generalization, but, rather, more specification. Roosevelt gloried in the Bill of Rights, as incorporated into the Constitution, but he felt that it was not enough for the conditions of the twentieth century. What was needed was a *second* Bill of Rights. As he explained in his State of the Union Message of 1944:

This Republic had its beginning, and grew to its present strength, under the protection of certain inalienable political rights—among them the right of free speech, free press, free worship, trial by jury, freedom from unreasonable searches and seizures. They were our rights to life and liberty.

As our nation has grown in size and stature, however—as our industrial economy expanded—these political rights proved inadequate to assure us equality in the pursuit of happiness. We have come to a clear realization of the fact that true individual freedom cannot exist without economic security and independence. "Necessitous men are not free men." People who are hungry and out of a job are the stuff of which dictatorships are made.

In our day these economic truths have become accepted as self-evident. We have accepted, so to speak, a second Bill of Rights under which a new basis of security and prosperity can be established for all—regardless of station, race, or creed.

Among these rights, he said, were the right of a laborer to a useful and remunerative job; of a farmer to a fair return for his produce; of a businessman to protection from unfair competition; of every family to a decent home; of every person to adequate medical care, good education, and protection against privation in old age.

His conception of economic security as a fundamental right traced back to his earliest experience in the New York legislature. Later, as governor, he pressed for wages and hour legislation and for extension of workmen's compensation laws. He regarded these proposals in 1929 as the minimum of what should be done to promote the welfare of the laboring classes. For, as he stated, "Modern social conditions have progressed to a point where such demands can no longer be regarded other than as matters of an absolute right." [21] As candidate for president, he told the Commonwealth Club of San Francisco that "Every man has a right to life; and this means that he has also a right to make a comfortable living. He may by sloth or crime decline to exercise the right; but it may not be denied him." Roosevelt's "Economic Bill of Rights" was officially presented in 1944, but he had openly subscribed to its contents more than a decade before.

The right to seek happiness was absolute in one sense, but limited in another. Roosevelt, like all others who have thought seriously about this problem, recognized that one man's rights may end where another man's begins. "We know," he said in 1932, "that individual liberty and individual happiness mean nothing unless both are ordered in the sense that one man's meat is another man's poison. . . . We know that liberty to do anything which deprives others of elemental rights is outside the protection of any compact. . . ." [22] At every level of society, from the family to the nation, the guiding principle was the same: no individual has a right to do things that hurt his neighbors. As society changes, new and different activities may become harmful in unexpected ways. But the *principle* remains constant.[23]

The difficulty of drawing the line between liberty and license was readily conceded by Roosevelt. He admitted that he himself did not know exactly where to draw the line, especially in relation to freedom of expression. At a press conference in 1938 he was asked to comment upon an action by the Federal Communications Commission, with reference to profane dialogue on the air. While avoiding a direct answer, he appeared to take a dim view of censorship of words that appear in the Bible. However, he observed that such words were regarded as very profane by some people, and who was to be the judge? Suppose somebody were to use words that were *really* outrageous, something which would shock even *him*. Ought there not be someone in the country to stop that sort of thing? "That," he remarked, "is the other side of it and nobody knows the answer." Continuing off the record, he pointed up an additional problem in connection with censorship. He recalled to the group a sizzling sketch, broadcast some months before, of "Adam and Eve"—featuring Mae West as Eve. The performance, in poor taste by contemporary standards, left a wake of indignant protest. But, as

Roosevelt confided to the reporters: "Now, the script was all right—if you or I read it, all right, but Mae West—my God, what she put into it! How do you censor intonation? Now, that is a nice question, How can you censor intonation?" [24]

The Good Life for Man

Though he did not study Aristotle, he would have agreed with the philosopher's view that there exists but one final end for man, namely, "happiness." This meant the "good life," but of what does the good life consist? Rexford Tugwell, who studied Roosevelt's thought processes more intently than any other of the brain trust believed that his definition can be put concisely. It meant for every individual a life of health and vigor; good education; decent work and reasonable income; freedom of enterprise under a fair set of rules; and the right to vote, to worship, and to behave as the individual wished, within an accepted national scheme. Tugwell, a skeptical man in most respects, was convinced that everything Roosevelt did was in the circumstances (or his understanding of them) aimed at bringing about one or more of these goals. He often did not know *how*, Tugwell added. The social problems he tackled were complex and his knowledge was limited. But Roosevelt's aim was simple and clear.[25]

While Tugwell's interpretation is amply sustained by general statements by Roosevelt, a further probing of his speeches and writings reveals a more precise definition of his concept of the good life. Again, he was in accord with Aristotle, who identified the happiness of each individual with *self-realization,* or the harmonious exercise of one's faculties, guided by reason. Such a life was dependent upon proper conditions and training. Roosevelt saw the individual's development commencing with infancy, "We must look at our civilization," he once advised, "through the eyes of children." The happy child should live in a home of warmth, food, and affection. He needs parents to nurture him and take care of him should he fall ill; he needs teachers to provide him with guidance and education. When he grows up there must be a job for him so that he will some day be able to establish a home of his own.[26] In maturity each person should be free to realize his capabilities and to express his individuality. But this did not mean egoism and selfishness; the good life was bound up with the Christian ideal of service to others. The desire to serve, Roosevelt believed, gave motive and value to life, regardless of one's years or physical condition.

Having devoted his own life to public service, Roosevelt had no doubt of the intrinsic rewards. Many individuals were reluctant to participate in community affairs (especially the toilsome business of government), and some of those who did wondered if they were receiving adequate return. But to Roosevelt, who had little appreciation of the lonely, contemplative life, it was enough simply to be a part of things, to help build, to "share in the great battles" of his generation. It was because of this feeling that he had such a strong affinity for his "Uncle Ted." He admired the man of action, and expressed his view best by repeating a classic statement of his illustrious relative:

It is not the critic who counts, not the man who points out how the strong man stumbled, or where the doer of deeds could have done them better. The credit belongs to the man who is actually in the arena; whose face is marred by dust and sweat and blood; who strives valiantly; who errs and comes short again and again; who knows the great enthusiasms, the great devotions, and spends himself in a worthy cause; who at the best knows in the end the triumphs of high achievement; and who at the worst, if he fails, at least fails while daring greatly; so that his place shall never be with those cold and timid souls who know neither defeat nor victory.[27]

He was convinced that the good life could be enjoyed by large numbers of individuals only if they had a fair chance to attain it. He had no illusions about equality of *ability*. "We know that equality of individual ability has never existed and never will, but we do insist that equality of opportunity still must be sought."[28] His so-called "soak the rich" schemes were intended, not to deprive wealthy men of a good life, but to make the good life possible for poor men. This was the true meaning of the words "New Deal" when spoken in their original context. In accepting the Democratic nomination in Chicago in 1932, he stated that "forgotten" men and women were looking to his party for more equitable opportunity to share in the distribution of national wealth. Those millions shall not hope in vain, he declared—"I pledge you, I pledge myself, to a new deal for the American people."

While he favored various measures to reduce economic disparities, he was opposed to a system of "handouts." He wanted to improve opportunity for the poor, but by this he meant opportunity to enjoy the good life through *work* and productivity. His belief in the value of work explains why he fought against the dole as a means of relief during the Depression. A dole would have been far easier to administer; it was also cheaper and appealed more to taxpayers than did work-relief. But as governor and as president he persevered against "handouts," whether by cash or grocery baskets. He insisted that, "we are dealing with properly self-respecting Americans to whom a mere dole outrages every instinct of individual independence. Most Americans want to give some-thing for what they get. That something, which in this case is honest work, is the saving barrier between them and moral disintegration." [29]

It was for the same reason that Roosevelt favored a *contributory* system of old-age pensions. The good life required a sense of earning whatever one received. He wanted a pension plan based on premiums paid by the individual, supplemented by payments from employers and government; the size of the annuity would be determined by the total amount paid in. Thus, individual thrift and saving would be rewarded.[30]

Savings, thrift, and incentives were essential to self-reliance, which Roosevelt regarded as a precious ingredient of happy living. He was no believer in "bread and circuses" for a restless, aimless, dependent population. "Self-help and self-control are the essence of the American tradition," he declared.[31] He encouraged the will to "get ahead"—with this qualification: he felt that the ambition of an individual to obtain a decent living for himself and his family was preferable to an appetite for great wealth and power. The good life for man was to be found in Aristotle's Golden Mean—the avoidance of excess or deficiency.

The Good Society

A good society, said Aristotle, is one which fosters the good life for man. In this view, and in his general social theory, there is a striking parallel between the philosopher and Roosevelt. These men were separated by a gulf of more than two thousand years. The Greek dwelt in the microcosm of the city-state, while the American viewed the panorama of the great globe itself. One was a teacher, the other a doer. Yet time, space, and function dissolve into a substantial unity of thought between these two men. Roosevelt was himself quite unaware of this long-range correspondence in ideas; it can be explained only by the existence of a common tradition, a common intelligence, and the eternal verities.

A social instinct is implanted by nature in man, taught Aristotle. The good life—in fact, really *human* life—cannot be lived outside of society. This view is thoroughly supported in Roosevelt's thought and action. He saw no separation, but only *relationship* between the individual and the group. Personal freedom does not mean solitary glory, but rather a harmonious functioning of the individual in the world of men.

And there were times when the good of each individual, even his survival, might depend upon the exercise of strict social discipline. In his First Inaugural, Roosevelt, facing a grave internal crisis, called

for such a spirit in the American people. "We now realize . . . ," he
said, "that if we are to go forward, we must move as a trained and
loyal army willing to sacrifice for the good of a common discipline,
because without such discipline no progress is made, no leadership becomes effective." It was something of this feeling that gave him appreciation of the training given in the Civilian Conservation Corps camps
and in the Boy Scouts. He was prompted to explain this in a letter to
Norman Thomas in 1940:

> I became the head of the Greater New York Boy Scouts about 1922 or
> 1923, and saw so much of their excellent camps that I favored some form
> of state-wide or nation-wide camps which would get every boy in the coun-
> try into the great outdoors for at least two weeks every year. This thought
> of mine was based not only on the health and recreational advantages but
> also on the very great advantage which comes to young people through
> having to get up when the bugle blows, come to breakfast when the break-
> fast call sounds (or get no breakfast), go to bed when told to do so, learn not to
> leave their belongings around, and getting in general certain elementary
> disciplines which a large percentage of American families fail to give to
> their offspring.[32]

Aristotle thought that the state (or the self-sufficient community)
was more important than the family, "since the whole is of necessity
prior to the part." Roosevelt would not have been bound by such a
logical stricture. Though perceiving the shortcomings in parental training, he regarded the family as the paramount social unit. Here the child
first learned confidence in his own powers, respect for the feelings and
rights of others, the sense of security and mutual good will, and faith
in God. "Here he should find a common bond between the interests of
the individual and the group. Mothers and fathers, by the kind of life
they build within the four walls of the home, are largely responsible
for the future social and public life of the country." Roosevelt saw that
the development of boys and girls was also bound up with institutions
outside the home, especially the school and church. He urged that the
work of all of these be harmonized, so as to give a rounded growth to
young people.[33]

Regarding the structure of society itself, that is, the larger order
which embraced individuals, families, and kinship groups, Roosevelt
departed further from the views of Aristotle, who saw society and societies as mainly *static*. Greeks were Greeks, and barbarians were barbarians; some races were born to rule and others to be slaves. Among
Greek citizens, classes were fairly rigid: there were the poor, the middle
class, and the rich. Roosevelt, of course, dismissed the idea of slavery;

and while admitting that classes existed in most societies, he did not agree that they were inherent or desirable. Some sort of gradation of condition was the inevitable outcome of varying tastes and talents, but natural gradation was a *fluid* not a static thing. In his good society all men would have equal opportunity, would start from the same line, and would push as far ahead in life as their merits carried them.

To him, America was a practical demonstration of the approach to this ideal. He rejected the notion of fixed "classes," or of any "class struggle" in the history of the United States. There was often a struggle for power among sundry aggregations of interests, which, as he pointed out, from time to time had gained control of the government itself. But this advantage was gained by various and temporary "groups of citizens"—groups which were not classes, as classes were known in Europe.[34] In the good society, as in America, individuals would be free to rise (or fall) in their rewards and position.

At the same time, he did not look upon society as a mere collection of free-wheeling egoists. There was, at any given time, a functional organization, in which individuals and groups performed specific tasks. As governor and during his first term as president, he pleaded for recognition of the "true harmony of interests." There was no inherent conflict among groups; all were naturally complementary, and the goal was co-operation for the general good. In closing the 1932 campaign in Madison Square Garden, he declared, "Today there appears once more the truth taught two thousand years ago that 'no man lives to himself, and no man dies to himself; but living or dying, we are the Lord's and each other's.'"

Like Jefferson, he had a deep-seated preference for country life, and believed that a rural foundation was the best for a good society. He did not consider the condition of city dwellers hopeless, but his ideal community was close to the soil. He told a midwestern audience in 1936, "In all our plans we are guided, and will continue to be guided, by the fundamental belief that the American farmer, living on his own land, remains our ideal of self-reliance and of spiritual balance—the source from which the reservoirs of the nation's strength are constantly renewed."[35] He thus remained pledged to what Richard Hofstadter has called the "agrarian myth" in America.

His association of the good life with rural society arose mainly from his love of nature. He expressed his feeling for the rich primeval elements in a speech at Charlotte, North Carolina. "Have you ever stopped to think," he asked his listeners, "that happiness is most often described in terms of the simple ways of nature rather than the complex ways of man's fabrications? Perhaps it is because peace is necessary to ultimate happiness. Perhaps, therefore, where we seek a symbol of happiness, we do not go to the rush of crowded city streets or to the hum of machinery to find the simile." Then, referring to the author of the Twenty-third Psalm, he went on, "The ancient psalmist did not use the parable of the merchants' camel train or the royal palace or the crowded bazaar of the East. . . . Be it remembered then, that those kings and prophets reverted, just as we do today, to the good earth and the still waters when they idealized security of the body and mind." [36]

But farming, as Jefferson knew, offered more than nature's peace. The interest in soil processes, the variety of activities, the satisfactions of harvest—these contributed solidly to the good life. There were vexations, discouragements, and frustrations, too, but even these gave depth and strength to human character. No wonder, then, that the gentleman farmer of Hyde Park looked with grave misgiving upon the ceaseless tread from farm to city. In 1926 he spoke of it with foreboding. "To me this idea of the abandonment or minimizing of country life in the days of our grandchildren is indeed the most cruel of prophecies." [37]

He understood the reasons for the move to urban centers, especially the "lure" of city life, conceding that there were some advantages, both social and mechanical, in the city, but arguing that the lure was in general false. He was further persuaded that the actual advantages were being reduced comparatively as modern conveniences were extended to the country. In 1933 he forecast that all this would soon be recognized and that the move to the city would at last be reversed.[38] By 1937 he saw that the "back to the farm" movement was failing; but he hoped, at least, that a shift would develop from large to smaller cities. He was convinced that the great cities were choking themselves on their own congestion and that a dispersal to outlying areas was the natural remedy.[39] And this movement, if it came, was of fair promise; for the good society must be near to the good earth.

He recognized that material standards influenced the character of men's lives and that a good society must have a sound economic organization. He believed that capitalism was the best system. Its weaknesses could be remedied, he thought, by minor adjustments and by improved behavior of those engaged in enterprise. While economists and businessmen tended to see the troubles of capitalism as technical or mechanical, he viewed them as primarily ethical and personal. He believed that business, like any other human endeavor, was essentially a moral undertaking. It could be aimed at the good of the community as well as at profits. Since business absorbed the principal talent and energy of a capitalistic nation, he hoped that it would be run that way in America.

As he thought that "good" men made capitalism good, he likewise believed that the machine could be directed to the welfare of society. Unlike some rebels of the twentieth century, he was not a primitivist, had no longing to destroy science or mechanical invention and return to the dubious bliss of handwork and scarcity. He saw the industrial revolution as the creation of a new vision: "the dream of an economic machine, able to raise the standard of living for everyone; to bring luxury within the reach of the humblest; to annihilate distance by steam power and later by electricity, and to release everyone from the drudgery of the heaviest manual toil." He knew, too, that there was a shadow over the dream. It brought evil with good, but, "So manifest were the advantages of the machine age, that the United States fearlessly, cheerfully, and, I think, rightly, accepted the bitter with the sweet." [40]

In his full view of the good society, he looked beyond technology and economic organization. These provided livelihood, even avenues of service and creativity; but the economic man could not be a whole man. To meet man's broader needs and higher aspirations, many other institutions had to be molded and had to function harmoniously. Prominent among these were churches and schools—and the arts and recreation.

While endorsing the separation of State and Church, he favored some kind of regular religious instruction for every child. The family, he felt, could not be entirely depended upon to discharge this responsibility.[41] Regular schooling, likewise, was a community obligation, and in the good society every person would have opportunity for the learning which his desires and capabilities permitted. (A broader analysis of his philosophy of education, freedom of inquiry, and communication of ideas is discussed in Chapter 7.)

His views on literature and the plastic arts were lively if not extraordinary. He was indeed an advocate of books and libraries, but was more of a collector than a reader. Among Chief Executives, he read less than Jefferson, Theodore Roosevelt, or Wilson—and more than Jackson or Lincoln. His literary tastes were fairly pedestrian, although he had such specialized interests as naval records and local history. He knew the influence and potentiality of books, but was too much a man of action to spend a great deal of time reading them.

He had a sound instinct for the value and function of art in society, though his personal taste and appreciation were quite conventional. "In encouraging the creation and enjoyment of beautiful things," he once declared, "we are furthering democracy itself." As he saw it, the arts were not exotic plants, tenderly nurtured for the benefit of "long-

hairs" (or eggheads). They were, on the contrary, an integral part of
the good society. He believed that the arts "ennoble and refine" life,
and that they, in turn, are brought to flower only by *free* men. ("Crush
individuality in society and you crush art as well." [42])

He knew that Americans were only gradually becoming conscious of
their rich inheritance and the relation of art to life. As president, he
called upon cultural leaders and institutions to aid in the spread of
understanding and appreciation. He stressed especially the importance
of traveling exhibits, which brought the latest and finest achievements
into far-flung communities. And such exhibits, he thought, should emphasize that the visual arts are more than just painting and sculpture.
The people should learn of the enormous importance of industrial design, architecture, the printed book, illustration, and photography. He
saw promise, too, in the inexpensive color reproductions that were coming into circulation; he felt that good reproductions of that sort would
substantially increase public appreciation of the masterpieces.[43]

Even more important to the growing popular awareness was the vi-
talization of an indigenous art. The view of art as something "foreign"
was being dispelled as the people saw (and heard) more and more
products of American artists. Roosevelt referred specifically to popular
appreciation of the mural art of the New Deal years—"some of it good,
some of it not so good, but all of it native, human, eager, and alive—all
of it painted by their own kind in their own country, and painted about
things that they know and look at often and have touched and loved." [44]
Similarly, in architecture, he favored designs and materials that suited
the historical background and resources of each locality. One of his pet
projects was to have federal buildings in the Hudson Valley built of
native fieldstone and in designs copied from early Dutch architecture
("which was so essentially sound besides being very attractive to the
eye" [45]). The visitor to Dutchess County will find these structures in
goodly number; the best known is the Roosevelt Library, standing near
his grave and river home.

His taste in painting, like that of the average American, was largely
restricted to natural representation. His attitude was no doubt influenced by long experience as a collector of prints (chiefly naval vessels),
which invariably "tell a story"; it also reflects, perhaps, his aversion to
all forms of abstraction. In any event, he revealed his bias simply and
decisively during a press conference in 1934. Commenting upon a dis-
play of some hundreds of examples of work-relief art, he observed with
satisfaction that they were "hopeful pictures." And what is more, he
said, "they are honest pictures; in other words, they depict American

life in an American way. There is very little of what some . . . call decadent foreign art. You can tell right away what the picture is intended to be." [46] Yet, he would leave the artist at liberty to choose his own style and subject: "As in our democracy we enjoy the right to believe in different religious creeds or none, so can American artists express themselves with complete freedom from the strictures of dead artistic tradition or political ideology." [47]

One has the feeling—it cannot be proved—that he had less inclination for music than the other fine arts. If asked about it, he would doubtless have accorded to music an important place in the good society. But in his speeches and writings, he does not reveal the enthusiasm for symphony or opera, for example, that he shows for first editions, rare prints, and scenic splendors. When his physical handicap is considered, the fact is all the more striking. For instinctive collector though he was, he was no collector of fine records. The only player in the home at Hyde Park was an ancient Edison wind-up model. With the exception of his professed enjoyment of Wagner (cultivated in childhood visits to Germany), his musical interests appear to have been commonplace. He liked popular and folk music, and loved chosen hymns, but the more serious forms yielded him little pleasure. It is, perhaps, significant that Dr. Hans Kindler, Director of the National Symphony, pleaded unsuccessfully with him to do something about a municipal concert hall for Washington. Roosevelt sympathized in a letter of reply to Dr. Kindler, but regretted that he could think of no solution to the problem of the struggling National Symphony.[48] The fact is that Roosevelt favored a concert hall, but did not consider it sufficiently important to push for.

The value placed upon sports at Groton made a lasting mark upon the youthful Roosevelt. While he proved to be no great athlete in either school or college, he responded vigorously to the challenge of physical competition. He tried out for almost every sport, but the only first place he won was in the "high kick" event at Groton. Football, baseball, and rowing were probably his favorite sports as a young man; later, until cut short by his illness, he played golf with enthusiasm and skill. His lifelong pleasure in sailing and fishing became well known to the American public. In any good society conceived by Roosevelt, there would be plenty of room for sports of all kinds—and the more lively ones, the better.

He believed that most people benefited from sports (either as participants or spectators) and that the benefit was moral and mental as well as physical. (Baseball, he thought, was rightly called the national pastime, because it stood for "fair play, clean living, and good sports-

manship, which are our national heritage.") He did not take a per-
fectionist view in athletics and enjoyed sand-lot ball almost as much as
that played in the majors. It was the *game* that mattered. He once made
an amusing and rather precise specification of the kind of contest he
liked best:

> When it comes to baseball I am the kind of fan who wants to get plenty
> of action for his money. I have some appreciation of a game which is fea-
> tured by a pitcher's duel and results in a score of one to nothing. But I must
> confess that I get the biggest kick out of the biggest score—a game in which
> the batters pole the ball to the far corners of the field, the outfielders scramble,
> and men run the bases. In short, my idea of the best game is one that guaran-
> tees the fans a combined score of not less than fifteen runs, divided about
> eight to seven.[49]

He was less interested in games played indoors than those played
in the open. No doubt one of the principal attractions of sports to him
was the fact that they generally brought folks outdoors; this was another response to his affection for nature. In the good society, all types
of outdoor recreation would be encouraged. But that which combined
the highest values, in his estimation, was camping—particularly by families. This was a subject especially close to Roosevelt's heart; combined
with thoughts on seeing the country, conservation, and state and national parks, it evoked the most consistent enthusiasm of all the topics
in his speeches. He was probably the most effective "back to nature"
propagandist since Rousseau—and certainly since Thoreau and Emerson.

As governor, he addressed the nation by radio in 1931, urging that
as many families as possible enjoy the advantages of camping during
the summer. In the course of that broadcast, he gave perhaps his most
complete exposition of the values of outdoor living. He attributed to it
the character of a national tradition, stating that since earliest colonial
days, "a very large proportion of our population was at all times engaged in camping out in one form or another." It was only with the
concentration of people in large cities, starting in the late nineteenth
century, that American families lost the habit of living "more or less
outdoors." But within the past several years, Roosevelt noted with satisfaction, a new understanding had developed. The joys of nature were
being rediscovered, and people were beginning to realize that the
strain of modern living required a complete change from city conditions at reasonable intervals.

Without enlarging on the health benefits offered, Roosevelt emphasized the value of camping as a social process. He believed that outdoor
living helped to break the narrow circle of one's everyday life and asso-

ciates; it provided a fresh viewpoint and a stimulus for better life at home and at work: "I like to think of the camper as one who is standing off at a little distance and looking at his normal and usual life. He is free to have the time for a little thinking, free to survey the conditions in which crowded humanity lives, free to ask himself questions as to whether improvement along various lines cannot be made in our much vaunted civilization. . . ."[50]

It is clear that he seriously believed in outdoor recreation as a necessity of the good society. It is equally clear that his concept of the good society was no cold abstraction, but a definite and realizable goal—the true object of American history and aspiration. For his ideals were nearly always cast in the frame of his own experience and that of his countrymen; so concrete was his habit of thought that he identified his idea of the good society with the higher values of American culture. His vision of the more abundant life was grounded in the soil, waters, and mountains of his homeland, and he believed that the youth of the nation had it in their power to realize this vision. In 1935, speaking to young Americans of their dream, better than that of their fathers, he said:

You place emphasis on sufficiency of life, rather than on a plethora of riches. You think of the security for yourself and your family that will give you good health, good food, good education, good working conditions, and the opportunity for normal recreation and travel. Your advancement, you hope, is along a broad highway on which thousands of your fellow men and women are advancing with you.[51]

In later years, when the destiny of America became linked with that of the United Nations, Roosevelt hoped that this American dream could become a *universal* aspiration, attainable in time by men "everywhere in the world."[52]

2

Unto Caesar What Is Caesar's

THE STATE, IN ROOSEVELT'S MIND, was merely an instrument for achieving the "more abundant life." During an age when the State in many lands became an idol, a devouring leviathan, Roosevelt clung to the view that it was a servant of individuals, not their master. There was no awe, no mysticism, in his concept. He would have accepted the simple and practical explanation of Aristotle—that the State originates in order to satisfy the bare necessities of life, and continues in existence for the sake of a *good* life.

The Nature of the State

His philosophy of government was long years in developing and reached maturity before he entered the White House. The fundamental ideas he held were his own—rooted in the tradition of Jefferson, shaped by association with Theodore Roosevelt and Wilson, and affirmed by his own political experience. The men who surrounded him later, such as Raymond Moley and other members of the brain trust, helped him to apply his ideas to the special conditions of the thirties; they did not give him any basic political concepts. These he already possessed. His definition of the State he had given to the New York legislature in 1931: "What is the State? It is the duly constituted representative of an organized society of human beings, created by them for their mutual protection and well-being. 'The State' or 'The Government' is but the machinery through which such mutual aid and protection are achieved."[1]

The State, like man himself, was part of God's plan, and in that sense might be regarded as of divine origin. It had no existence, however, apart from society, and its actual creation and form were the result of human intelligence and will. It is significant that Roosevelt preferred the word "government" to the more cryptic "state," although he regarded the two terms as synonymous.

He saw the origin of modern government in the rise of the European nation-state. It came about because there was powerful sentiment for the building of a centralized force, strong enough to impose peace upon the feudal barons. This was accomplished after a prolonged struggle, led by ambitious and ruthless men. The state-makers were justified in their methods, he thought, because they relieved individuals from insecurity and local tyranny. "The people preferred the master far away to the exploitation and cruelty of the smaller master near at hand." But when the development of nation-states had been completed, there was growing resentment against the continuance of despotic privilege and power. Out of this feeling arose new forces to check the authority of the monarchs: town councils, trade guilds, parliaments, and constitutions. Above all by the seventeenth century, the idea took hold that chiefs of state were limited in power, and bore a responsibility for the welfare of their subjects. Thus, the way was opened for Jefferson's doctrine of the "unalienable rights" of man, rule by consent, and the American theory of representative government.[2]

The Functions of Government

There was no question in Roosevelt's mind that the State should serve the welfare of the individuals who created and supported it. The only issue was: *what* functions were beneficial to the people? In seeking the answer to this, he began by rejecting Jefferson's maxim that that government is best which governs least. (He excused Jefferson for this teaching on the ground that it reflected a residual antipathy to British "tyranny"; he was sure that, a hundred years later, Jefferson would have cast off the dogma.) The best government was not necessarily the "leastest" or the "mostest." The problem was a variable and utilitarian one, answerable only in the complex of human experience. "Your Government," said Roosevelt, referring to his first Administration, "has had but one sign on its desk—'Seek only the greater good of the greater number of Americans.'"[3]

The actual trend, he observed in 1930, was toward increasing activity by local, state, and national governments. He opposed an unplanned drift of this sort, pushed by "expediency" or "popular demand," because it threatened to empty the public purse and create an intolerable tax burden. He called for a careful study of the situation, in order to determine the "right" functions of government and to eliminate those which belonged properly to private enterprise. And the test of whether a particular function belonged to private or public enterprise was simply, "which can do it better." [4] He believed with Lincoln that, "The legitimate object of Government is to do for a community of people whatever they need to have done but cannot do at all or cannot do so well for themselves in their separate and individual capacities." [5]

As the complexity of technology and human relations increased, the ability to solve problems by private means was narrowed. Roosevelt gave these principal reasons: private parties looked at a problem from the point of view of their own business and locality; they had no adequate machinery for harmonizing their views; and they had no authority to bind the "inevitable minority" of non-co-operators. [6] This situation made it imperative that citizens look to their government as a dynamic force, adaptable to the needs of the times. "New conditions impose new requirements upon government and those who conduct government." [7]

He made clear, in Albany, what he thought were the legitimate responses of government to the challenge. In messages to the legislature from 1929 to 1933 he called for measures in fields where he later urged appropriate federal action. These included welfare legislation, protective labor reforms, relief of unemployment, social insurance, regulation of banks and utilities, housing, electric power, and conservation of resources. As president, he operated on a different level and with a national point of view; but his broad objectives were the same.

The expansion of government functions, he thought, went hand-in-hand with the new concept of social responsibility. This idea distinguished the civilization of his generation from civilizations of earlier times. It was an outgrowth, he explained in 1929, of a new sensitivity—so dominant that the era should be named "The Age of Social Consciousness." State, church, and private associations were taking care of the sick, the crippled, the mentally deficient; people in general were more alive to humanitarian issues, race problems, maintenance of peace, and a hundred other social questions.

Roosevelt heartily approved of the new spirit, and he declared that its goals conformed more truly to Christian teachings than any objective of previous centuries. He added significantly that this age, with its impact upon government, had its dangers. It might result in too much organization, enormously increased powers over the individual, and a narrowing of control into the hands of a few. To escape this, men might ultimately have to revolt to a simpler existence. But, notwithstanding the risks of the new era, "We are married to it for better or for worse; we are a part of it, and whatever may be our doubts and fears we can do no good to our fellow men by sitting idly by or seeking to dam the current with a brick." [8]

It was the crash of 1929, with its train of unemployment, foreclosures, and privation, that expanded his idea of social welfare into the concept of *social justice*. In earlier thinking, he thought of government as lending a hand to the widow, the orphan, the aged, and the sick. But he now conceived of a broader responsibility—one extending to every man, woman, and child. As candidate for president in 1932, he presented this view in a key address at Detroit. He contrasted his philosophy of social justice through social action with the rival philosophy of "letting things alone." The latter doctrine, which had prevailed "from the days of the cave man to the days of the automobile," had resulted in the jungle law of survival of the so-called fittest. But his philosophy aimed at "the fitting of as many human beings as possible into the scheme of surviving." Here, indeed, was an ambitious project of social engineering! It was no more so, however, than the ideal with which Roosevelt identified it. "The thing we are all seeking," he declared in 1935, "is justice—justice in the common sense interpretation of that word—the interpretation that means 'Do unto your neighbors as you would be done by.' " [9]

The idea that it was the function of the State to promote social justice vastly increased the possible range of government activities. But he did not fear this prospect. The fact that the State could act did not mean that it *would* act in violation of good sense and basic human rights. He put his trust in democratic processes while conceding that the new circumstances required greater vigilance than ever before. In his Annual Message of 1936 he pointed out that he had helped to build up new instruments of public power. These were wholesome and proper in the hands of a people's government; but in the hands of an oligarchy, they would be "shackles for the liberties of the people."

As he developed new instruments of power, Roosevelt gave vigor to a traditional function of the State. This was the function of regulation—not of a particular enterprise or enterprises, but of the basic interests which compose society itself. In a campaign speech of 1932, he expressed agreement with James Madison, who had shrewdly written (*Federalist*, No. X): "A landed interest, a manufacturing interest, a moneyed interest, with many lesser interests, grow up of necessity in civilized nations and divide them into different classes, actuated by different sentiments and views. The regulation of the various and interfering interests forms the principal task of modern legislation. . . ." Roosevelt went on to observe that Madison's theory applied especially to America, where men from many states and of many interests sought to achieve, through government, the necessary harmony of forces. "This is the American system," he declared.[10]

The State, in his view, should achieve a subordination of private interests to the general welfare and supply leadership when private leaders fail. It was on this ground that he saw the need for decisive intervention by government on March 4, 1933. General distress had befallen the nation, he declared in his First Inaugural, because the rulers of business had failed and abdicated: "The money changers have fled from their high seats in the temple of our civilization. We may now restore that temple to the ancient truths." It is significant that when addressing the "money changers" (bankers) in the following year, he chose to elaborate his view on the relation of the State to the constituent groups of society:

> You will recognize, I think, that a true function of the head of the Government of the United States is to find among many discordant elements that unity of purpose that is best for the Nation as a whole. This is necessary because government is not merely one of many coordinate groups in the community or the Nation, but government is essentially the outward expression of the unity and the leadership of all groups. Consequently the old fallacious notion of the bankers on one side and the Government on the other side as being more or less equal and independent units has passed away. Government by the necessity of things must be the leader, must be the judge of the conflicting interests of all groups in the community, including bankers.[11]

One can only speculate upon the thoughts and feelings of the assembled bankers as they heard these words from "*That* Man."

Comparative Political Systems: Dictatorship and Democracy

During the thirties, with the sickening collapse of democracy and democratic spirit abroad, many Americans did some political soul-searching. It was rather fashionable, at least in some circles, to view representative government as a "noble experiment," a system which had become obsolete in the world of technology and power politics. The "wave of the future" was something foreign, efficient, and exciting. It was dramatically personified in the strutting Mussolini pacing his balcony on the Piazza Venezia—or in the half-wild, ascetic Fuehrer, standing gravely beneath the giant swastikas. It was an era when various forms of government were being analyzed and considered as possible alternatives. Democracy, on the defensive, was the object of "agonizing reappraisal" by its votaries in the United States.

Roosevelt shared the interest of his countrymen in rival political systems though his own faith never wavered. He believed that constitutional democracy was the system best suited to his homeland. At the same time, he recognized that no single type of government was the best for *all* peoples. He held with Edmund Burke that political institutions should be rooted in a nation's history. In keeping with this, he insisted that every people had the right to choose their own form of government, with but one reservation: their choice should be predicated on certain freedoms which are essential everywhere. "We know that we ourselves shall never be wholly safe at home unless other governments recognize such freedoms." [12]

He regarded as regressive the "new" orders of Mussolini, Hitler, and Stalin. By denying freedoms which had been painfully won over the course of centuries, they were turning back the clock of civilization. He readily conceded that these systems appeared efficient and acted swiftly, but this was because they had destroyed the safeguards of an independent legislature and judiciary. Discussing these points with the press in 1940, Roosevelt regretted that there were some Americans who were willing, on account of more efficiency, to favor the corporate state.[13] He was thankful, though, that most of his fellow citizens had a sounder sense of values:

> Dictatorship . . . involves costs which the American people will never pay: The cost of our spiritual values. The cost of the blessed right of being able to say what we please. The cost of freedom of religion. The cost of seeing our capital confiscated. The cost of being cast into a concentration camp. The cost of being afraid to walk down the street with the wrong neighbor. The cost of having our children brought up, not as free and dignified human beings, but as pawns molded and enslaved by a machine.[14]

He saw little difference between the corporate Fascist state and the corporate Communist state. He interpreted the former as a "plutocratic" dictatorship, supported by vested interests as a means of perpetuating their power; the latter he described as a "proletarian" dictatorship, established by men who were willing to bid for Utopia by a reckless and violent seizure of power.[15] In the early days of Mussolini, Roosevelt was inclined to be somewhat sympathetic—or at least to withhold judgment. Even after becoming president, his official correspondence with *il Duce* revealed a cordial tone. Until the day in 1940 when the would-be Caesar cast his die against France, Roosevelt regarded him as a reasonable man, through whom he might check the madness of Hitler.

The historian, Douglas S. Freeman, once asked Marvin McIntyre if he could secure a confidential statement of Roosevelt's attitude toward Mussolini and Italian Fascism prior to 1933. (Freeman was planning a book about F.D.R.) Roosevelt's response, in a memorandum to his secretary, describes his initial hopefulness: "It should be remembered that during those years Mussolini still maintained a semblance of parliamentary government, and there were many, including myself, who hoped that having restored order and morale in Italy, he would, of his own accord, work toward a restoration of democratic processes." The memorandum also suggested that if Nazism had not sprung to power in Germany, Mussolini would have been unable to push toward greater absolutism at home. On the contrary, thought Roosevelt, he would have been compelled sooner or later to establish genuine representative government. To sum up, he stated that Fascism before 1933 was "still in the experimental state"—and might have taken another direction.[16]

He had a similar disappointment in connection with the Russian "experiment." He freely admitted this in 1940 while addressing the pro-Communist American Youth Congress. During the first years of the Bolshevik revolution he had been deeply sympathetic with the Russian people, he said. The Communists, he believed, were doing something to improve the education, health, and opportunities of millions who had been neglected and oppressed by the harsh rule of the czars. He abhorred some features of the new government—the regimentation, violence, and banishment of religion. Nevertheless, he had hoped that Russia would eventually become a peace-loving, popular government with a free ballot. But if he had once been a foolish dreamer, he was now wide-awake: "That hope is today either shattered or put away in storage against some better day. The Soviet Union, as everybody who has the courage to face the facts knows, is run by a dictatorship as absolute as any other dictatorship in the world."

Three years later, when the United States and the Soviet Union were joined in a common struggle against the Fascist powers, Roosevelt had a more friendly attitude toward his fighting ally. But he did not allow wartime sympathies to alter his revised estimate of Russian communism. In fact, by 1943 he reached the conclusion that the inherent evils of Marxism were such that no regime based upon its principles could long endure. He regarded the doctrine of materialism as the underlying defect—the ignoring of spiritual values. Communism did not recognize the dignity of man, and it emphasized hate rather than love. In spite of desperate purges and suppression, Stalin and the Party had been forced to give up much of the original Communist program. It was more than likely, thought Roosevelt, that Russia would desert Marxist principles altogether, and swing back to the fervid nationalism and imperialism of the czars.

His concept of democracy, which stood opposed to the corporate state, was broad and flexible. It included not just the American system, but a great variety of political structures—from the stable British Constitution (with its Crown) to a turbulent Latin republic (with its *junta*). To Roosevelt, democracy was essentially a matter of spirit, rather than form. The structure of government and extent of popular participation would depend on the level of education and other conditions in each country.

By the word democracy, he meant representative government, a republic. And this was its hallmark: free and frequent choice by citizens of their officers of government. He emphasized the qualification "free choice," which meant liberty of expression and the absence of force or undue influence over the voter's decision. He favored the broadest possible franchise; but he believed that even where voting was restricted, representative government obtained so long as "the cardinal principle of free choice by the body politic prevailed." [17] He regarded the "rigged" elections of the corporate states as contemptible travesties upon a sacred political right. Yet the glaring contrast in the two kinds of elections served to highlight the essential difference between democracy and dictatorship: "No dictator in history has ever dared to run the gauntlet of a really free election." [18]

For him, the question of what constitutes a republican form of government was not just a theoretical one. The Constitution states that "The United States shall guarantee to every State in this Union a republican form of government. . . ." (Art. IV, Sec. 4); it was the responsibility of the Chief Executive to enforce the guarantee. Roosevelt was faced with this problem early, as the Huey Long regime had become fastened upon the state of Louisiana. Critics of Long clamored for federal intervention on the ground that the "Kingfish" had created a corrupt, dictatorial machine. Roosevelt handled this subject gingerly, as it was a "no man's land," both in politics and in constitutional law. Although he directed his Attorney General, Homer Cummings, to investigate the situation in Louisiana, he did not find sufficient evidence to warrant federal action. Roosevelt regarded Long as a menace, but he saw the legal problem as limited to one question only. A reporter, at a press conference in August,

1934, put that question directly to him: "Are you satisfied that there is a republican form of government in the State of Louisiana?"

Roosevelt replied, "I should say that, if there was a free franchise in the State of Louisiana . . . and we haven't gotten to that." [19] He was obviously reluctant to act and faced a hard decision in determining whether the voters of Louisiana were freely exercising their right to vote. One year later an assassin's bullets stopped the "Kingfish" and relieved Roosevelt of making that decision.

He knew that a free franchise meant more than control over the machinery of government. All the democratic rights depended upon it, "For such elections guarantee that there can be no possibility of stifling freedom of speech, freedom of the press and the air, freedom of worship." [20] And he believed that democracy, where the people were capable of self-rule, was preferable to alternative systems. He was familiar with its weaknesses: the pressure groups, the political machines, the selfishness, ignorance, and prejudice that enter into democratic processes. Indeed, he had his moments of discouragement. Exasperated by Congressional "politics as usual" during the war, he wrote to James M. Cox: "Sometimes I get awfully discouraged when I see what is going on on the Hill. The truth of the matter is that neither we nor the Republicans have fighting leadership there." But then, as if to catch himself, he added, "*However, however, however*—I still believe in representative democracy!" [21]

He admitted that democratic governments made mistakes, but he kept his perspective. When critics found fault with management of the war effort in 1943, he suggested that they "look at some of the blunders made by our enemies in the so-called 'efficient' dictatorships." [22] And a year afterward, as American production and manpower drove the Japanese toward destruction, he could be pardoned for an exultant remark to his press conference. A reporter had asked why American soldiers were able to beat the enemy at his own game of jungle and atoll fighting. Roosevelt answered: "Perhaps it sounds like a little bit of boasting, but it is the difference between our type of civilization and our type of fellow, and their type of civilization and fellow. We will take them on at any game, war or pleasure, and beat them at it." [23]

The trend of history, he felt, was on the side of democracy, and he was impatient with those who thought the future belonged to the corporate state. "Whatever its new trappings and new slogans," he declared, "tyranny is the oldest and most discredited rule known to history." [24] He denied the assertion that democracy could not meet the problems of the twentieth century; the swift action of the Hundred Days and the conduct of a global war were proof of its adaptability. "No," he replied to those men of little faith, "democracy is not dying. . . . We know it because, if we look below the surface, we sense it still spreading on every continent. . . . The democratic aspiration is no mere recent phase in human history. It is human history." [25]

Faith in the Majority

Roosevelt's confidence in democracy sprang from his faith in the wisdom of the majority. So basic is this premise to the idea of representative government, that it requires the most searching examination. May sovereign power rest safely with the people, or (as the cynics say) does good government consist in circumvention of the popular will? Roosevelt held that there could be an honest difference of opinion on this question and that the issue in America traced back to the Founding Fathers. There were those, after the American Revolution, who were frightened by the public confusion which attended the years of struggle and who "surrendered to the belief that popular Government was essentially dangerous and essentially unworkable." Hamilton was the most brilliant and forthright spokesman for this point of view. He was convinced that the safety of the republic lay in a strong central government, directed by a small group of able and public-spirited citizens. [26]

But Jefferson, turning his mind to the problem, took a different view. He wrote in his *Notes on Virginia* that, "Every government degenerates when trusted to the rulers of the people alone. The people themselves therefore are its only safe depositories." The historic political duel thus opened between Hamilton and Jefferson left a cleavage which has persisted to the present day. While Roosevelt admired the practical accomplishments of Hamilton, he took his stand with the Sage of Monticello. He did not object to the ideal of aristocratic government, which called for unselfish service by the best educated and most successful citizens. But he believed that because of human frailty, the Hamiltonian theory would lead in the long run to goverment by selfishness.

He was familiar with the classical arguments for aristocracy; and he once refuted the views of Thomas B. Macaulay, the British historian and statesman. Macaulay had written that democratic institutions, such as those in the United States, would sooner or later destroy liberty and civilization. "The day will come," he had predicted in 1857, "when . . . a multitude of people, none of whom has had more than half a breakfast or expects to have more than half a dinner, will choose a legislature. . . ." In a time of adversity such people could not be trusted to exercise restraint: "you will act like people who should in a year of scarcity devour all the seed corn and thus make the next year a year, not of scarcity but of absolute famine. . . . There is nothing to stop you. Your constitution is all sail and no anchor." Macaulay's anchor was supreme power in the hands of a numerous but *select* class, deeply interested in the security of property and order. But to this, Roosevelt replied, "Mine is a different anchor. . . . My anchor is democracy—and more democracy." [27]

For he believed that the wisdom of the whole was greater than the part. Majorities could make mistakes; but any minority makes *worse* mistakes—for the simple reason that it takes counsel from itself and fails to heed the problems and welfare of all kinds of men. He stated, for example, that on general political issues, he would rather trust the aggregate judgment of all the people in a factory—the president, vice-presidents, board of directors, managers, foremen, and laborers—than the judgment of the directors alone.[28] He declared his faith in the final speech of the 1940 campaign: "The opinion of all the people, freely informed and freely expressed, without fear or coercion, is wiser than the opinion of any one man or any small group of men."

His unabashed faith in the judgment of the majority has led, understandably, to caricatures of his conception of government. But a man does not just "believe in democracy"; he must have in mind certain specifications. Roosevelt, in the first place, put several qualifications upon his faith in the voters: they should have a decent standard of living, a reasonable amount of education, free access to information, and full opportunity for expression and discussion. The people of America, he thought, were gaining steadily in political wisdom, for they enjoyed increasing advantages of education and communication. They were listening to "both sides," and were "thinking for themselves." [29] But he admitted that an ignorant vote still existed in certain areas. He confided to a group of editors in 1938 that "The South, because it is still educationally behind the rest of the nation, is peculiarly susceptible to the demagogue." [30]

In the second place, Roosevelt's faith in the majority did not mean that he would put the "common man" in positions requiring special skills or education. He had high respect for rare talents (including his own!) and did not believe that the democratic principle required a "leveling" of qualifications for office. On the contrary, he insisted upon high standards of proficiency in government and supported the principle of a civil service based upon training, experience, and merit. Roosevelt did not favor the "average man" as a legislator, either. His own experience had led him to conclude that a legislator could be free in making decisions only if he were financially independent, or had a profession to which he could easily return. He did not mean that only men of affluence should stand for public office; he felt, on the contrary, that individuals in government should represent a cross-section of community interests. By his standard, however, only a small minority of citizens were in a position to serve as lawmakers.

What Roosevelt wanted was government by honest and competent representatives of the people. His faith in the majority of citizens extended to their wisdom of judgment on general political issues and in selecting responsible officeholders. In the exercise of this function, one citizen might show more or less intelligence than another, but it was the decision of the *majority* that Roosevelt believed in. Moreover, in the high enterprise of government, sovereign decision-making could not be regarded as just an intellectual proposition. It represented a grand accommodation of interests, values, and aspirations. Since the lives of all were bound up in the consequences, the people themselves should choose.

One question remains: What of the rights of the individual, of the minority? Did majority rule remove the protection of their "unalienable rights"? Roosevelt apparently felt no difficulty on this issue although his critics did. Political attacks upon him during his years as president centered on the charge that he had interfered with "personal liberty." He did not see it that way. On Constitution Day, 1937, he declared: "No one cherishes more deeply than I the civil and religious liberties achieved by so much blood and anguish through the many centuries of Anglo-American history. But the Constitution guarantees liberty, not license masquerading as liberty." Here was the nub of the matter. Roosevelt insisted that no man had an absolute right to act or to use his property in such a way as to damage his neighbors. He offered as an example the wasting of the nation's resources by careless private use of the soil and forests. "The day has gone by when it could be claimed that government has no interest in such ill-considered practices and no right through representative methods to stop them." [31] It was the century-old question of the meaning of "due process of law," of the distinction between "liberty" and "license." He liked to quote Lincoln's view of this problem:

The world has never had a good definition of the word liberty, and the American people, just now [1864], are much in want of one. We all declare for liberty; but in using the word we do not all mean the same thing. . . . The shepherd drives the wolf from the sheep's throat, for which the sheep thanks the shepherd as his liberator, while the wolf denounces him for the same act, as the destroyer of liberty. . . . Plainly, the sheep and the wolf are not agreed upon a definition of the word liberty; and precisely the same difference prevails today among us human creatures. . . .[32]

For interpretation of the word "liberty" and the answer to the question of individual and minority rights, Roosevelt would turn, once more —to the judgment of the majority of citizens. He felt, as did Rousseau concerning the "General Will," that there could be no real conflict between the decision of the majority and the rights of individuals. For personal liberty could be seen, by the light of sense and reason, to be a paramount value. How could the majority, whose basic judgment was sound, oppose so obvious a good for its individual members? If this kind of logic seemed specious, proof could be found in the record of history. For, as Roosevelt often stated, no civilized people, by a really free choice had ever surrendered their individual liberties. In time of mortal crisis or under duress, they might yield to temporary encroachments, but their long-term judgment sustained the core of freedom. Laws of the people, evolved through constitutional processes, could be trusted; and, as Aristotle taught, true liberty consists of freedom to act *within the laws.*

Revolution and Political Stability

Roosevelt would not have taken literally the counsel of Jefferson that there should be a new constitution every generation. He favored a dynamic government that met change with change and thus made revolutions obsolete. He agreed that the people had a reserve right of revolution (should they be faced with a "long train of abuses"), but he was conservative by instinct and considered a major task of statecraft to be the *preservation* of the government and of social order. This became his legal responsibility when he took the oath to "defend the Constitution against its enemies, foreign and domestic."

How could revolution be averted? He reduced the problem to simplest terms: a government, if it is to endure, must *succeed*. That is to say, it must solve problems and afford broad satisfaction to the great majority of the population. In modern times, he thought, social and economic problems were the root of revolution around the globe. "After the World War [1918], there arose everywhere insistent demands upon government that human needs be met. . . . In some countries, a royalist form of government failed to meet these demands—and fell. In other countries, a parliamentary form of government failed to meet these demands —and fell." The threat to democracy was in those lands where statesmen had not met human needs. "People have become so fed up with futile debate and party bickering over methods that they have been willing to surrender democratic processes and principles in order to get things done." [33] But in America democracy had not failed, and would not fail, if the people gave support to effective action by the State. "History proves that dictatorships do not grow out of strong and successful governments, but out of weak and helpless ones." [34]

A statesman could not afford to ignore the threat of revolution. He must *do* something about it, but Roosevelt was convinced that the action must be positive, not negative. It would not do simply to "batten down the hatches," suppress propaganda, bring out the tear gas, and put people in jail. He made a point of this in relation to the danger of communism in America. There was no difference between the major parties, he insisted, in what they thought of the Communist system. But there was a very great difference in what the two parties did about it. The Republicans, by "letting things alone" during the twenties, had permitted economic conditions to deteriorate to the point where radicalism became a threat. But the Democrats sought a positive program:

> Early in the campaign of 1932 I said: "To meet by reaction the danger of radicalism is to invite disaster. Reaction is no barrier to the radical, it is a challenge, a provocation. The way to meet that danger is to offer a workable program of reconstruction. . . ." We met that emergency with emergency action. But far more important than that, we went to the roots of the problem, and attacked the cause of the crisis. We were against revolution. Therefore, we waged war against those conditions which make revolutions—against the inequalities and resentments which breed them.[35]

Roosevelt believed that the wisdom of his course was proved by the events of the thirties. Revolutionary groups, though noisy and troublesome, gained little popular support during those years. Even the demagogic appeal of Huey Long, with his "Share-the-Wealth" scheme, was held in check. All this resulted, claimed Roosevelt, because the New Deal was in existence—with a program of wiser remedies. He told Arthur Krock of *The New York Times* that Long would have proved a real menace if Hoover had won the election in 1932.[36]

Government Policy Toward Radicals: The Communist Party

It is a fact that there was no revolution or social disruption during Roosevelt's tenure in the White House. His plan for maintaining political stability through progressive action appears to have been successful. Somewhat less certain, however, was the efficacy of his policy in dealing with the radicals themselves. Though the bulwarks of American democracy were not breached, some cracks did appear in the underground defenses. What was Roosevelt's attitude and policy toward the Communists at home? How did he view the irrepressible issue of "Reds in government"?

Roosevelt accepted the notion, generally endorsed by "liberal" opinion in the thirties, that the Communists and other radical groups had a legal right to organize and to form political parties. He explained his viewpoint in an address to the Youth Congress in 1940:

> It has been said that some of you are Communists. That is a very unpopular term these days. As Americans you have a legal and constitutional right to call yourselves Communists, those of you who do. You have a right peacefully and openly to advocate certain ideals of theoretical communism; but as Americans you have not only a right but a sacred duty to confine your advocacy of changes in law to the methods prescribed by the Constitution of the United States—and you have no American right, by act or deed of any kind, to subvert the government and the Constitution of this nation.

He thought that a clear distinction could be drawn between "propaganda activities" (permissible under a system of free expression) and acts of sabotage and espionage. He admitted to reporters in 1938 that "foreign spying" had increased considerably during the preceding ten years and was a problem of serious concern to him. He did not suggest, however, that espionage was related to legitimate activities of the Communist Party; the principal need, he felt, was for improved co-ordination of the government's counterintelligence agencies.[37]

Many thoughtful observers during the thirties were uneasy and uncertain about the threat of subversion. The Communists in America represented, beyond reasonable doubt, a *conspiracy* to seize control of the State. Was it sensible or safe to allow such a group to masquerade as a legal party in the American sense? Was it realistic, in reference to Communists, to maintain the nice distinction between "legal" activities and overt subversion? Roosevelt believed that the whole tradition of American law and justice required such a course, even though the course be distasteful and risky. He also thought, as did many experts on the subject, that outlawing the Communist Party would aggravate the danger by making surveillance more difficult.

The issue was sharply raised during the 1940 campaign by a letter from Representative Martin Dies to Roosevelt and to Wendell Willkie, the Republican nominee. Dies was chairman of the House Committee on Un-American Activities and had become a principal leader in the move toward a "tougher" policy with Communists. He wanted to know if the presidential candidates would back his proposal to outlaw Communist, Fascist, and Nazi organizations "which have been shown by evidence before our Committee to be linked with foreign governments." [38] Roosevelt, in a letter drafted by his Attorney General, Robert Jackson, expressed agreement with moves to protect the country from "foreign hostile attacks." But he stated that the "broadness and generality" of Dies' proposal did not permit a categorical answer. "Furthermore, there are the questions of whether outlawing such organizations constitutes the most effective method in this field and whether such a step is consistent with the preservation of the rights of the citizens of a Democracy." In closing, he indicated that he favored the idea of registration of such organizations, rather than outlawry, although his attitude would depend upon the nature of specific proposals. [39] Roosevelt's position was apparently endorsed by the majority of Americans at the time, and four years later public opinion still inclined that way. It was not a party issue; Governor Dewey, the Republican candidate in 1944, and Senator Taft also opposed outlawing the Communist Party.

What *was* a party issue was the question of "Reds in government." Roosevelt's opposition charged that his Administration was infiltrated by Communists, "pinks," and "fellow travelers." Some held that the President was deliberately using the powers of his office to place radicals in high position (as part of a grand plot to subvert American institutions); others, more charitable, asserted that he was merely being hoodwinked by the scheming revolutionaries. The first allegation was hardly worthy of consideration to those who knew Roosevelt's philosophy and record. As he wrote in 1936 to Bishop James H. Ryan of Omaha, "The charge that I am a communist or sympathetic with communist principles is as false as it is malicious. It is a calumny circulated by those who have forgotten the ancient injunction against the bearing of false witness." [40]

On the other hand, there is some foundation for the belief that Roosevelt did not fully perceive the character of the Communist conspiracy and its adherents. There were two chief reasons for this: one was his natural tendency to attribute decent motives to people; the other was his long experience of seeing reform leaders falsely labeled Reds. While talking with Rosenman during the gubernatorial campaign of 1928, Roosevelt remarked, "You know, things today are not very different from the days when I was in the Senate back in 1911 and 1912. Al Smith and Bob Wagner and Jim Foley were there then, plugging for social and labor legislation as I was. I remember they used to call us socialistic and radical in those days." [41] Time and again, he reverted to this theme. What had been called socialism in 1911 had become "solid Americanism" by 1928; what was called communism and radicalism in 1933 became part of the Republican platform by 1944!

It is easy to see how Roosevelt developed a kind of sympathy for any man labeled as "radical." It is also easy to see why, after hearing the cry of "Wolf!" for so many years, he did not spring into action when members of his Administration were called Reds. In cases where he knew the individuals personally he was convinced beyond doubt of their decency and loyalty. He tended, from this, to discount similar charges against the hundreds of subordinate officials whom he could not know. He concluded that the allegations were a "red herring," drawn across the political path by an opposition that had no positive program to offer. The herring fooled the voters to some extent; and to some extent, it may have led Roosevelt off the trail of real subversives.

Political expediency was an additional (though minor) factor in Roosevelt's policy toward the radicals. He was fully informed that some of his supporters, especially in the labor unions, were tagged by the F.B.I. as "left-wingers" or "fellow-travelers." He had learned, through a report of J. Edgar Hoover, that the American Youth Congress (which he saluted by a special conference and address) was "understood to be strongly Communistic." [42] But he regarded the radicals as moving in the same direction that he was, and therefore useful as an auxiliary force in achieving reforms. In order to overcome the political opposition, he felt that he could ill afford to ignore any source of aid; and he was confident that he could keep control of the "progressive" coalition. Roosevelt did not court the vote of radicals, but he gained some support by his liberal policy toward them.

Still, when all is said and done, the total Communist influence in his Administration was negligible. A few radicals gained rather important positions in government departments, but there is no evidence that any policies were engineered by them which did not conform to the general aims of the Administration. And it might be added that the few "big names" who did fool the President fooled their conservative associates as well. Jesse Jones, though he had close dealings with Harry Dexter White, never suspected him of devious activities, and John Foster Dulles was a character witness for Alger Hiss. The "pumpkin papers," it must be said, made a great many people feel like pumpkin *heads*.

And there was, of course, still another side to the problem of "Reds in government." Sterner measures than those approved by Roosevelt might well have reduced subversive infiltration to *zero*. But at what price? American experience since World War II has demonstrated that a stricter program of investigation and lesser allowance for individual rights will eliminate a number of people from government service. But the climate of repression and fear which it generates may reduce substantially the effectiveness of all government workers, and turn from public service the more capable and original minds of the country. Finally, what kind of procedures for ferreting out subversives (or "security risks" and "undesirables") is *just?* How may the basic rights of the individual be protected? (The very questions have a quaint ring in today's H-bomb era.)

Roosevelt, in a frank but off-the-record discussion, explained his own attitude before a press conference in 1940. He said that the F.B.I. supplied plenty of information on individuals to indicate that they might be dangerous. But the information was usually insufficient to warrant conviction in a court of law, and it was often difficult to decide whether to discharge a person right away or keep him under surveillance. No hard-and-fast rule should be followed:

> Every case has to be determined on its merits. Let me give you an illustration: it was suggested in talking this whole subject over. . . . Just what is a Communist? Well, there are probably some people in this room that have signed Communist nominating petitions—I should not be a bit surprised. Does that make you a Communist? . . .
>
> I will give you another example: There have been a number of cases, as you know, where people are not only suspected of subversive activities but where we have probably got an open-and-shut case against them. All right. Now, it may be advisable not to arrest them but to leave them right there, because by watching them we may get information as to connections with other people. It is a matter for discussion; it is a matter for the law-enforcing agents of the Government.

A reporter then asked him what could be done about a subversive employed in a factory doing government work. He answered that if there were substantial evidence that the man threatened sabotage or were connected with "some kind of plot," there were indirect ways to secure his discharge. "But," the questioner pursued, "suppose he is merely a member of the Communist Party and they have no case on him?" To this the President replied, "It would depend upon the individual case. He might be a perfectly innocent little fellow that you would never suspect of hurting a fly." [43]

Roosevelt, in a manner that now seems quite old-fashioned, was generally averse to investigations of private lives. In 1937 he appointed Senator Hugo Black to the Supreme Court of the United States; within a few days, a nation-wide furore blew up with the revelation that Black had once joined the Ku Klux Klan. Roosevelt was no doubt embarrassed by the disclosure of this fact, previously unknown to him. Newsmen, seeking a headline at the next White House press conference, posed a leading question for him: Would he require, in the future, a Department of Justice report on each individual before announcing an appointment? He answered without hesitation:

> No, certainly not. Here is the simple way, off the record. A man's private life is supposed to be his private life. He may have had certain marital troubles which, if they came out, might be pretty disagreeable. It certainly is not incumbent on the Department of Justice or the President or anybody else to look into that, so long as it does not come out and a fellow has led a perfectly good life. . . . You must assume that the man, if he has led a decent life up to the present time, is all right. You cannot go and ask him about it. . . . You would have to investigate a man's check book and his accounts and things like that.[44]

This was Roosevelt, the Grotonian, speaking—out of a bygone era of gentlemen, when certain personal things "just weren't done"—and one man could trust another. It seems almost as remote today as the age of chivalry. But the squire of Hyde Park did not live to see the time when his kind of respect for private rights would be brushed aside by men less sensitive and more fearful than he. It was a different breed, product of a rougher school, that was to lead the American people into a changed atmosphere of human relations. The prototype was Martin Dies, whose antisubversion program was rejected by Roosevelt, but afterward became the law of the land. The "Dies Committee" proposals, a subject of bitter controversy in 1940, have since been accepted and exceeded by a resigned and hardened people: virtual outlawry of the Communist Party; loyalty pledges for all government employees; and voiding of the "outworn principle of waiting for an overt act." [45] Dies passed the torch, in the fifties, to McCarthy and McCarran; but, as he rightfully claimed, the new order and spirit were his.

This new spirit has not proved wholly triumphant. The widespread reaction against it has shown that our historic respect for the individual —upheld by Roosevelt—is potent still.

3

Government and the Economy

THE CENTRAL ISSUE of the New Deal philosophy was the relation of the State to economic life. Roosevelt believed that government had responsibility for social welfare and social justice, and that these aims were closely tied to the production and distribution of wealth. His wish to "interfere with business" was not capricious, but was the logical outgrowth of his concept of the welfare state.

It is not surprising that the New Deal provoked cries of interference, regimentation, and dictatorship. Most businessmen, farmers, and workers do not object to the *idea* of social justice, but it is another matter when government tells them what wage to pay, or how much corn to plant. The economic measures of the New Deal brought the Administration into bruising contact with the great interests of the country, as well as millions of "little fellows." It is small wonder that the government-and-business issue became a source of strife during the thirties—and left scars still visible a generation later.

General Economic Philosophy

There is a rather widespread notion that Roosevelt was ignorant on the subject of economics. He may well have appeared so to a theoretical economist, such as John Maynard Keynes—or to a practical merchant who knew that selling price must cover costs. However, Roosevelt had a better grasp of economic facts than most of his critics. He cared little about theory and the so-called "laws." But his long experience in government (as well as his short experience in business) gave him opportunity to learn about a wide variety of economic activities.

He was familiar with banking, investment, corporate structure and control, insurance, and real estate. For years he gave study to public utilities and holding companies, especially in the power field. He represented a rural district as state senator and knew from experience the problems of agriculture and forestry. While Assistant Secretary of the Navy, Roosevelt was principal business officer of the department and had extensive contacts with industry and labor. As governor and as president he encountered the mysteries of public finance and had final responsibility for fiscal administration. One has only to read through the record of his press conferences, in which he was often called upon to discuss economic affairs, to be impressed by the range and depth of his understanding. He did not know, perhaps, so much as he pretended, but he was exceptionally well informed. In an open discussion of the economic facts of life, there were few professors and still fewer businessmen who could hold their own with him.

His views seldom conformed with those of orthodox economists, who were "going by the book." This did not bother him, for in his opinion the experts "changed their definition of economic laws every five or ten years. . . ." [1] A fat file of letters in the Library at Hyde Park points up the contrasting approach of Roosevelt and the professional economist. A prominent New York banker, Fred I. Kent, accepted Roosevelt's invitation to write to him regularly about economic and business affairs. From 1933 to 1945, he sent a stream of criticism of New Deal policies. Some of these were lengthy essays, a mixture of theoretical argument and specific proposals, which the President could hardly have read in full. Occasionally, however, he dictated replies in defense of his actions. He usually explained that a given *theory* would simply not solve a particular *problem,* and on occasion he hinted that the "theoretical" approach was a devious means of putting off a solution. As he wrote Kent in 1940: "I find on the part of many of my theoretical friends in New York and elsewhere that they are wholly in favor of improved conditions, improved pay and the ending of certain abuses—but they pray to God that their ideals will not be brought about until after they have passed to the Great Beyond." [2]

While he did not believe in any body of economic laws, he saw the necessity for working concepts and an intelligible rationale of the eco-

nomic system. He knew that individual business problems could not
be approached as isolated affairs; they could be successfully dealt with
only in relation to the general system, generally understood. The numerous programs of the New Deal—for banking, industry, agriculture, labor
—were not unrelated to each other or to the whole.

Raymond Moley has written that the substance of New Deal policies
was plainly outlined in the candidate's speeches of 1932. Every important venture from 1933 to the middle of 1935 was forecast, except the
gold policy, deficit spending, and the NIRA.[3] It was during this campaign that Moley, with his team of "experts," helped Roosevelt to develop a definite plan for each problem area—to be explained in successive addresses. The speech which best revealed the candidate's general approach to the economy, and his over-all plan of reform, was that
delivered in September, 1932, to the Commonwealth Club of San Francisco. It was as "clear and unambiguous a statement of what was to
come" as Roosevelt, with all his advisers, could make it. Yet slight attention was paid at the time to this philosophic and "dull" speech of the
campaign. Some pundits would still write that Roosevelt was just a
"pleasant young man who wanted very much to become President." If
they read the Commonwealth Address, they did not give it credence.[4]

In the address, Roosevelt placed the American system in a broad context of time and place. It had opened, in politics, a new day of human
freedom, when the State was turned to the service of the individual. It
had brought a new day in economics, too, made long and splendid by
vast resources and an open frontier. So long as those conditions prevailed, there could be no serious economic trouble in America: "Traditionally, when a depression came a new section of land was opened in
the West; and even our temporary misfortune served our manifest
destiny."

The industrial revolution made possible the exploitation of the continent at an unprecedented rate. Captains of enterprise, wasteful and
ruthless, pushed forward with the aid and blessing of government: "As
long as we had free land; as long as our population was growing by
leaps and bounds; as long as our industrial plants were insufficient to
supply our own needs, society chose to give the ambitious man free
play and unlimited reward provided only that he produced the economic
plant so much desired." But the turn of the tide came with the turn of
the century. Free land was running out, and individual entrepreneurs
were being supplanted by huge industrial combinations—"uncontrolled
and irresponsible units of power within the State."

The contemporary situation looked to Roosevelt like this: "Our industrial plant is built; the problem just now is whether under existing conditions it is not overbuilt. Our last frontier has long since been reached. . . ." The opportunity to develop enterprise had narrowed; a few hundred corporations dominated the main fields of production and were expanding in power. "Put plainly, we are steering a steady course toward economic oligarchy, if we are not there already."

All this called for a reappraisal of values. A mere builder of *more* industrial plants, much as he had been needed in the nineteenth century, was now as likely to be a danger as a help. The day of the promoter was over; the task was no longer exploitation and more production, but the "soberer, less dramatic business of administering resources and plants already in hand." The giant corporations, once a servant of national desire, were now a menace. They should not, however, be broken up; they should be modified and controlled in the public interest. "As I see it, the task of Government in its relation to business is to assist the development of an economic declaration of rights, an economic constitutional order. This is the common task of statesman and business man."

The assertion in 1932 that the American industrial plant was built makes strange reading in the second half of the twentieth century. Roosevelt's view derived from his uncritical acceptance of the "frontier thesis" and failure to grasp the potentiality of capital development. By the wisdom of hindsight, his error is plain to see; but in the thirties his belief was shared by many economists and industrialists. Indeed, the "observable facts" gave powerful support to an "overproduction" theory. Wherever one looked there seemed to be more than needed: too much wheat and too many pigs; idle mills and too much steel; too many farmers, teachers, lawyers—and too many unemployed. Roosevelt was influenced by this short-run view to see the future in terms of a "limited" economy.

The demographers contributed to the mistaken outlook of the thirties by predicting a stationary population by 1960. World War II upset their calculations and radically altered the economic situation. Today we think of a dynamic production machine geared to the needs of an expanding population. But the present economy is driven by "defense" spending which, alone, exceeds the total national income of 1932! Without the war, hot and cold, the economic concepts of the thirties might seem less strange.

Roosevelt believed that the situation in his day required strong action by government. The Depression had taught that no private group, however powerful, could safeguard even its own security, let alone that of the community. What was needed, he wrote in 1934, was a complete reorganization and "measured control of the economic structure." [5] He confessed that he had not foreseen these imperative changes before 1929. Though concerned about the impact of declining farm income upon business, it was not until the crisis struck that he realized the fundamental weaknesses of the old economy.

As governor he supported measures, within the competence of state government, to deal with the deepening distress. But it soon became evident to him that effective and parallel action by forty-eight states was impossible, and that the problems of a national economy must be met primarily by the *national* government. One of the principal tasks, he became convinced, was restoration of purchasing power to the mass of consumers.

Roosevelt's "purchasing power" theory of recovery grew out of his analysis of the Depression. He believed that the crisis had resulted from the overbuilding and overselling of the preceding ten years. During that time little of the high profits went into increased wages or dividends; instead, there was a piling up of surpluses, "the most stupendous in history." These surpluses were used to build new and unnecessary plants (and for speculation in Wall Street). Productive capacity thus outran the buying power of consumers.[6] At Columbus, Ohio, in August, 1932, Roosevelt satirized the economic policies of the twenties by placing them in the familiar terms of Alice in Wonderland:

I agree that Alice was peering into a wonderful looking-glass of the wonderful economics. . . .

The poorhouse was to vanish like the Cheshire cat. A mad hatter invited everyone to "have some more profits." There were no profits, except on paper. A cynical Father William in the lower district of Manhattan balanced the sinuous evil of a pool-ridden stock market on the end of his nose. A puzzled, somewhat skeptical Alice asked the Republican leadership some simple questions—

"Will not the printing and selling of more stocks and bonds, the building of new plants and the increase of efficiency produce more goods than we can buy?"

"No," shouted Humpty Dumpty. "The more we produce the more we can buy."

"What if we produce a surplus?"

"Oh, we can sell it to foreign consumers."

"How can the foreigners pay for it?"

"Why, we will lend them the money."

"I see," said little Alice, "They will buy our surplus with our money. Of course, these foreigners will pay us back by selling us their goods?"

"Oh, not at all," said Humpty Dumpty. "We set up a high wall called the tariff."

"And," said Alice at last, "how will the foreigners pay off these loans?"
"That is easy," said Humpty Dumpty, "Did you ever hear of a moratorium?"

The only way to end this Humpty-Dumpty state of affairs was to correct the underlying imbalance of the domestic economy. The experience of the twenties had proved, thought Roosevelt, that production did not automatically guarantee consumption. The government must lead in steps toward adjustment of the economy—in such a manner that productive capacity would be matched by consumer buying power. This was admittedly a complex problem. Mere relief "handouts" and public works would not be sufficient. What was required, primarily, was the lifting of the economic condition of some "fifty or sixty million" people, whose earnings were dependent upon agriculture. When farm income recovered from the low point to which it had fallen, the market for industrial products would be restored.

Such an economic program, Roosevelt knew, could be appealingly conjoined with his political platform. For the building up of mass purchasing power also meant a "New Deal" for the poorer citizen; it meant doing something for the "Forgotten Man." As early as April, 1932, Roosevelt glimpsed this two-edged sword and grasped it by the hilt. He charged that the Republican leaders had built an economic system from "top to bottom," instead of "bottom to top." In the challenging "Forgotten Man" address, he made use of this analogy:

It is said that Napoleon lost the battle of Waterloo because he forgot his infantry—he staked too much upon the more spectacular but less substantial cavalry. The present administration in Washington provides a close parallel. It has either forgotten or it does not want to remember the infantry of our economic army. These unhappy times call for the building of plans that rest upon the forgotten, the unorganized but the indispensable units of economic power, for plans . . . that put their faith once more in the forgotten man at the bottom of the economic pyramid.

In a speech at Oglethorpe University, Georgia, Roosevelt insisted that the economic order could not endure for long "unless we can bring about a wiser, more equitable distribution of the national income. . . . In such a system, the reward for a day's work will have to be greater, on the average, than it has been, and the reward to capital, especially capital which is speculative, will have to be less."

On this point he ran into a head-on argument with many economists, financiers, and businessmen. The banker, Fred Kent, for instance, tried to persuade the President that it was the "Haves," not the "Have-nots," who created wealth and jobs. The government should encourage large returns on risk capital, because investment was the principal drive wheel of the economy.[7] But Roosevelt replied to this orthodox argument that it was exactly such a policy which had led to the smashup of 1929. He often referred to it disdainfully as the "trickle-down" theory—that profits put in at the top will trickle down to the little fellow. He favored building prosperity the opposite way—from bottom to top.

Even today the experts do not agree on the cause and cure of depressions. Roosevelt stubbornly opposed, and to some extent distorted, the "investment" theory of recovery. But his policy is considered to have been correct by at least one school of economists. According to their interpretation, productive capacity in the thirties was too far out of line with consumption ability. Large capital outlays were therefore unlikely, regardless of government attitudes, and might even have aggravated the problem. Purchasing power had to catch up before private investment could play its normal role. As John Galbraith pointed out, New Deal measures boosted the *market power* of large groups, especially farmers and wage-earners. This tended to correct the grave imbalance in the economy.

Fiscal and Monetary Policy

Roosevelt's general economic philosophy was the foundation of his ideas about fiscal and monetary policy. The government should manage its financial affairs, he thought, in such a way as to promote a stable and prosperous economy. Taxes, for example, must not fall too heavily upon consumers, for that would defeat the aim of building up purchasing power. On the question of government spending and debt, probably the most talked-about fiscal issue of the thirties, Roosevelt at first took a conservative stand. For he was, by temperament and logic, a strong and sincere advocate of a "balanced budget"; he believed that economy and efficiency were indispensable to good government. It is a striking irony that this man, who was a frugal manager in private and public life, was cast in the role of history's greatest spender.

As governor he earned the reputation of an economy-minded executive. In one of his early radio reports to the people of New York, he insisted upon a policy of limiting expenditures to current income. He held that long-term investments in roads, public works, and state institutions might properly be financed by bond issues; this conformed to the practice of private enterprise. But for current operations, the budget should balance.[8] In September, 1931, he criticized the Hoover policy of

borrowing and said that it afforded a poor example to the state governments. "I think we would be very foolish and recreant to our trust if we
should follow any such precedent." [9]

A perusal of his *Papers* during the four years in Albany provides many
illustrations of his effort to reduce spending. Some of his actions appear
picayune. He entered a personal objection, for example, to a proposal
for *per diem* compensation to the mosquito extermination commission
of Nassau County; on another occasion he eliminated a small salary
boost for the supervisors of Lewis and Madison counties. He scrutinized
personally the budgets of state institutions and sometimes vetoed such
items as a small land purchase or salary adjustment for an individual
clerk.

As candidate for president in 1932, he accepted his party's "economy"
plank with the zeal of a crusader. "For three long years," he told the
Convention, "I have been going up and down this country preaching
that government—Federal and State and local—costs too much. I shall
not stop that preaching." Afterward, in discussing the platform by radio,
he emphasized the goal of a twenty-five percent reduction in the cost of
the federal government. In words that were to mock him a few years
later, he urged, "Let us have the courage to stop borrowing to meet continuing deficits." [10]

But the worst was yet to come. In October, 1932, he gave a full dress
exposition on the budget at Forbes Field, Pittsburgh. In an effort to
reassure conservatives on his fiscal soundness, Roosevelt did something
that was rare for him: he committed himself so definitely that he left
little room for maneuver. After bemoaning the unbalanced Hoover
budgets, he discoursed at length about the burden that taxes had placed
upon individuals and business. He indicated that reducing government
expenditures and balancing the budget would be a *paramount* object
of his Administration—and that every Cabinet officer would have to give
him a personal pledge of economy. He left himself but one opening—
the budget might have to go unbalanced, "if starvation and dire need
on the part of any of our citizens make necessary the appropriation of
additional funds. . . ."

In writing an explanatory note to this speech for the *Public Papers
and Addresses,* he pointed out in 1938 that he *did* institute drastic economies during his first year in office. "The great increase in the expenditures of Government came," he wrote, "from the new extraordinary
agencies of Government created to meet the emergency, and from the
necessities of meeting the widespread needs of the unemployed. Neither
the platform nor the speech intended, in letter or in spirit, to permit the

emergency and the distress of the unemployed to go on without assistance from the Government's treasury." [11]

All of which was quite true. But what he did not mention in his note was that his concept of fiscal policy had changed substantially after 1933. He found that retrenchment worsened the deflation which was holding down the economy. Believing that recovery was his most important objective, he decided that balancing the budget must give way to larger spending. Four years after his 1932 speech at Pittsburgh, he drew a different picture of the fiscal problem:

No one lightly lays a burden on the income of a nation. But the vicious tightening circle of our declining national income must be broken. The bankers and the industrialists of the Nation cried aloud that private business was powerless to break it. They turned, as they had a right to turn, to the Government. We accepted the final responsibility of Government, after all else failed, to spend money when no one else had money left to spend.

At the same time he hastened to assure his listeners that fear of the national debt was "foolish." It would not be paid off by oppressive taxation of future generations; it would be taken care of by the increased revenue from a rising national income. "The truth is that we are doing better than anticipated in 1933. . . . The national debt today in relation to the national income is much less than it was in 1933, when this Administration took office." [12] For the rest of his years he tried to discount the weight of the debt upon "generations yet unborn." In 1939 he was explaining it as merely "an internal debt owed not only by the nation but to the nation. If our children have to pay interest on it they will pay that interest to themselves." [13] This rationalization comforted some Americans, but most of them are still worried about the debt.

Although Roosevelt had outgrown his early qualms about red ink and had learned to live with it, he did not lose his hankering to balance the budget. By 1937 he was within a step of achieving the goal, but then came a decisive reversal. The stock market break of October, 1937, according to Henry Morgenthau, was the turning point. As business activity began to spiral down into the "Roosevelt Recession," the President's advisers urged upon him two alternative policies. The one (favored by Morgenthau, Garner, and Hull) was to meet the crisis by "restoring business confidence"—through the orthodox method of balancing the budget. The other (supported by Hopkins, Henderson, Corcoran, and others) was to follow the principle of "compensatory expenditure" by government as a means of stimulating the economy. Roosevelt was temporarily undecided—to try the old way which had failed in 1932, or to try the "new" theory. Morgenthau related that the Cabinet prevailed upon Roosevelt to "reassure business." When he protested wearily that he had done this repeatedly, Morgenthau said, "Do it again."

"All right," replied Roosevelt, "I will turn on the old record."

But the fact is that business leaders made a contemptuous response to his reassurance. Consequently, Roosevelt swung to the alternative course—"priming the pump" by a resumption of deficit spending. From this time forward, he was in the camp of the "new economics." [14]

John Maynard Keynes, noted British economist, is generally regarded as the father of this school of thought. The core of his theories is that government spending should be used to balance the activity of the economy. When business is going full tilt, government should retrench and retire debt; when business is slow, government should compensate by increased expenditures and borrowing. This approach to the national budget, in place of the traditional insistence upon a balance for each fiscal year, was revolutionary in the thirties.

How much influence Keynes had upon Roosevelt has been a matter of speculation. His major study, *The General Theory of Employment, Interest, and Money*, was not published in America until 1936. It is doubtful whether Roosevelt read the book, though he talked with Keynes in 1934 and corresponded with him afterward. The politician and the economist did not quite understand each other. Nevertheless, the pragmatic method of the New Deal led to policies which *coincided* with Keynesian principles. Arthur Smithies, economic analyst for the Bureau of the Budget, has stated that the planned use of deficits as a recovery measure first began in 1938—after Roosevelt made the decision related by Morgenthau.[15]

The Annual Message to Congress, in 1939, reflects Roosevelt's developed idea about the relation of the budget to national prosperity. "We suffer," he said, "from a great unemployment of capital." In order to get enough capital at work to absorb the pool of unemployed, numerous improvements in economic understanding and practices were required. But these were long-term objectives. The instrumentality which could provide the greatest *immediate* help was "Federal investment." Bringing the budget into balance by curtailment of expenditures would tend to hold the nation down to its current income level; a boost in spending would push the national income upward. Here was a definite, though limited, statement of the "new economics." It went as far in the direction of Keynesian theory as American thought and prudence would permit at the time.

While Roosevelt came to accept the idea of deficit spending, he remained set against spending *wastefully*. He urged Congress again and again to shun "opportunist appropriations" and to provide for long-range planning of valuable public works. But in the popular mind, and in the tale of history, his penchant for sound expenditure was submerged in the larger fact of the spending itself. Roosevelt, conscious of his place in history, was aware of this. When he signed the appropriation bill for fiscal 1943, he remarked to his secretary, William Hassett, "This is the biggest appropriation bill in the history of the world—forty-three billions. . . . I shall be remembered by the historians as the great spender. What the historians won't know, what the public doesn't know now, is the enormous sums I have been able to save by careful scrutiny of bills, paring down extravagant and unnecessary expenditures. If I hadn't done that, we would have gone broke long ago." [16]

Yes, Roosevelt is remembered as a spender. He is remembered for the national debt. And, almost as if he had *invented* them, he is remembered for taxes. For the New Deal raised taxes as well as deficits. There were two reasons for this: he sought to keep revenues as high as practicable in order to check the amount of borrowing; secondly, he regarded taxation as a proper means of balancing wealth—an instrument of "social justice."

Roosevelt's philosophy of the good life and the good society was the foundation for his views on use of the tax power. Some equalization of economic condition was the only practical means of giving a fair chance to the "underprivileged." He felt, however, that the term "redistribution of wealth" did not correctly describe his aims. He drew a distinction between "old" or "accumulated" wealth and "new" wealth in the process of creation. He would not take away the old, he said, but the lion's share of new wealth should go toward raising the standards of low income families (rather than increasing the luxuries of the rich).[17]

In June, 1935, Roosevelt submitted to Congress a formal statement of his tax views. He endorsed the principle, inherent in the Income Tax Law of 1913, that levies should be made in proportion to the "ability to pay" and to "benefits received." *Income* was the best measure of both. Although various types of taxes were necessary in a balanced revenue system, income should remain the "governing principle" of federal taxation. He justified progressive rates on this ground: "Wealth in the modern world does not come merely from individual effort; it results from a combination of individual effort and of the manifold uses to which the community puts that effort." Therefore, notwithstanding the great contribution of unusual individuals, the people in the mass have helped to make large fortunes possible. As Andrew Carnegie put it, "Where wealth accumulates honorably, the people are always silent partners."

In addition to favoring higher surtaxes on large incomes, Roosevelt asked for (and got) increases in rates on estates and gifts. In support of this request, he argued that huge accumulations were not essential to personal or family security; they served only to perpetuate an undesirable concentration of control over the economic life of the nation. "The transmission from generation to generation of vast fortunes by will, inheritance, or gift is not consistent with the ideals and sentiments of the American people." He did not believe that creative enterprise would be discouraged by a heavy tax upon great fortunes; it was not a deterrent to thrift or industry, as a tax on small estates might be.

He gave special attention to taxation of corporate income and was chiefly responsible for the substitution (in 1936) of a graduated tax in place of uniform rates. In his 1935 statement to Congress, he explained his theory of federal taxation of corporations. A corporation enjoyed special advantages, conferred by the state which granted its charter and allowed it to operate within state boundaries. But the most important advantages, especially to a large corporation, came from *interstate* commerce; and the interstate character of the business protected it in some measure from the taxing and regulatory power of the states. "As the profit to such a corporation increases, so the value of its advantages and protection increases." Furthermore, the great corporations had stronger reserves and could withstand financial strain better than smaller companies. The recognized principle in individual taxation should apply as well to corporations: tax rates ought to be geared to economic capacity and advantages received.

During his press conferences Roosevelt often discussed the problem of tax evasion; he liked to tell reporters of the devices by which wealthy men and smart lawyers "beat" taxes. The tax beaters took moral refuge in the rationalization that high taxes were an offense to natural and divine law, but he insisted that their tactics were unethical and unpatriotic. Large portions of great incomes escaped taxation by one gimmick or another, he complained; and it was necessary to alter revenue laws continually in order to catch up with the ingenuity of tax lawyers. But the charges for this ingenuity came high. He once explained to newsmen that there was a big difference between tax evasion and tax avoidance. "In the latter case," he cracked, "you retain a lawyer for $250,000 who changes the word from evasion to avoidance for you." [18]

Conservative businessmen (whether or not they sought tax loopholes) were generally opposed to the New Deal tax and fiscal policies. They were also shocked (or outraged) by Roosevelt's monetary manipulations. Particularly among bankers, the "gold standard" had long been held as the holy of holies. When Roosevelt, in 1933, laid irreverent hands upon it, the inner sanctum of finance thought that the end of all might be precipitated. The repudiation of the "gold clause" in government obligations, devaluation of the gold content of the dollar, and the establishment of a stabilization fund for influencing the exchange value of the dollar—all these became highly controversial subjects in the world of finance.

Roosevelt believed that exclusive control over the monetary standard was an indispensable and sovereign power of the State. It should be a major instrument in the government's relation to the economy, because monetary control, like fiscal policy, was a means of influencing general business affairs. It was from this base of thought that Roosevelt looked at the existing gold standard. Was it actively promoting prosperity and social justice? For both of these goals, he thought, were the concerns of modern government.

According to his economic analysis in 1933, the principal need of the time was an increase in consumer purchasing power. But related to this was the enormous weight of private debts—debts accumulated when prices were high and which now were payable when prices were low. If bankruptcies and failures were to be avoided, with resulting further shrinkage of credit, something had to be done about the price level. He expressed himself frankly, in April, 1933, to his intimate friend, Colonel E. M. House. While agreeing that public confidence had been restored by his dramatic actions of the preceding month, he noted that his measures had given the country more of deflation than of inflation. "It is simply inevitable," he wrote, "that we must inflate and though my banker friends may be horrified, I still am seeking an inflation which will not wholly be based on additional government debt." [19] He was looking, of course, in the direction of Fort Knox.

His decision to "tinker" with gold was related to the theory of Professor George F. Warren of Cornell University. Warren persuaded Roosevelt that if the price of gold were raised in terms of dollars, the effect would be to raise prices in general. Here was a simple, attractive program, which he thought deserved a try. Accordingly, in October, 1933, the government began bidding up the price of gold by purchases in the open market. This experiment did not, however, achieve the desired end of raising other prices. In the following year, a different technique was attempted. After receiving authorization from Congress,

Roosevelt announced a reduction in the gold content of the standard dollar, holding in reserve the power to decrease it still further. The Warren theorists believed that this measure would do the trick. A given quantity of wheat, for example, *should* require in exchange a larger number of the "reduced" dollars—in other words, a higher price. But it did not work out that way, and after January, 1934, Roosevelt abandoned further manipulation of gold and the content of the dollar.

He did not, however, give up his aim of raising prices. He continued to search for effective methods of influencing them, seeking a level which would make debt settlements more equitable and which would bring all segments of the economy into balance. He thought that the 1929 level, for example, was too high for real estate and too low for farm commodities. The inflation must be directed and controlled as individual conditions required.[20]

This "quarterback" technique, by which he made up price plays on the snap of the economic ball, was upsetting to businessmen. They complained of uncertainty about future costs and values, and urged return to a "sound" dollar. But Roosevelt insisted that his basic price goal was clear enough and that he *had* a sound dollar. As he told Congress in 1934, "Our national currency must be maintained as a sound currency which, insofar as possible, will have a fairly constant standard of purchasing power. . . ."[21] Reporters were forever asking him if his policies might not lead to runaway inflation. On one occasion, pressed for a definition of "sound" currency, he came back with a very simple answer: "Now, the real mark of delineation between sound and unsound is when the government starts to pay its bills by starting printing presses. That is about the size of it." And he repeatedly assured newsmen that he had no intention of starting the presses; the idea was "silly."[22]

His views on money precipitated the issue of "national" versus "international" approaches to the economy. Hoover had taken the stand that the Depression was of European origin and that recovery depended primarily upon measures of international collaboration. In the campaign of 1932 Roosevelt had scathingly attacked this theory, and suggested that the Republicans were merely trying to pass the blame to foreign countries. While accepting the importance of world trade, he asserted that our central problem was *domestic* and that we should not be hampered by "internationalists" in taking necessary steps for our own relief. During 1933 he accordingly concentrated upon reforms which did not depend upon the co-operation of other countries.

A crisis of policy arose in connection with the World Monetary and Economic Conference, meeting at London in June, 1933. A number of issues, including the reduction of tariffs, was on the agenda, and great hopes of success had been built up. But it soon developed that the real interest of the British and French negotiators was in currency stabilization, and they virtually refused to consider related problems until this was settled. Roosevelt believed that since England had already devalued the pound, American interests would suffer if stabilization were achieved on the basis of current exchange rates. Furthermore, an international agreement would restrict his freedom in trying to lift the domestic price level, and he felt that inflation was essential to American recovery. He therefore balked on stabilization and urged the Conference, in a special radio message, to study what he thought were more fundamental economic measures among the nations. His statement hit London like a bombshell (the pundits called it a torpedo). It became instantly apparent that progress in international economic collaboration was now stalled. Roosevelt was pleased, rather than dismayed, by the furor. He believed that he had proved himself no "sucker" for the British bankers and that he was, in truth, putting first things first.

Throughout the thirties he pursued an economic policy which was predominantly *national* in aim and procedure. As he saw it, the major field of international co-operation lay in the reduction of tariff barriers. He believed that trade must be a two-way movement, and that America must work with other nations to achieve the advantages of enlarged world commerce. Cordell Hull's reciprocal tariff program therefore received his steady support. But while Hull tended to believe that this program, if achieved, would solve most of the world's ills, Roosevelt viewed it as only one of many facets of economic policy.

The Idea of Interdependence and Partnership

Roosevelt's long-term program for economic stabilization involved an idea more fundamental than tariffs, monetary controls, or fiscal policy. He believed that the day of unguided business competition was passed; the facts of technology and economic interdependence demanded a new era of industrial co-operation. But mere voluntarism in enterprise would not suffice; government had the responsibility to lend a directing hand. The desired relationship of government to business was therefore one of partnership.

The concept was long years developing in Roosevelt's mind. It traced back at least to the time when he was a New York State senator. In March, 1912, before the "Peoples' Forum," in Troy, the young politician made a challenging address on the idea of social co-operation. He sought the underlying cause of the "present discontent among the working classes," and found it in the sense of failure of traditional economic competition. Just as Western man had struggled for centuries to attain individual freedom, he was now groping for a solution to a new set of economic conditions. "To state it plainly, competition has been shown to be useful up to a certain point, but cooperation, which is the thing we must strive for today, begins where competition leaves off."

The new interdependence placed the individual in a changed relationship to the group. Farmers, for example, could no longer engage in wasteful soil practices, because the results injured not themselves alone, but society as a whole. The time was not far distant, Roosevelt predicted, when the government would make farmers "pay something back to the land" and institute controls over crop production. This idea, he insisted, should not be called "Un-American" or "dangerous"; the right word was "cooperation." [23]

As governor, he repeated again and again this central theme; he believed the new social fact must be clearly grasped before measures of co-operation could be placed in effect. Interdependence was the keynote of his gubernatorial Inaugural in 1929. He was cheered, he declared, by the growing willingness of citizens to aid various groups in the larger community who needed support. But this spirit represented more than humanitarianism:

It is the recognition that our civilization cannot endure unless we, as individuals, realize our personal responsibility to and dependency on the rest of the world. For it is literally true that the "self-supporting" man or woman has become as extinct as the man of the stone age. Without the help of thousands of others, any one of us would die, naked and starved. Consider the bread on our table, the clothes upon our backs, the luxuries that make life pleasant; how many men worked in sunlit fields, in dark mines, in the fierce heat of molten metal, and among the looms and wheels of countless factories, in order to create them for our use and enjoyment.[24]

More specifically, he wished to bridge the gulf between farm and city; between stockholder and laborer; between East and West, and North and South. He tried to drive home the point that each group depended for its own prosperity upon the well-being of the others. When he sponsored state aid to farmers through highways, bridges, and schools, he said the cost should not cause friction between cities and rural districts. "We are all in the same boat, and if we put too large a burden on the rural sections, the cities must and will inevitably feel the reaction, just as too heavy a burden on the cities will in the long run retard the progress and prosperity of the farms." [25]

Roosevelt held to this philosophy when he moved upon the national scene. Reporters in the White House sometimes asked this question: how could he justify the huge sums spent by the federal government (and paid for by citizens of all the states) to aid development of certain regions? The TVA, for instance, involved large expenditures and was of primary benefit to the South. Such programs were justified in Roosevelt's mind by the interdependence and mobility of the American people. A more prosperous South would provide a growing market for the products of North and West. And, as he explained at Grand Coulee Dam, the government knowingly spent disproportionate sums in areas with the greatest potential for development. "We did it," he said, "because out here in the Mountain States and in the Coast States you have unlimited natural resources; you have vast acreage, capable of supporting a much larger population than you now have." Projects, such as dams and irrigation canals, would benefit not only the people of those states, but the people of more populous areas who could move there and share in the new opportunities.[26]

Because of his lifelong belief in the need and practicability of industrial co-operation, it was natural for Roosevelt to place fond hopes in the National Industrial Recovery Act. Here was a mechanism by which the managers, workers, and consumers of each industry could, in co-operation, work out decent and sensible business plans. Here was the means by which government, representing all the people, could enter into the planning and provide the necessary enforcement. Labor exploitation, unfair competition, overproduction, and the general chaos of "rugged individualism" would be superseded by a new order of economic well-being. In signing the measure he declared, "History will probably record the National Industrial Recovery Act as the most far-reaching legislation ever enacted by the American Congress."

But serious troubles developed in the administration of NIRA. Code making was often dominated by the large units of an industry, to the detriment of smaller competitors. It was also feared that the codes were being used in a way contrary to traditional antitrust principles and laws.[27] Even more serious, however, was the fact that no agreement could be reached, by leaders in industry or government, upon fundamental economic policies. There was wide support of the general aims of NIRA, but no accepted program for over-all integration and direction of industry.[28]

While NIRA did much good as a temporary measure, and some features of it survived as permanent economic reforms, the central idea proved a failure. This was apparent even before the Supreme Court delivered the *coup de grâce* in May, 1935. The concept of government partnership with business in a self-regulated economy was, perhaps, a sound one, and it may some day return in another form. But no one in the thirties had the knowledge and technique to carry the idea through successfully.

Roosevelt himself did not lose faith in the general objective. After the court decision he was not prepared to ask for another grand experiment, but he remained convinced that his aim was sound—and that it was being realized in other more limited ways.

The Break with Business: Attack on Monopoly

The year 1935 marked a crucial turning point in Roosevelt's relations with business. Up to that time he had hoped to evolve a partnership, based on a true "concert of interest." But his disillusionment with the NIRA codes, and the mounting attacks upon him by business groups, brought a switch in his thinking. He began to feel that a change in tack was necessary for accomplishment of his social aims.

He never quite appreciated the psychology and viewpoint of businessmen. A subtle but persistent reason for this was his own social orientation. Although he sought to transcend local and class bias, it was impossible to cut it away completely. As a Hudson Valley squire, he inherited a submerged antipathy toward the profit-seeking entrepreneur. Documentary evidence for this feeling is scarce, though it is suggested in a confidential letter to Roosevelt in 1938. An intimate Hyde Park neighbor, of the same social standing, assured him that the people of the country supported him—" in spite of all the Bourgeois attack. I want to help you to prevent them from committing suicide. . . ."

Whatever his social attitude, Roosevelt thought that the attack was mean ingratitude for the "rescue" of business which he had led in 1933. His irritation was heightened by the falsity of most of the charges— that he wished to "destroy business," bankrupt the nation, or "make himself a dictator." He did not object, he said, to constructive criticism, and he knew that a politician must have a tough skin. He had one. But it wore thin under the barrage of misrepresentation. He felt that such tactics were not criticism at all, but pure abuse—"just plain, downright sabotage." [29]

As early as the Congressional campaign of 1934, Roosevelt became aware of the alignment of "vested interests" against the New Deal. It was not, however, until the following year that he was confronted with a political crisis of the first magnitude. The adverse Court decisions of 1935 threw a block across the road of reform and gave aid and comfort to his opponents. He shrewdly sensed that the New Deal, as well as his own career, was at a fateful pass. On the side of the opposition was economic power, community prestige, control of the press, and the Supreme Court of the United States. He concluded that the only chance of winning through against this formidable combination was to open a hard-striking offensive. His subsequent speeches and actions aroused "class spirit," the antagonism of the poor against the rich. His opponents did not counter with an open appeal to "class"; wealth was already on their side, and instruments of power were in their hands.

The break with business—this shift from partnership to conflict— came as a disappointment and shock to many of Roosevelt's moderate supporters. Raymond Moley, for example, deplored the turn of events and suggested that it figured heavily in his drift away from the Administration. There is no doubt, from the standpoint of social harmony, that the new direction was ominous. But Roosevelt's militant tactics proved a smashing political success. He overwhelmed Alfred Landon in the bitter campaign of 1936 and emerged confident that the New Deal program had been saved.

The program, to be sure, was somewhat changed. The NIRA was dead, and the break with business seemed complete. In place of the earlier policy of partnership with enterprise, the government now turned to the role of policeman. This shift of attitude was not quite a contradiction of his earlier theories. Roosevelt had always held that there were some situations which called for the government to "sit around the table," in collaboration with business, and other situations which required regulatory action by government, in its authoritative role. Since the area of collaboration had sharply narrowed, the principal action left was regulatory.

Roosevelt had long been conscious of the menacing trend of concentration; this was apparent in key speeches of his first presidential campaign. He was now in a mood to do something about it. In March, 1935, he had told Congress,

It is time to make an effort to reverse that process of the concentration of power which has made most American citizens, once traditionally independent owners of their own businesses, helplessly dependent for their daily bread upon the favor of a very few. . . . I am against private socialism of concentrated economic power as thoroughly as I am against governmental socialism. The one is equally as dangerous as the other; and destruction of private socialism is utterly essential to avoid governmental socialism.[30]

He made it clear that he was against not only the abuses of monopoly, but the principle of Bigness itself. During a press conference a newsman once asked him why. He replied that one reason was that when a business became too large the men at the top did not know enough about it. But more serious than this was the *control* inherent in Bigness: "We are a great deal better off if we can disseminate both the control and the actual industrial set up as a whole."

He held that too much control from one source usually led to "uneconomic concentration" of certain industries. Pittsburgh was overly dependent upon steel, Detroit on automobiles. These cities were facing the headaches that came to one-crop agricultural sections. A bad year in a single industry could cripple the economy of a great city like Detroit. The community would be sounder if it had a "group of industries." [31]

His principal objection was to the political consequences of Bigness. Speaking at Dallas in June, 1936, he asserted that free government depended upon a "line of defense" held by the yeomanry of business and industry and agriculture. Any policy which eliminated the small man and centered control in the hands of a few was directly opposed to the stability of government and to democracy itself. Later in the year, in a campaign address at Boston, he claimed that his Administration had begun the "first real offensive in our history" against concentrated wealth and monopolistic power. The steps taken included taxation of the intercorporate dividends of holding companies, graduated taxes on corporation income, and higher surtaxes on large personal incomes and estates. The New Deal had also brought under regulation the financial markets, through which "mergers and consolidations and monopolies are created with other people's money." [32]

After his triumphant re-election, Roosevelt wanted to intensify the attack. But it remained more a posture than a program. The old antitrust weapons had proved ineffectual in checking concentration, and he was unable to forge new ones. He was at grips with two of the most baffling problems of our time: how can a competitive economy be maintained, and how can political democracy coexist with economic oligarchy? In April, 1938, he placed the issues before Congress in a forthright message. He stated that the ultimate choice before the people was either to diffuse economic power or transfer its control to government. He favored the first alternative, but believed that successful means could be developed only with greater understanding of industrial policies and practices. To that end, he asked for a comprehensive economic study.

Congress complied with his request, and the Temporary National

Economic Committee (T.N.E.C.) was created a few months afterward. The Committee held lengthy hearings, directed an impressive series of analyses, and submitted recommendations for a wide range of measures. The reports were helpful in giving a clearer picture of the workings of the American economy, but the practical effects upon concentration were negligible.

The fact is that no man or nation has solved this politico-economical puzzle. Roosevelt's views and fears were well formed in 1938, but the answers eluded him. Moreover, the lengthening shadow of international aggression drew his attention to other objects. As early as the fall of 1938 (after Munich) he saw the need of building stronger internal unity—and undertook a policy of conciliation toward business. He told Anne O'Hare McCormick of *The New York Times* that the framework of the New Deal had been completed; he contemplated no more "surprises." This could only mean that the attack on Bigness had been called off—for the duration.[33] As the United States assumed its role of the Arsenal of Democracy, businessmen, on their side, became friendlier toward the White House. For Roosevelt no longer called them to task— but to arms.

Business leaders, furthermore, have themselves developed a partial answer to the problem of concentrated control. Never before has economic power been exercised with such a sense of responsibility; the "public be damned" attitude has been disavowed by a new generation of business statesmen. This enlightened view is partly the outcome of experience and education during New Deal years. It is possible that what Roosevelt could not accomplish directly, he achieved, to some degree, indirectly.

The Idea of Planning and Conservation

In another sphere Roosevelt's ideas were translated into more definite results. He said in 1934 that national planning had been one of his "pet children" for many years. It went back to the time of the Harding-Cox campaign, when he was a strenuous but unsuccessful candidate for vice-president:

During three months in the year 1920 I think I spent eighty-nine out of ninety-two days on a sleeping car. I went to forty-two states in the Union. I drove literally thousands of miles by automobile, and I got to know the country as only a candidate for office or a traveling salesman can get to know it.

In that trip, the one great impression I got of our country was that it had grown like Topsy, without any particular planning. People over a period of three hundred years had been wandering around from one section to another, opening up new territory, starting new industries, haphazardly.

And because the country was so vast, during nearly all of those three hundred years nobody seemed to suffer very much, because there were plenty of new opportunities in the way of new land and new industries available for generation after generation of our forebears. But as I went over the country I became impressed with the fact that in these latter days we had come, to a certain extent, to the end of that limitless opportunity of new places to go to and new sources of wealth to tap, of new industries to start almost anywhere, and new land to take up. I realized that the time was ripe, even overripe, for the beginning of planning—planning to prevent in the future the errors of the past, and planning to meet in the future certain perfectly obvious economic and social needs of the nation.[34]

Nine years after that tour, when he became governor, he had the opportunity to do something about planning in the most populous state of the Union. His papers during the four years at Albany show continuing interest in various types of planning and provide a backdrop for his policies in Washington. He was interested in laying out roads that would make a rational state-wide network; he promoted studies of land use and population distribution; he supported systematic resource conservation, reforestation, and park development.

After his election as president, the idea of planning formed an important part of his First Inaugural. Addressing himself to the baffling problem of unemployment, he suggested planning on a grand scale as a means toward its solution. The people must recognize the "overbalance of population" in industrial centers and engage in redistribution on a systematic basis. Necessary population and economic adjustments would be facilitated, he went on, by related plans for transportation, communication, and public utilities. Later, he recommended a special study on the impact of industrial technology. "Family, church, community, state, and all industry are subject to its influence," he declared. "Study and investigation of technological advances and their social implications constitute one of our most important American planning problems." [35]

Attempts to provide acceptable national policies on technology, population distribution, and industrial organization proved fruitless; a monument to this failure was the sepulcher of the Blue Eagle. In a more limited field, however, Roosevelt's ideas were realized with striking success. This was the area of resource conservation and development. As early as June, 1934, he appointed a National Resources Board to prepare an inventory of national assets; he later hailed its report as the "foundation for what we hope will be a permanent policy of orderly development in every part of the United States." He expressed his resource philosophy in these words: "We as a nation take stock of what we as a nation own. We consider the uses to which it can be put. We plan those uses in the light of what we want to be, of what we want to accomplish as a people." It was an error, he concluded, to say that men have "conquered" Nature. Rather, men should begin to shape their lives in greater *harmony* with Nature.[36]

Resource conservation required the construction of large works by man; it opened up what Roosevelt called an "era of rebuilding" in America.[37] He recommended to Congress in 1937 the creation of regional "authorities" in the major watersheds of the country. Their main work would be to draw integrated plans for use of water, water power, soils, forests, and other resources entrusted to their stewardship.[38] This ambitious proposal was not approved, but hundreds of conservation works were authorized and built across the face of the land. The project which best exemplified Roosevelt's broad approach was the Tennessee Valley Authority.

As the NIRA had been the object of his most serious concern, TVA was his greatest enthusiasm. For it embodied most of his ideas concerning the role of government in the life of people. It aided thousands of poor families and contributed to the economic uplifting of an entire section of the nation. TVA made giant strides in conservation of land and water and in development of recreational areas. It served, too, as a king-size test of public power and as a measuring stick for utilities. All in all, it represented planning on an unprecedented scale and a bold experiment in human engineering. On the tenth anniversary of the project Roosevelt could write in sincerity to David Lilienthal: "As I have said before, I glory in the development of this enterprise as one of the great social and economic achievements of our time." [39]

The Idea of Protection and Parity

The economic responsibility of the State, thought Roosevelt, extended not only to the development of natural resources, but to the safeguarding of its citizens. This idea was related to his aim of "social justice." He felt that some groups in society were sufficiently well off to provide for themselves, but there were others whose welfare depended upon State intervention. He believed that they could be aided by means which would strengthen the economy as a whole.

Rich and poor alike were entitled to protection in their role as consumers. Roosevelt followed the view of an earlier generation of "progressives" on the need for pure food and drug laws, meat inspection, and the like. Similarly, he believed that public utilities must be regulated to ensure adequate service and reasonable rates. On the general matter of regulation he reiterated this key point: regulatory bodies should not consider themselves as mediators between the public and the utilities; they should represent the public position one hundred percent, and act accordingly.

Few people in the thirties objected to the regulation of chartered monopolies. But cries of protest went up when the New Deal sought to extend protection of consumers to areas like the stock market. Though harboring a chronic suspicion of bankers and speculators, Roosevelt did not favor investment regulation before 1932. The Wall Street collapse brought a swift change of mind, however, and during his last year as governor he urged enactment of a "Blue Sky" law for New York. Defeated in the legislature, he took the issue with him to the Democratic Convention in Chicago. He was now convinced that *federal* regulation was the only adequate answer. In a magazine article he criticized the Hoover Administration for taking no steps to prevent unsound promotions. "The government," he wrote, "must protect its citizens against financial buccaneering. No Federal Administration can prevent individuals from being suckers, but our government has the right as well as the positive duty to dissect, for the benefit of the public, every new form of financial action." [40]

Hoover admitted later that the orgy of stock buying during the twenties was dangerous to the nation. He had met the threat with efforts of persuasion, which proved useless. Beyond that, however, he refused to go: "The initial difficulty was a lack of government authority, except such as could be exerted by the Federal Reserve System. To ask Congress for power to interfere in the stock market was futile and, in any event, for the President to dictate the price of stocks was an expansion of Presidential power without any established constitutional basis." [41]

There was not, of course, any suggestion that the President should "dictate the price of stocks," but Roosevelt pressed for regulation which would protect the buyer from deception. In his campaign address at Columbus, in August, 1932, he laid down the principles for such regulation. He called for "truth telling" about every issue of securities—its purposes and terms, condition of the issuing corporation, and the commissions and interests of the sellers.

During his first month in the White House, Roosevelt sent a message to Congress urging appropriate legislation. "This proposal," he explained, "adds to the ancient rule of *caveat emptor*, the further doctrine 'let the seller also beware.' It puts the burden of telling the whole truth on the seller." In the following year, he moved to protect the public against unsound market practices. He recommended and approved the Securities Exchange Act, which created a commission to regulate the principal exchanges. These were its aims, substantially achieved: requirement of financial information about companies whose securities were listed; prevention of stock manipulation; and publicity on all "inside" trading by corporation officers.

Protection of consumers was good as far as it went, but it did not reduce unjust disparities in group incomes. Roosevelt believed that government should lend a hand to those who were not sharing in the upsurge of national wealth. It was natural in this connection that his first concern should be for farmers. He liked to think of himself as an agriculturist, and during most of his political life he was close to farm problems. This was especially true during the twenties as corp surpluses piled up and falling prices left farmers stranded in debt.

The idea of "parity" developed in Roosevelt's mind long before it became news in Washington. He was saying in 1928, "I want our agricultural population to be put on the same level of earning capacity as their fellows Americans who live in cities." [42] Later, when seeking the presidency, he stressed the point in a major speech at Topeka. The root of the country's economic difficulty, he said, was in the lack of equality for agriculture: "Farming has not had an even break in our economic system." The articles which farmers bought cost nine percent more in 1932 than before World War I; the things they sold brought them forty-three percent *less*. Here was the kernel of an economic and moral problem which government could not ignore.

How to solve the problem had stumped the experts for over a decade. When Roosevelt came to power on the national scene, he sought widely for advice—from government specialists, farm groups, and his own brain trust. He knew that he was tackling a tough, stringy problem. Before sending his farm recommendation to Congress, he explained to reporters, "Obviously a farm bill is in the nature of an experiment. We all recognize that. My position is that we ought to try to do something to increase the value of farm products and if the darn thing doesn't work, we can say so quite frankly, but at least try it." [43] The resulting Agricultural Adjustment Act aimed, by a combination of measures, to lift prices and the economic position of farmers.

Agriculture seemed to Roosevelt to be the chief interest in need of support. With the swelling unemployment of the early thirties, however, another large group appeared to be in trouble. Labor, organized and unorganized, was his second major concern. He was familiar with the problems of wage earners; as governor he had carried forward the social legislation begun by Alfred E. Smith. But the primary aim of those laws was *minimum* protection, applying mainly to women and children. After becoming president, he began to feel that this was not enough. If industrial workers were to achieve a satisfactory standard of life, and substantial parity with other economic groups, the general level of their income must be raised.

Roosevelt was one of the first men in public life to point out that seemingly high hourly rates did not necessarily mean good annual wages. Looking back, even to experiences in Navy shipyards during World War I, he often spoke of the difference between the two. It was "what a man accumulates by December 31" that counts, he used to say. He called upon industry to spread work more evenly through the year and at least to give attention to the problem of a guaranteed annual wage. "What we want from all of you people," he said to a group of industrialists in 1936, "is realization that this thing can be worked out, and can be worked out without calling people names. Don't call the union names." [44]

It is significant that even with the interruption of World War II, he did not put aside the annual wage idea. Two weeks before his death, he opened his last White House press conference with this statement: "I think the most important thing I have [as news] is setting up an inquiry into the new question of guaranteed wage plans. As some of you know, I have been talking about it for ten years. . . . And it is only lately that the trade unions have become interested in the question. Therefore it's new." He had requested the advisory commission on War Mobilization to make a study of American experience with such plans. "You will know more about it when this commission reports." [45]

He did not intend, of course, that government should become involved in annual wage guarantees; he wished to stimulate private plans by an expert investigation of the subject. He knew that government could bolster the minimum pay of workers through measures like the Fair Labor Standards Act. But the principal means of raising earnings was by free negotiation between employers and employees. It was chiefly in this light that Roosevelt saw the value of unions. The State should not attempt by fiat to lift the general level of wages; rather, it should protect legitimate union activities, encourage collective bargaining, and promote responsible leadership in labor-management relations.

He expressed his philosophy of labor-management relations in a letter to the A.F.of L. in 1935. Industrial co-operation could best be achieved, he thought, through highly developed organization of both employers and employees. He hoped that relations might rest upon patient discussion, conciliation, and arbitration—with frank recognition of the "inescapable community of interests" within each industry.[46] He opposed legislation, litigation, and all forms of industrial warfare as a means of settling disputes; collective bargaining (in good faith) could solve the issues between capital and labor. He held that those who worked, openly or covertly, against effective bargaining power for labor were endangering national unity. They, not the union organizers, were promoting attitudes that would put industrial relations on a European "class" basis.

Roosevelt was ready to admit that there were defects in the Wagner Labor Act, which compelled employers to bargain collectively. But this did not invalidate its basic principle, or call for radical changes in the law. He observed, in a special conference with newspaper editors in 1938, that statutes in England were put on the books with full knowledge that alterations would be made "every year or so." As a basis for review, the British used the Royal Commission method, which Roosevelt admired. "If we had that temperament over here," he concluded, "we would have improved the Wagner Act this year and improved the Social Security Act this year, keeping them out of politics." [47]

Sound negotiation depended upon *responsible* leaders on both sides of the bargaining table. Yet he knew that this quality of leadership could not be attained overnight. When his attention was called to occasional union excesses, broken contracts, and flaunting of the public interest, he always gave the same answer: the labor movement in this country was young; it would have to learn through such experience; it *was learning*. This attitude applied to the nasty breach between the A.F.of L. and C.I.O., which he deplored. When asked, in 1938, where the split was leading, he replied:

> Oh, I don't know. When you get that kind of a very personal row, it will end in two wings of labor that will become fairly well established and become fairly permanent, or it may end in their working out some kind of a compromise and agreement between the two. In other words . . . this is in the evolutionary process, similar to that which organized labor was going through in other countries twenty and thirty years ago. It is evolutionary. Probably five years from now we shall not recognize or shall have forgotten the existing situation.[48]

He did not like strikes and hoped that they could be held to an absolute minimum. He understood, however, that the strike was the reserve power which made collective bargaining effective. He was also aware of the motivation behind work stoppages. In 1934, when prices and business activity were beginning to rebound from the depths of the Depression, he said to reporters: "You all know that in any period of this kind . . . you are bound to have more strikes. I look for a great many strikes in the course of this summer. . . . It is a normal and logical thing." There were many causes of strikes, he observed, other than wage demands. Sometimes they resulted from an accumulation of grievances—when workers simply got "sore" at individual business owners. The attitude of certain employers was often provocative. As an example, Roosevelt referred to a certain Toledo industrialist who reputedly had said that he would be "demeaning" himself by sitting in the same room with William Green. "Now that kind of autocratic attitude on the part of a steel company official does not make for working things out. On the other hand, there are people on the other end of the camp, the labor end, who are just as autocratic." [49] He had little patience with stoppages due to jurisdictional disputes, but hoped that the unions could end them without the necessity of legislation. If they failed to do so, however, "something will have to be done." [50]

The big strike year was 1937, culminating in the drawn battle between Tom Girdler of Republic Steel and the Steel Workers Organizing Committee, C.I.O. The issue at Republic, as at most other places, was simply union recognition. Reviewing the unhappy time, several years later, Roosevelt explained this period of strife as a time of labor's "growing pains." Subjected to exploitation in the past, the workers were beginning to feel their new power, "under the impetus of favorable legislation and a sympathetic Government." In some quarters leadership had fallen to racketeers and to irresponsible individuals, but the history of capital and of finance showed similar periods of rapid expansion and the same kind of faults. He opposed the hysterical demands for "curbs" on labor and for use of troops to put down strikes. The calling of troops, except in a national emergency, he held as dangerous to democracy. Roosevelt remained convinced that his policy of restraint during that troubled year proved, in the long run, the best for industrial relations and for the public welfare.[51]

As to the wave of sit-down strikes in 1937, Roosevelt had no illusions. He steadfastly refused, however, to commit himself in public either to approval or disapproval of the sit-down. In doing this, he was following what he believed to be the wisest course, notwithstanding legal and emotional aspects of the problem. He wanted the workers themselves to learn the obvious lesson.

He explained his strategy in a confidential session with editors and publishers. He observed that the "experience mentality" in an organization such as the United Automobile Workers was still (1937) on an adolescent level, but he felt that the strikers were beginning to recognize that the sit-down was illegal—"no question about that." What complicated the problem was the fact that their officers could tell them that their offense (technically a misdemeanor) was not nearly so serious as defying a federal statute, like the Wagner Act, as some industrial leaders were doing. Nevertheless,

They are beginning to realize that a misdemeanor is a wrong thing, and they are beginning to realize that sit-down strikes are damned unpopular, and finally they will realize that labor cannot get very far if it makes itself unpopular with the bulk of the population of the country.

It will take some time, perhaps two years, but that is a short time in the life of a nation and the education of a nation.[52]

The Roosevelt Administration, because it believed that wage earners were entitled to a higher economic status, looked benevolently upon organized labor. Roosevelt knew that gains by unions tended to raise the level of *all* wages, including those of unorganized labor. But wage rates, even annual income, were only one side of the coin. Workers wanted and needed protection against loss of income due to unemployment and old age. And this could be provided on a general basis by no union or private organization; it thus became, in Roosevelt's view, a responsibility of government. This idea was the germ of the New Deal venture into social insurance, which today is an accepted feature of our national life.

Unemployment had begun to mount while he was governor. Roosevelt saw how it sapped prosperity everywhere, making it a problem not of the individual alone, but of the whole community. He believed at first that a solution could be found by businessmen themselves. With this in mind, he appointed a committee of industrialists to recommend voluntary measures for stabilization of employment, based on "authentic American business experience." [53] When this approach failed, the Governor took care of displaced workers through state work-relief; at the same time, he suggested that some form of state unemployment insurance be devised and placed in operation for the future.

When he took office in Washington, the problem before him dwarfed what he had faced in Albany. In spite of large numbers on relief, however, he held that the economy could be so managed as to eliminate most of the unemployed in the years to come. "I stand or fall," he told the people in a Fireside Chat of 1934, "by my refusal to accept as a necessary condition of our future a permanent army of unemployed. . . . I do not want to think that it is the destiny of any American to remain permanently on relief rolls." [54] Only reluctantly did he retreat from this position. In 1937, while not abandoning hope of a solution, he advised his fellow citizens that unemployment was "one of the bitter and galling problems that now affect mankind. . . . It is a problem of every civilized nation, not ours alone. It has been solved in some countries by starting huge armament programs but we Americans do not want to solve it that way." [55] Ironically, it *was* solved that way; the choice, however, was not made by Americans, but by the Nazis.

Linked with the problem of unemployment, which Roosevelt at last accepted as chronic, was the question of income security in old age. Roosevelt had made a fighting issue of this question in New York State; he favored modest living allowances for needy old folks and the beginning of a contributory system of pensions for all wage earners. "What do the American people want more than anything else?" he asked the Democratic Convention in 1932. "To my mind, they want two things: work . . . and security." [56]

He did his best, according to his lights, to attain those goals during his tenure in the White House. While he did not solve the underlying dilemmas of the economic order, he made a start toward providing much-needed "cushions" in the system. Through the Social Security Act, individual wage earners became entitled to unemployment and old-age benefits as a matter of right. These payments not only aided them, but helped to steady the economy. Roosevelt summarized the significance of the new legislation when he signed the measure in 1935:

Today a hope of many years' standing is fulfilled. The civilization of the past hundred years, with its startling industrial changes, has tended more and more to make life insecure. Young people have come to wonder what would be their lot when they came to old age. The man with a job has wondered how long the job would last. . . .

We can never insure one hundred percent of the population against one hundred percent of the hazards and vicissitudes of life, but we have tried to frame a law which will give some measure of protection to the average citizen and to his family against the loss of a job and against poverty-ridden old age.

This law, too, represents a cornerstone in a structure which is being built but is by no means complete. It is a structure intended to lessen the force of possible future depressions. . . . The law will flatten out the peaks and valleys of deflation and of inflation. It is, in short, a law that will take care of human needs and at the same time provide for the United States an economic structure of vastly greater soundness. [57]

4

A More Perfect Union:

The American

Constitutional System

POLITICAL CONSTITUTIONS AND STATECRAFT held a special fascination for Roosevelt. Naturally, his main interest was in the American system, and his commentary upon it is the fruit of long service and reflection. Few men of the twentieth century have had the opportunity which was his: to observe, from the grass roots to the heights of power, the spectacle of American government and politics.

The Founding Fathers and the Constitution

On the river side of Poughkeepsie's Market Street, at the corner of Main, stands the brick County Court House of Dutchess. The building today attracts no more than ordinary notice, but a bronze plaque, fastened to the outer wall, calls softly to history. For on this site, in a long-departed courthouse, delegates to the New York State Convention gathered to deliberate upon the Constitution. The Federalists, led by Hamilton, argued there, in the hot summer of 1788, against Clinton and the Anti-Federalists. At long last (with "full faith and confidence" that a Bill of Rights would be adopted), the Convention voted to ratify. Thus, the participation of New York, vital to success of the federal venture, was assured. It was ever a source of pride to Roosevelt that his great-great-grandfather, Isaac, sat in that ancient courthouse and cast his vote with Hamilton.

Roosevelt identified himself and the tradition of his family with the Constitution (as with the War of Independence). He felt that he understood what the Founders were seeking. Thirteen states could not individually provide for the safety and welfare of their citizens. What was needed was a "more perfect union"—a *national* government resting upon a charter of fundamental law. The Constitution, Roosevelt believed, was the "best instrument ever devised" for this high purpose.[1]

He knew that the Framers wished to establish, and did establish, a representative government—"not democracy by direct action of the mob," but democracy "under the Constitution."[2] Having studied the record of the Constitutional Convention and the *Federalist* papers, he appreciated the task of the Framers and the compromises forced upon them. Their central problem was to create effective government, while insuring against tyranny by any man, class, or party. The division of powers between the states and the national government was in itself a protection; and as Madison shrewdly observed, the form, as well as the size, of the new republic was further assurance against faction. For triple safety, the Founders provided for "separation of powers" within the national establishment. The legislative, executive, and judicial powers were vested in independent branches—with built-in checks and balances.

While Roosevelt did not share the fears of the more conservative Fathers about possible tyranny of the people, he warmly endorsed the Constitutional pattern created in 1787. He felt, moreover, that it was a duty of the officers in each of the three branches to remain vigilant toward possible encroachments upon their assigned spheres. As governor, he fought against interference in executive functions by both the legislature and the judiciary. After a skirmish with lawmakers over control of state expenditures, which carried into the courts, he hailed the outcome in these words: "The Court of Appeals upholds in its decision the sacred time-honored principle of the separation of the judicial, legislative and executive departments of Government. Every school child has been taught that this is the fundamental division of our governmental powers. Many attempts have been made in the past to break this clear division down. The highest court of the State of New York sustains this sacred American principle. . . ."[3]

In 1929 he appreciated the ruling of the Court, but found a few years later that the justices themselves might violate the spirit of the separation of powers. During the proceedings against Mayor James J. Walker in 1932, Justice Staley of the New York Supreme Court upheld Roosevelt's prerogative to investigate the Mayor's conduct. However, in the course of his opinion, the Justice criticized the Governor's handling of the case and implied that it should have been brought before the jurisdiction of the court. In Roosevelt's view, this criticism was "altogether exterior to the Court's appropriate business," and called for an answer.

The answer was included in a special memorandum on the Walker case, prepared some months after the Mayor's resignation. In words of high dudgeon, Roosevelt insisted that he had followed the guides of conscience, reason, and legal precedent. He resented the "offensive implication" of Staley's advice and, with his Dutch definitely up, declared: "In no aspect of his own duty or decent regard for discharge of the Governor's duty could intervention by the learned Justice be permissible." He went on, returning fire with fire, to lecture the Justice upon his conduct. By expressing himself on the conduct of the proceedings, Staley had been guilty of "judicial encroachment upon the performance of executive duties." This was so, because,

His utterances could have no effect except the possible one of influencing public opinion adversely to the Executive in the discharge of the latter's duty and so bring implication of blame upon a coordinate branch of the government. It is incumbent upon public officers, under our system, to respect the constitutional division of authority and to remain within the limits prescribed for their own action. Failure to do so, if repeated, would create suspicion of intentional misuse of power.[4]

One may feel that Roosevelt was a bit overjealous and overzealous in his rebuke. Less than five years later the tables were turned, and Roosevelt was himself casting stones at a co-ordinate branch, the Supreme Court of the United States.

The Federal Idea and Practice

Perhaps the most curious feature of American government, as seen by European observers, is the federal relationship. Foreigners are confounded by our overlapping jurisdictions and the proliferation of political seats, from town hall to national capitol. Their bewilderment is due, no doubt, to the fact that Europeans have seldom reckoned with the vastness and diversity of our land and life.

The American system, with its stress upon local autonomy, was a response to the variety in colonial condition and culture. The states reflected these differences and have played a significant role in the history of the nation. Lord Bryce once declared (before World War I), at a dinner in Washington which Roosevelt attended, that the United

States government would outlive all other existing regimes. Why? Because modern conditions had brought to the world new problems requiring unknown solutions. And, while most European countries had but *one* political laboratory in which to operate, the Americans could experiment in forty-eight. Out of these trials and errors, thought Bryce, national remedies would be successfully evolved.

Roosevelt often recounted Bryce's observation.[5] He had a strong feeling for the individual states and abhorred the notion of unitary government for America. He believed that the existence of separate states gave elasticity to our institutions and permitted peaceful accommodation wherever it was needed. As governor he told the legislature in 1932 that this happy condition contrasted with the political rigidity of many other countries, where "reconstruction has been possible only by revolution." [6]

There was a price for all this. Successful operation of the federal system required a high degree of tension—to hold in balance the state and national powers. Officials in Washington and in state capitals had to remain jealously on guard; relaxation might open the way to usurpations by one authority or the other. And the line between the two could never be fixed, because the welfare of the American people required a moving equilibrium, adjusted to changing conditions. In 1861 the tension within federalism erupted into Civil War, and the soul of Lincoln was tried in preserving this "last, best hope on earth." The Union was saved by his heroism and the blood of brothers, but the tension over State rights remained—persisting in countless forms to the present day.

Roosevelt endorsed Lincoln's theory that the Union was a perpetual compact, created by "We, the People," and not subject to nullification by individual states. On the question of national-state relationships, however, he was less definite. The record shows that his point of view was not constant and may be divided between two periods of his career. During the governorship he appeared as a vigorous spokesman for State rights, whereas in the presidency he personified the idea of a powerful central government. (The campaign of 1932 may be seen as a transition between the two periods.) It can be argued that there was no change in his theory at all—that Roosevelt simply bolstered whichever authority he happened to hold. This would have been natural and was no doubt partially true. But there was a genuine shift of view, too, and it resulted from his education in office.

In 1929 Roosevelt was lamenting the gravitation toward Bigness in America—in industry, education, and government. At Hobart College he praised the small school as a symbol against the trend. He urged students, and young people everywhere, to enlist in a crusade against the growing centralization of authority in Washington. They had the right to tolerate this drift if they wished, he declared, but "Every previous great concentration of power has been followed by some form of great disaster." [7]

A month later, in an address to the Conference of Governors, Roosevelt again emphasized the theme of State rights. He attributed the historical success of American democracy to the fact that the individual states had zealously guarded their sovereign prerogatives. "But there is a tendency, and to my mind a dangerous tendency, on the part of our national government, to encroach, on one excuse or another, more and more upon State supremacy. The elastic theory of interstate commerce, for instance, has been stretched almost to the breaking point to cover certain regulatory powers desired by Washington." [8]

Yes, that was the voice of Roosevelt in 1929—not Hoover or the American Liberty League in 1936. The Governor believed that the remedy was to revitalize state government, for he conceded that much of the trend toward concentrated power in Washington resulted from local defaults. When health, education, and welfare were inadequately managed under home rule, the people naturally turned to the central authority. That was the "easy" way; but good government called for action, whenever possible, by the political unit closest to the people. The states must regain the initiative and demonstrate the will and ability to satisfy modern needs.

Pursuing this theme in a radio speech of 1930, Roosevelt said that preservation of home rule was a "fundamental necessity" to the life of the nation. He pointed, for illustration, to the mining states of the Rockies, the fertile savannas of the South, and the prairies of the West—each with problems that have no existence in the others. "It must be obvious," he concluded, "that almost every new or old problem of government must be solved, if it is to be solved to the satisfaction of the people of the whole country, by each State in its own way." [9]

Later, he was sensitive to the charge that he had reversed his position after entering the White House. In the Introduction to his *Public Papers and Addresses* (written in 1938), he endeavored to square what he had preached as governor with what he practiced as president. He admitted that he had spoken on many occasions in favor of home rule. He held, however, that his stand applied only to problems which could be handled properly by state legislation. It was not inconsistent, he argued, with his support of federal legislation on "such subjects as cannot be adequately and properly dealt with by forty-eight States separately." [10]

But the fact is that he changed his mind considerably as to what subjects belonged in the latter category. After coming to Washington he discerned the national scope of many matters that once seemed local, and he grasped more fully the impact of recent technological advance. By 1936 he saw that the major social and economic problems of his day raced across state lines; they were "reflected with the speed of light" from border to border.[11]

Constitutional Growth and Interpretation

Roosevelt believed problems of national scope called for solution by the national government. And he was confident that the national government could fulfill its new responsibilities within the framework of the Constitution. The Founders had been wise enough to foresee that circumstances would change in the future as surely as they had in the past. They therefore prepared a charter suitable to their particular needs, yet broad enough to meet the requirements of generations to come.

Amendments to the Constitution were one means of keeping it up to date, but Roosevelt did not view this as a sound general practice. The document was not a mere compilation of statutes, requiring change to meet every passing situation. It was fundamental law, and its flexibility was inherent. A long list of amendments would transform the character of the document and make it rigid and awkward as a governing instrument.

The major growth of the federal Constitution was achieved, properly, by *interpretation*. Its broad, even vague grants of authority were constantly reviewed as the basis for fresh legislation and executive acts. The "interstate commerce" clause, for instance, had a different concrete application in each generation from 1800 onward. As Roosevelt wrote to Carroll Miller, Chairman of the Interstate Commerce Commission,

I am reliably informed that . . . the founding fathers . . . were wholly ignorant of the terms "railroads" and "automobiles," for the very good reason that the first did not come into existence until half a century later, and the second were not manufactured until over a century later. The Interstate Commerce Commission is, indeed, fortunate that interpretations of our charter of liberties have allowed it to function during the past half century, through recognition of the fact that an obviously national need can be met only through obviously national action.[12]

Few statesmen or political theorists have denied the principle of constitutional growth through interpretation. But there has been a wide difference of opinion as to how strict (or liberal) the construction should be. There is no doubt that Roosevelt, after becoming president, represented an extreme degree of liberal interpretation. And he knew that, for practical purposes, there were *two* constitutions—the one which he saw and the one seen by a strict, legalistic mind. After his Second Inauguration (which occurred only a few weeks before release of his Court Reorganization plan) he confided to Samuel Rosenman, "When the Chief Justice read me the oath and came to the words 'support the Constitution of the United States,' I felt like saying: 'Yes, but it's the Constitution as I understand it, flexible enough to meet any new problem of democracy. . . .'" [13]

Because his kind of Constitution was so elastic, Roosevelt never felt the need for appealing to a "higher law," as did Seward in the crisis over slavery. Facing the Depression emergency, he declared in his First Inaugural:

Our Constitution is so simple and practical that it is possible always to meet extraordinary needs by changes in emphasis and arrangement without loss of essential form. That is why our constitutional system has proved itself the most superbly enduring political mechanism the modern world has produced. It has met every stress of vast expansion of territory, of foreign wars, of bitter internal strife, of world relations.

Later, he could take time for a more explicit analysis. He found the occasion in March, 1937, during the fight over reform of the Supreme Court. In a carefully prepared Fireside Chat, he drew attention to the Preamble. The leading purposes stated there, plainly and simply, were to form a more perfect union and to promote the general welfare. The powers assigned to Congress to carry out those purposes were not enumerated by Roosevelt; he preferred to sum them up in this way: "they were all the powers needed to meet each and every problem which then had a national character and which could not be met by merely local action." He believed that the Framers provided for future unforeseen problems by granting to Congress broad powers "to levy taxes . . . and provide for the common defense and general welfare of the United States." He quoted those words from the Constitution itself; but, by omitting the phrase, "to pay the debts" (as indicated by the ellipsis), he altered the construction and meaning of the clause as a whole. He thus gave the impression that a grant dealing solely with *tax* powers included *general* powers as well. [14]

This was, to say the least, a careless interpretation of the authority delegated to Congress. Roosevelt was no doubt aware of this misreading and never insisted upon using the tax clause as ground for "general" legislation by Congress. A better, more rounded statement of his view was given in his Constitutional Day Address, in September, 1937. A lawyer by training, he shunned the lawyer's approach to the great charter:

> The Constitution of the United States was a layman's document, not a lawyer's contract. *That* cannot be stressed too often. Madison, most responsible for it, was not a lawyer; nor was Washington or Franklin, whose sense of the give-and-take of life had kept the Convention together.
>
> This great layman's document was a charter of general principles, completely different from the "whereases" and the "parties of the first part" and the fine print which lawyers put into leases and insurance policies and installment agreements.
>
> When the Framers were dealing with what they rightly considered eternal verities, unchangeable by time and circumstance, they used specific language. In no uncertain terms, for instance, they forbade titles of nobility, the suspension of habeas corpus and the withdrawal of money from the Treasury except after appropriation by law. With almost equal definiteness they detailed the Bill of Rights.
>
> But when they considered the fundamental powers of the new government they used generality, implication and statement of mere objectives, as intentional phrases which flexible statesmanship of the future, within the Constitution, could adapt to time and circumstance. For instance, the Framers used broad and general language capable of meeting evolution and change when they referred to commerce between the States, the taxing power and the general welfare.

"So we revere it," he concluded, "not because it is old but because it is ever new, not in the worship of the past alone but in the faith of the living who keep it young, now and in the years to come."

The Supreme Court Crisis

After his astonishing triumph of November, 1936, Roosevelt had returned to the White House with a new lease of power. The Second Inauguration saw him at the height of his prestige, influence, and audacity. With an overwhelming mandate behind him, it seemed that nothing could stop the onward roll of his New Deal. Yet, only six months later, the Democratic coalition was rent; Roosevelt had suffered a humiliating defeat by his own party; and the brightness of his armor was tarnished. The political opposition, heartened by this surprising turn, redoubled their attack upon him and his program.

All this was the price—a high price—for a war over the Constitution. He joined battle, knowing his forces to be at high strength, and knowing that the casualties would be heavy. For the adversary was the most formidable one in American political life: the Supreme Court of the

United States. And it appeared, on the surface, that Roosevelt's sacrifices proved vain because his plan for reorganization of the Court became stymied in Congress. Deeper examination, however, indicates that he *did* win his strategic objective, and the victory was vital. Roosevelt himself believed that the year of the Supreme Court fight, 1937, "marked a definite turning point in the history of the United States." If the judiciary had continued to block essential reforms, American democracy might have given way to "some alien type of government." For that reason, he wrote in 1941, the outcome of the Court battle ranked among the most significant achievements of his first two terms.[15]

He may have exaggerated the crucial nature of the issue. But it is certainly true that over a period of years the Court and the elective branches of government had moved to an impasse. There was, indeed, a Constitutional crisis: whether the judiciary, in defiance of executive leadership, legislative enactment, and public opinion, could stand unmoved upon a narrow interpretation of fundamental law.

Between January, 1935, and June, 1936, the Court struck down a series of key enactments in the field of industry, agriculture, and labor. Some legislation, it is true, was spared; but when it is considered that the New Deal program had to function essentially as a whole, the full damage of the Court decisions can be understood. What was ominous to Roosevelt and his followers was the language of the decisions. While new laws could have been drawn to meet most of the specific legal objections, the majority of the Court had taken a firm stand against the basic idea of national solutions to economic problems. It was not a matter of patience and more skillful draftsmanship. As Roosevelt explained, "the whole question of the power of the federal government to handle these problems in an effective, decisive way had been placed not only in doubt, but in positive jeopardy."

Beyond that issue loomed another, equally vital one: the nature of the Constitution and the American political system. For the Court decisions, in Roosevelt's belief, abrogated the principle that an act of Congress must not be disturbed by the judicial branch, "unless the act was beyond all reasonable doubt unconstitutional." The Court had brought about "a complete breakdown of the system of government by three independent but theoretically cooperating branches."[16]

He pondered the problem and the most effective way of dealing with it. His conservative advisers, hoping to pass around the crisis, counseled that he do *nothing* about it. Roosevelt's personal popularity was high; his name was magic over the land. Why not play the role of national Hero, and pass the blame for evil consequences upon the Court? It was in this vein that Norman Davis wrote to him in June, 1935 (just a week after the NIRA had been declared unconstitutional). "I hope that you don't try to make an issue of constitutional reform," he warned, "for I fear it would be the only thing now on which you could lose." He thought that "real recovery" was taking place and that Roosevelt should simply sit back and watch it. If he did that, Davis concluded, "the opposition wouldn't have a foot on which to stand." [17]

But Roosevelt would not back away from a fight on this issue, and he did not agree with his friend's analysis of the economic situation. "Things are not so well economically and socially as they appear on the surface," he replied to Davis. In the long view, it would be wiser to *use* his present political strength in an effort to insure better economic conditions for the future. "These are reasons," he concluded, "why a campaign of inaction would be bad for the country as well as for the party!" [18]

Thus, in June, 1935, more than eighteen months before submitting the Court reorganization plan, Roosevelt confidentially implied that he would act. What he would do, and when, remained a guarded secret. Not so guarded were his comments on the actions of the high tribunal. He declared that the NIRA decision was one of the most important ever made—more important than any since the Dred Scott Case. The key point was the narrow definition given by the Court to "interstate commerce" as a source of Congressional authority. If the commerce clause were sliced down by an obsolete interpretation, the power of government to act effectively in economic affairs would be virtually paralyzed. "The whole tendency over these years has been to view the interstate commerce clause in the light of present-day civilization," he told his press conference. The country was in the "horse-and-buggy age" when that clause was written, and by the Court decision, "We have been relegated to the horse-and-buggy definition of interstate commerce."

"Can we use the direct quotation on that horse-and-buggy stage?" asked one reporter, quick to spot a catch-phrase.

"I think so," replied the President.[19]

Within minutes, "horse-and-buggy" was on the wires; and, jerked out of context, it became a potent weapon in the war of words about the Court.

By the end of 1936 Roosevelt was convinced that he must tackle the Court head-on. During the presidential campaign he did not make a leading issue of the problem. But he believed that his decisive re-election signaled beyond doubt that the American people wanted the New Deal program. As popular leader, his responsibility now seemed clear. He would meet the challenge of the Court to the will of the majority.

Two main courses of action lay open to him. He might support some kind of constitutional amendment as a means of removing the impasse, or he could recommend legislation. He rejected the former possibility for these reasons: there was insufficient time, and ratification could be too easily blocked. "Therefore," he explained afterward to reporters, "we came down to the other category, which was legislation." Out of a great many proposals, he selected the one which seemed most effective and at the same time was clearly constitutional.[20]

On February 5, 1937, he solemnly read a message to Congress, discussing and transmitting a plan for reorganization of the judicial branch. There had been no advance notice or rumor of the spectacular content of this message. Although he discussed at length the need for speeding the work of the lower federal courts and for reforming various procedures, the core of his proposal was aimed at the Supreme Court itself. He proposed that the high judges be allowed to retire (at age seventy) on full salary, as lower court judges were already entitled to do. But—and here was the lever—a *new* justice would be appointed for every one on the bench who passed retirement age. The old judge could stay or leave as he pleased, but in either event the President would appoint another justice.

The message was met by stunned silence—then uproar. The Supreme Court had become sacrosanct in American tradition, and even Roosevelt's supporters fell into division over this proposal. In theory, as Roosevelt insistently argued, a solid case could be made for the principle of his plan: a younger Court could do more work and might be more in step with the times. But these arguments, as well as the associated recommendations for lower court reforms, could not mask the heart of the matter. In the circumstances his plan appeared to be an expedient by which one branch of government sought to circumvent one of the historic checks of the Constitution. Since six of the nine high judges were past seventy at the time, adoption of the measure would have allowed the Executive to dominate the Court through new appointments. It was a constitutional plan, and not inherently unsound, but it appeared to the American people as a disingenuous strategem. It was quickly named the "Court Packing" plan, and the label stuck.

A bitter fight ensued in Congress and the country, with some prominent Democrats leading the attack upon the proposal. (Republicans could lean back and enjoy the struggle.) At last, in June, 1937, the Reorganization Bill was reported unfavorably by the Judiciary Committee of the Senate. The contest, for all practical purposes was ended—with apparent defeat for the President.

But meanwhile things had been happening across the plaza from the Capitol—in the halls of the august Court itself. In a series of historic decisions, from March through June, 1937, the liberal interpretation of freedom of contract, interstate commerce, and the tax power became the majority opinion. According to Roosevelt, "The Court yielded. The Court changed. The Court began to interpret the Constitution instead of torturing it. It was still the same Court, with the same justices. No new appointments had been made. And yet, beginning shortly after the message of February 5, 1937, what a change!" [21] The new front on the old Court undermined support for Roosevelt's reorganization plan, but it meant fulfillment of his basic objective.

He was willing to let historians draw the ultimate conclusions as to why the Court shifted to a liberal interpretation. For his own opinion, he thought in December, 1937, that the election of 1936 had been the principal influence on the justices.[22] But in a later view (1941) he considered that the decisive cause was the "frontal attack" which he had launched on February 5, 1937.[23] The fact of overwhelming importance, as he saw it, was that the Court crisis had been resolved. He frankly admitted that he "lost the battle." But he had "won the war."

Skeptics might cast doubt upon Roosevelt's frequent assertions of victory in the Court fight. It is seldom good politics to admit defeat, and Roosevelt was probably the most reluctant man in America to confess that he was beaten. Even as a boy at Groton, he always wanted to win. When his team lost the "Big Game" to St. Mark's in 1899—by the margin of the extra point-after-touchdown—he wrote to his mother that the score did not in the least prove St. Mark's superiority. Groton had played as well, if not better, and had gained more yardage. Years later, at the peak of manhood, he was tragically stricken with paralytic polio. His response, through anguish, was characteristic: "I'll lick this thing!"

Yet there is reason to believe that Roosevelt's assessment of success in the Court issue was more than bravado; it is likely to be sustained by the judgment of history. The eminent Constitutional scholar, Edward S. Corwin, has concluded that the Court indeed reversed itself. Beginning in the spring of 1937, he observes, the justices approved a new line of power for the central government in dealing with nation-wide social problems. The *laissez-faire* approach of earlier decades was definitely dropped in favor of increased government intervention, greater concentration of authority in Washington, and more power for the Chief Executive. The switch was accomplished, Corwin explains, by a facile means within the prerogative of the Court. The high judges chose, "among the formulas, rules, or devices of constitutional law . . . those . . . which favored New Deal legislation. . . ."[24] (Actually, this was easily done, as the majority simply adopted the legal guides which a minority of the Court had developed over a period of years.)

Corwin points out that the reversal of the Court's view was the result not of events in the New Deal era alone, but of a trend going back to about 1890. The actual shift was precipitated, however, by Roosevelt's proposal for judicial reorganization. It is Corwin's opinion that Chief Justice Charles Evans Hughes was mainly responsible for the Court's response to Roosevelt's threat. Hughes exercised his influence to shift the position of the majority. In doing so he was prompted by two considerations: his wish to preserve judicial independence, and his fear that chaos would ensue if the national government lacked power to meet critical problems.

So Roosevelt's view of the Constitution, the Court, and American democracy prevailed. He did not succeed in imposing an organic alteration upon the Court, and he was not certain, therefore, that his effort had achieved a permanent solution to the problem. It appears probable that his campaign will have enduring effect. Though his proposal was at the time thought improper and was, happily, turned down, the Court was taught a crucial lesson. It should prove as lasting as that taught by Herbert Asquith to the British House of Lords. When the Lords blocked the Parliament Act in 1911, the Prime Minister threatened to ask the King to create enough new peers to carry the measure. The pressure of this "packing" plan (English style) induced the Lords to yield to the will of the people.

5

The People's Choice:
The Presidency

No MAN BUT ROOSEVELT has been elected president more than twice; no other has served longer than two terms. Under the Twenty-second Amendment to the Constitution, none will have the chance to equal his tenure as president.

Although he knew much of the judicial and legislative branches of government, Roosevelt was pre-eminently a specialist in the executive process. Counting his service as Assistant Secretary of the Navy, he spent twenty-four years in the executive branch—including sixteen as Chief Executive (of state or nation). His long hold on the presidency and the drama of history enabled him to know that office from alpha to omega. It has been said, rightly, that "a President is many men," and Roosevelt played every role.

Conception of the Office

When he was inaugurated in 1933, he had a well-developed conception of the presidency. As a child he had once sat on Grover Cleveland's knee. His first vote for president was for his dynamic relative, "Uncle Ted." As Assistant Secretary, he served with enthusiasm under Wilson. He deeply admired these three, and they formed in his mind a highly personal, composite model of what a president should be.

Cleveland, Theodore Roosevelt, and Wilson were Chief Executives of the "strong" type. These were men whom Franklin had seen and known, but he was aware that their idea of the office was inherited from earlier times. The development of the presidency had been left open by the Constitution; it stated simply, "The executive power shall be vested in a President of the United States of America" (Article II). Washington, by personal example, set the mold: a Chief Magistrate, dignified, restrained, and above faction. But even before the close of his Administration, it became evident that the office could not remain insulated from partisan contention. It was soon to become the most sought-for prize in American political life.

Jefferson leaned toward the idea of legislative primacy, and as president he usually deferred to Congress. With his left hand, however, he exercised (as party chief) a controlling influence over the legislative branch—thus combining in his person a powerful leadership. His immediate successors, men of lesser force, were unable to play the dual role; as a result the presidency fell to a subordinate position, and Congressional leaders became dominant. It was Jackson who overturned this order of things. His election in 1828 signaled a new epoch; he assumed the position of leader of the "democratic" section of the community against the business and landed "elite." The majority instinctively looked to him, rather than Congress, for protection and advancement.

After the retirement of "King Andrew," Congress resumed the upper hand for the balance of the nineteenth century. (Lincoln was a "strong" type, but he was a *war* president; Cleveland reasserted executive independence, but hardly in the positive manner of Jackson.) One of the critics of this period of "Congressional government" was Professor Woodrow Wilson, who believed that the leadership provided by legislative committee chairmen was inadequate for a great nation like the United States. At the turn of the century, Theodore Roosevelt began the kind of aggressive leadership which Wilson thought was needed. In the spirit of Jackson, the "first Roosevelt" felt that he embodied the popular will, and that therefore he should do anything, not expressly forbidden to him, that would serve the public interest.

Wilson was prepared to carry on in the same tradition when he came to the White House in 1913. The president, he believed, could be as influential as his capabilities would permit. He was the only spokesman for *all* the people; and having once gained public confidence, he was in position to supply irresistible leadership. Though his Republican successors reverted to the concept of the "weak" executive, Wilson's exercise of presidential powers was a lasting contribution to American political practice.

While a difference of opinion persists regarding *how* strong the modern president should be, it appears that this general conception of the office has taken hold. Popular government and truly national leadership requires that the Chief Executive play an active role in sensing and guiding the public will. Franklin D. Roosevelt subscribed wholeheartedly to this idea. He conceived, further, that under the separation of powers, someone should assume the initiative in co-ordinating the branches of government; he agreed with Wilson that "leadership and control must be lodged somewhere." The White House appeared to both men as the logical and rightful place.

Presidential Roles and Functions

When Roosevelt regarded the presidency, he thought of the wholeness of its powers. For it was through a combination of roles that the President was able to give the nation effective and responsible leadership. He was, of course, the Chief Executive, which, in the narrow sense, means administrator of the federal departments. In addition, the Constitution assigned to him a legislative function, which an aggressive President could readily exploit. He was, too, Commander-in-chief of the armed forces, with uncharted powers in time of war. As Chief of State, the President conducted foreign relations and was the symbol of national strength and character. Finally, there was his extraconstitutional role as *vox populi:* the chosen instrument of the people's needs and aspirations.

In evaluating Roosevelt's service as president, most observers seem to agree that he was least successful in the role of administrator. Even among his admirers there is admission that his philosophy and practice of administration left much to be desired. Pundits described Washington, in the heyday of the New Deal, as a "madhouse," a "merry-go-round," or "alphabet soup." During the war there was further grumbling about divided authority, offices without men, and men without offices. How much of this was due to the exigencies of the times and to inexperienced personnel? How much may be traced to inadequacy on the part of the Chief Executive himself?

As governor and as president, Roosevelt gave substantial attention to administrative detail and repeatedly stressed the importance of efficiency in government. He often held up the example of New York State, where over one hundred separate agencies had been consolidated (by Alfred E. Smith) into some twenty departments, reporting to the governor. He tried to make a similar overhaul of the federal administration, but Congress balked at giving him the necessary authority. Within the limits allowed, Roosevelt made some important executive reforms. He knew, however, that effective administration requires more than a sound *structure,* for "Government is not a machine, but a living organism." [1]

Here, indeed, was the core of Roosevelt's philosophy of administration. He saw government, with its millions of public servants, as a pulsating, creative instrument of a free people. The managerial experts, who taught from the book, were likely to regard Roosevelt's methods as haphazard and inefficient. Perhaps they were right. He did not always follow "straight-line" administration, in the manner of the military. But his technique, evolved from long practice and deliberation, was related to a unique human enterprise. The problem of administration in government cannot properly be compared to that of an army, of a business, or of any private undertaking.

A peculiar handicap which Roosevelt faced in building a successful administration was the paucity of able executives ready to serve his cause. As Raymond Moley remembers,

> We stood in the city of Washington on March 4th like a handful of marauders in hostile territory. . . . The Republican party had close to a monopoly of skillful, experienced administrators. To make matters worse, the business managers, established lawyers, and engineers from whose ranks top-drawer governmental executives so often come were, by and large, so partisan in their opposition to Roosevelt that he could scarcely be expected to tap those sources to the customary degree.[2]

A reform wave like the New Deal seemed to attract men of another sort—amateurs, world-savers, and *prima donnas.* Such men were often of high individual quality—even genius. But they were not always of balanced temperament, easily molded into a smooth-working, professional team. To appreciate this, one has only to survey the New Deal memoirs, or to reflect for a moment upon several of the best-known personalities—Ickes, Hopkins, Wallace, Richberg, and Johnson. But Roosevelt had to take his material as he found it and hold it as he could. He had no power, like that of a corporation president, to purchase talent at whatever price; or, like a general, to keep his subordinates under discipline.

The New Deal memoirs are a principal source for the notion that Roosevelt was a poor administrator. Each author tended to regard his own show in the Administration as the main one, and complained that the President did not always see it that way. Some, like the irascible Ickes, were more peevish on this score than others. But the limitation upon all of these accounts is that no subordinate was ever in a position fairly to judge the Chief. Each adviser saw the President from a restricted angle: labor (Perkins), conservation (Ickes), relief (Hopkins), loans (Jones), or party regularity (Farley). As General Marshall has remarked, all theater commanders suffer from "localitis"; each believes that the war will be won or lost in his theater alone. This is a desired spirit in a field commander or a subordinate; but in a sense, it is the job of the Chief of Staff (and President) to frustrate their commanders and department heads—and so gain the over-all objective.

Roosevelt's advisers and aides often felt frustrated. Marriner Eccles has written that they frequently found their conferences with the President unsatisfactory—subject to interruptions or inattention on his part to the problems which weighed so heavily upon them. But in retrospect, Eccles found a perspective that eluded some of his colleagues: "When I recall the din in which he lived as we vied for his support and attention, I marvel that he was able to see, not just single administrators, but the world; that he was able to fill not just one role of the Presidency, but all its roles." [3]

Henry Stimson conceded that Roosevelt's general direction of the war was good, but grumbled about his administrative practices. He found most objectionable the absence of clear-cut lines of authority among executives in the government, which sometimes resulted in nasty disputes over jurisdiction. The President was at fault, he thought, because he often "placed his bets on two subordinates at once." [4] Donald Richberg confirmed this "fault." He wrote that Roosevelt repeatedly made assignments in such a way that he could double-check his administrators. Richberg, as general counsel for the National Recovery Administration, reported to *both* Roosevelt and Hugh Johnson (the Administrator). [5]

One reason for the President's method is suggested in the example cited by Richberg. Roosevelt did not have complete confidence in Johnson. In other situations, where he found it distasteful or politically unwise to fire an administrator, he might divide the power with another man in whom he had more faith. But there was a deeper reason for his reluctance to delegate exclusive or final authority. It reached to the center of his concept of office and his understanding of human nature. He viewed the presidency not as an administrative job, primarily, but as a place of high *political leadership*. He could not assign, and dismiss from thought, functions of importance to the American people. He must look personally to their needs and desires—and keep in his own hands the power of decision on vital matters. Harding might entrust the Treasury to Mellon and the Department of State to Hughes. But this did not

fit Roosevelt's idea of presidential responsibility. It was tacitly understood by those in his Administration that questions of policy required
his approval.

His precise mode of procedure was flexible. He might accept the
policy proposed by a subordinate, without change; he might restate a
policy, leaving details to the department; or he might approve a policy,
but order new details. The method depended upon his relation to the
subordinate and his confidence in him, the nature of the problem and
his knowledge of it, and the elements of time and pressure that bore
upon him. For Roosevelt there could be no cut-and-dried method of
decision, no copybook rule for running the government of the United
States.

He believed, too, in the old-fashioned American principle of competition—especially the competition of ideas. He found that two or more
men, approaching the same problem from different points of view, gen-
erated more ideas for solution than did a solitary individual. His advisers were often discomfited to learn that a "special" assignment was
in fact shared by others, but the information usually spurred them to
greater efforts to outthink their rivals. A few men, it is true, quit the
President because of such tactics. But the large result was a free-for-all
atmosphere of ideas, in which no adviser had a sacred or reserved prov-
ince. His was a technique, trying upon subordinates, which pressed
them to great exertions.

Roosevelt had little faith in the old-line departments when it came to
meeting new and challenging problems. For this reason he usually favored creation of special boards and commissions to administer key programs of the New Deal and the war effort. He was convinced that the
departments were too much bound by red tape and fear of irregularity
to act quickly and successfully. Stimson objected to the independent
agencies, preferring that all government functions be under the supervision of Cabinet officers.[6] The President agreed with this as an administrative principle and desired to have the boards report to him
through the departments. He would keep them free, however, in their
mode of operation.

In addition to creating boards for special purposes, Roosevelt sometimes by-passed regular departments and channels in other ways. Secretary Hull, though satisfied in his general relationships with the President, resented direct communications between the White House and
his Undersecretary, Welles. Hull was also miffed by the activities of
Roosevelt's special representatives abroad, who reported directly to
the President, rather than through the State Department. But these

means fortified Roosevelt's power of decision and furthered the implementation of his policies.

Henry Morgenthau recounted, as an illustration, his work for the President preliminary to recognition of the Soviet Union. Why was Morgenthau, rather than the State Department, asked to make these overtures? The answer is that influential officers in the State Department were unsympathetic toward recognition. Roosevelt believed that the venture would enjoy a better prospect if entrusted to a close personal friend, who would loyally carry out his wishes.[7] Every Chief Executive is, in a sense, the prisoner of a vast bureaucracy and the political appointments he is obliged to make. He does not have the freedom, enjoyed by top corporation executives, to hire and fire freely— and so to build his *own* official team. Two basic choices are therefore open to him: he can plod along within the official framework and lay claim to "regularity" in administration—or he can jump the traces when necessary and get results by "irregular" methods.

Roosevelt did not shrink, because of compunctions about orthodoxy, from following the course he thought best as to *ends*. He could, indeed, be his own Secretary of State, Navy, or Treasury. For, as Chief Executive, he had the ultimate responsibility and chose to exercise the corresponding power. The consequences of this approach to administration may be judged in the perspective of Harold Smith, Director of the Budget from 1939 to 1946. During those years he was associated with the President in managing the federal establishment, and he regarded him at the time as a "very erratic administrator." But afterward, in looking back, he took a different view. As he explained to Robert Sherwood,

People like me who had the responsibility of watching the pennies could only see the five or six per cent of the programs that went wrong, through inefficient organization or direction. But now I can see in perspective the ninety-three or -four or -five per cent that went right—including the winning of the biggest war in history—because of the unbelievably skillful organization and direction. . . . Now I'd say that Roosevelt must have been one of the greatest geniuses as an administrator that ever lived. What we couldn't appreciate at the time was the fact that he was a real artist in government.[8]

Roosevelt appreciated the importance of effective administration, but he knew that it was only one part of the President's functions. In keeping with his concept of the "strong" type of Executive, he felt an obligation to provide legislative leadership as well. The authority of the President in relation to lawmaking is stated by the Constitution in negative terms: the veto. The early presidents, deferring to Congress in legislative matters, felt constrained to use the veto but rarely. (The first six leaders exercised the prerogative a total of only nine times.) Jackson, however, had a different opinion of his duty. Regarding himself as the people's champion, he thought he should use the veto (and every other power) *actively* in the public interest. Accordingly, he issued twelve vetoes.

Jackson's precedent was followed by the succeeding "strong" presidents, who embraced his concept of office: Cleveland, Theodore Roosevelt, Wilson, and Franklin Roosevelt. Franklin took pleasure, in 1941, in sending to Cleveland's widow (Mrs. Thomas J. Preston) a summary of presidential vetoes from the time of Washington. He observed that no other president approached the number of vetoes recorded by either Grover or himself. It was also true, he added, that Grover's veto record while governor of New York was approached only by his own. "I am happy in the association which this record brings out," he concluded cheerfully.[9]

Roosevelt added a wrinkle of his own to the exercise of the veto. In one of his early press conferences, in June, 1933, a correspondent asked him if he intended to use the time-honored method of "pocket veto" on a bill then pending in Congress. To which he replied, "I don't believe in pocket vetoes. I believe in good, worded vetoes." [10] Roosevelt considered that the legislators and the public were entitled to know the reasons for the withholding of the President's signature from any important bill. The innovation became standard practice during his Administration.

A large measure of influence over legislation was not to be derived from vetoes, whether worded or silent. In addition to the right of veto, the Constitution provides a source for leadership by the president in Congress. It is not, strictly, a legislative power, but it forms a springboard for suggestion and political leverage: "He shall from time to time give to the Congress information of the state of the Union, and recommend to their consideration such measures as he shall judge necessary and expedient. . . ." (Article II, Sec. 3.) Roosevelt, pursuing the example of Wilson, made effective use of this provision as a means of focusing attention upon his proposals. He thus gave force to the idea that lawmaking is not an exclusive domain of Congress, but a joint enterprise of Capitol Hill and the White House. According to this concept, the president is expected to take the initiative in fashioning a well-rounded program.

Roosevelt's first two terms were given in large measure to legislative promotion; most of this was related to domestic problems. But as the shadow of war fell across Europe, he became more concerned with foreign affairs and his role as commander-in-chief. Of all the powers granted to the president by the Constitution, the war power is potentially the greatest—for no man has yet fixed its boundaries. Lincoln, as Civil War leader, pushed the authority of his office further than any other president. He freed the slaves by proclamation, increased the armed forces beyond statutory limits, and spent public money without appropriation. He did these things, knowing them to be of doubtful legality. Lincoln was sworn to preserve the Constitution, but he knew that to do this, he must first save the *nation*.[11]

Yet if Lincoln's position was valid, who could define and limit the powers of a president at war? Lord Bryce, in his *American Commonwealth*, reported the unvarnished facts: ordinary law during the Civil War had been practically suspended, and would have to be similarly suspended in similar cases. This, concluded Bryce, makes the president a "sort of dictator." [12]

Even when the nation was not legally in a state of war or rebellion, the powers of the commander-in-chief were formidable. Bryce observed, shrewdly, that when foreign affairs become threatening or internal disorders developed, "everything may depend upon his judgment, his courage, and his hearty loyalty to the principles of the Constitution." [13] Roosevelt took up the problem frankly during a press conference in 1939. The definition of war, he said, was very difficult. He referred, as an illustration, to the American naval expeditions (directed by President John Adams) against privateers in the West Indies: "There was no war declared [1798]. It was, of course, actual warfare. This business of carrying on war without declaring a war, that we think is new, is not new. There are a lot of examples all through history." There was no doubt in the President's mind that, in case of attack on the United States, he had a constitutional duty to defend the country without waiting for a declaration of war.[14]

After Pearl Harbor, the President had the full legal powers arising from a state of hostilities. He made ample use of his wartime authority but did not go to the furthest extreme. In a message to Congress (September, 1942) requesting authority to stabilize prices, he referred to the powers which he held in reserve. "The President," he declared, "has the powers, under the Constitution and under Congressional Acts, to take measures necessary to avert a disaster which would interfere with the winning of the war." What he had in mind specifically was inflation, and he considered that he had the authority, if he chose, to deal with it "without further reference to Congress." It was his decision, however, to ask Congress for the legislation; this course was "consistent with my sense of responsibility as President in time of war, and with my deep and unalterable devotion to the processes of democracy." But he warned that unless Congress took action within the month, he would be left with an "inescapable responsibility" to see to it that the war effort was not imperiled by threat of economic chaos. He went on to explain, further:

> The responsibilities of the President in wartime to protect the nation are very grave. This total war, with our fighting fronts all over the world, makes the use of executive power far more essential than in any previous war. . . .
> I cannot tell what powers may have to be exercised in order to win this war.
> The American people can be sure that I will use my powers with a full sense of my responsibility to the Constitution and to my country. The American people can also be sure that I shall not hesitate to use every power vested in me to accomplish the defeat of our enemies in any part of the world where our own safety demands such defeat.
> When the war is won, the powers under which I act automatically revert to the people—to whom they belong.

As he stated, he favored the processes of democracy even in time of emergency. Consequently, he asked for legislation and followed customary procedures in the general conduct of the war. However, he knew that the game with the Axis was for keeps. And like Lincoln, he knew that the nation must survive if the Constitution was to be preserved. He therefore made it clear that in order to gain victory, he would not hesitate to use *any* power at his command. There was no concealment of his principle; he would act by authority of statute, the Constitution, and the law of self-preservation.

Some observers were profoundly disturbed by the magnitude of presidential power during the emergency. To be sure, there were a few checks upon the Commander-in-chief: Congress still controlled the purse, and the President could hardly succeed in a major undertaking without support by both Congress and the public. But persons close to the White House became a little frightened by what they saw. Robert Sherwood expressed the hope that the nation would never again be in the position of placing "so much reliance on the imagination and the courage and the durability of one mortal man." He came out of his five years of experience in wartime Washington with "alarmed awareness of the risks that we run of disastrous fallibility at the very top of our Constitutional structure." Roosevelt, he thought, was not to blame for this situation; his example had merely brought the problem out into the open. The "extraordinary and solitary" constitutional powers were inherent in our political system; and in time of crisis, "they are going to be asserted for better or for worse." [15] Other men share this apprehension, but none has offered a solution. What Sherwood has written is true: the President at war has terrifying powers. But, for the present, this thought leads no place except to a sobering concern regarding the character and preparation of candidates for the White House.

While Roosevelt never feared the exercise of his own power, it is doubtful if the role of commander-in-chief was the one he preferred. There is little question that the role he liked best, and to which he was most suited, was that of popular leader. This function of the presidency was not prescribed in the Constitution. It *evolved*, chiefly through the example of Jackson, and became a vital part of the office as conceived by the "strong" executives. According to this conception, the President was indeed the People's Choice—an instrument of their mind and will.

In delivering the nominating address for Alfred E. Smith at Houston in 1928, Roosevelt called special attention to this role. A president, he declared, must have that "rare ability to make popular government function . . . , to reverse the present trend towards apathy and arouse in the citizenship an active interest—a willingness to reassume its share of the responsibility for the nation's progress. So only can we have once more a government not just for the people but by the people also." [16] When Roosevelt, rather than Smith, made it to the White House, he reaffirmed his idea of executive leadership. He concluded his audacious Second Inaugural with these words:

> To maintain a democracy of effort requires a vast amount of patience in dealing with differing methods, a vast amount of humility. But out of the confusion of many voices rises an understanding of dominant public need. Then political leadership can voice common ideals, and aid in their realization.
>
> In taking again the oath of office as President of the United States, I assume the solemn obligation of leading the American people forward along the road they have chosen to advance.
>
> While this duty rests upon me I shall do my utmost to speak their purpose and to do their will, seeking Divine Guidance to help us each and every one to give light to them that sit in darkness and to guide our feet into the way of peace.

Essentials of Executive Leadership

No ordinary man, untutored in the arts of statecraft and human relations, could make the imprint which Roosevelt left upon his nation and the world. What are the qualities and practices that make for effective leadership in the presidency? From the well of his political experience, he developed a rather complete set of views on this question. And the question, in view of the awful responsibility of the president today, could be the most critical of our times.

Roosevelt would have given a grin and a nod to the sketch drawn by Merriman Smith, veteran White House reporter. Referring to the president, Smith has written:

> He should be an excellent actor, a better-than-average financier, have administrative ability superior to that of a big corporation executive and be quite a fair student of the military sciences. He should know geography as well as a university professor. He ought to know a lot about farming. He should have been an avid student of international affairs before going to the White House.
>
> In other words, he should know something about every phase not only of American life, but of the economies and thoughts of other nations of the world. And all this in addition to maintaining the best possible balance between the party platform on which he was elected, his own principles and the propriety of the moment.[17]

While Smith was writing from the outside in, Roosevelt could speak from the inside out. He expressed the basic requirements in these terms: broad knowledge of affairs, political experience, appealing personality, firm character, and idealism. The specifications for each of these may be found in the words and deeds of his career.

He spoke often of the importance of wide knowledge, especially that acquired from personal observation. In a tribute to Washington, he gave high place to this characteristic of the First President. His grasp of facts, said Roosevelt, was "the foundation stone of his superbly realistic statesmanship." No other president brought to office a greater comprehension of the country—"and most of it acquired on horseback at that!"[18] Government could be competent only when its leaders kept abreast of conditions. The gravest danger, he warned, was for any administration to "lose touch with reality."[19]

By travel and study a man could aspire to the knowledge that a successful president must have. Roosevelt was not a scholar, but by various means he became an expert in several fields. Herman Kahn, Director of the Roosevelt Library, has spoken to this point. From personal association and from the mass of Roosevelt records he has surveyed, Kahn has expressed the belief that there were three main subjects in which Roosevelt had outstanding proficiency: geography, naval history, and politics.[20] All three proved exceedingly useful to him in the White House.

He realized that an individual could be an expert in only a few fields, at most. His technique as president, therefore, was to place himself at the center of a far-reaching network of information. It consisted of thousands of advisers, continuous news analysis, special reports, and an unending stream of communications from people of all stations and places. This network was an indispensable supplement to his own general knowledge, personal observation, and intuition.

The public was aware of only one limited group of advisers to Roosevelt—the so-called brain trust. All previous presidents had made use, in varying degrees, of expert counsel; but Roosevelt developed the practice in a more comprehensive and systematic way. As a matter of fact, the basic idea originated with him long before he went to Washington. He found, as governor, that he could learn what he needed to know quickly by the method of "picking brains." Consequently, he kept a flow of visitors coming to the Mansion in Albany. In addition, he drew regularly upon certain individuals for particular kinds of advice. He leaned rather heavily upon academic experts, valuing the thoroughness of their training and their disinterestedness.[21]

His use of experts did not mean that he trusted them without reservation. He took a perverse pleasure in telling stories about specialists who had gone wrong. It made him uneasy, he often remarked, to hear optimistic reports from diplomatic officials abroad; all the experts had insisted in 1914 that there would be no war in Europe. Since then he had felt safer when the experts were scared! Roosevelt believed that specialized advice was indispensable, but it had to be weighed—and tested against common sense and judgment. He would have been the last to suggest that the government be turned over to a brain trust—his, or any other. (He wanted the experts on tap, not on top!) Roosevelt never forgot his faith that the people should rule, and in the final decision he spoke for *them*.

Few people knew the wide range of general advice which came to him. A conservative associate, John L. Saltonstall, suggested in 1938 that he find "mature and experienced" counselors, instead of relying upon the views of "a number of young men with revolutionary ideas in whom business men as a whole have no confidence." [22] Roosevelt replied sharply that such an impression derived from partisan news interpreters. He ridiculed the idea that any adviser or clique had special influence in the White House. He saw more people each day than "any two previous Presidents combined"—and they came, he insisted, from "literally every walk in life, with just as high a percentage of rich as of poor, of conservatives as of liberals, of old men as of young men." [23]

His answer was actually an understatement. A study of his appointment calendar (and of his personal correspondence) leads to the conclusion that a disproportionate amount of advice came from conservative business and professional men.

Roosevelt knew that in order to keep his office close to the people, he had to have more than advisers; he needed specialized information services. He was the first Chief Executive to establish an organization for gathering and gauging facts and views of all kinds. Not the least valuable among his keys to public opinion was the analysis of White House mail—the "public response" file. He received more than four thousand letters daily, which gave him a fair cross-section of what people were thinking. This was in keeping with his thought that the presidency should become a great "clearing house for exchange of information and ideas, of facts and ideals, affecting the general welfare." He was not exaggerating when he said, in 1940, "In the White House today we have built up a great mosaic of the state of the union from thousands of bits of information—from one man or woman this thought; from another, data on some event, a scrap here perhaps and a scrap there; from every Congressional district in the Union; from rich and poor; from enthusiast and complainant; from liberal and conservative; from Republican and Democrat." [24]

The mosaic was kept current, but Roosevelt believed that a public leader must also keep in mind the facts of the past. He had a romantic interest in history (especially American), but he was impressed mainly by its usefulness. "It is necessary," he declared in 1926, "to look back before we look at today or the future; in this lies the truest value of the study of history." [25] In writing the Introduction to the published volumes of his gubernatorial papers, he stated that the record should be preserved primarily for its utility to public officials. "Reference to the Public Papers of former Governors has been of great assistance to me, and it has been surprising to me often to find that many matters of apparently new present day policy have some parallel or precedent in bygone years. . . ." [26]

A reading of his press conferences, after he came to Washington, reveals the constant reference in his thought to experience and history. His first reaction to almost every question was in terms of some previous encounter—usually in Albany. Whether discussing soil conservation, utilities, or old-age pensions, the point of departure generally was, "When I was in New York State . . . " As he penetrated more deeply into national problems, the attention paid to earlier experiences lessened, but he never lost sight of them or discounted their relevance.

He was distressed by the loss of many of the public papers of former presidents; he felt that those records would be of inestimable help to their successors in office. He determined to keep his own papers intact, for use both by scholars and public officials. This was the primary motive in his establishment of the Library at Hyde Park and of his wish to make the papers there accessible as quickly as possible. He was a collector and preserver by instinct, and he saw history as a living force for progress in a democracy.

From history, from studies and reports, from correspondence and personal advice, the Chief Executive should form in his mind a broad panorama of the nation and its problems. The quality which he, more than any man, must possess is the capacity to see the whole rather than the parts. He must, in other words, aspire to be a *generalist*. Roosevelt himself never lost sight of this; he regarded it as a definite obligation of office. In a Fireside Chat of April, 1938, he gave this "personal word" to his constituents:

> I never forget that I live in a house owned by all the American people and that I have been given their trust. . . . I want to be sure that neither battles nor burdens of office shall ever blind me to an intimate knowledge of the way the American people want to live and the simple purposes for which they put me here. . . .
> I can hear your unspoken wonder as to where we are headed in this world. I cannot expect all of the people to understand all of the people's problems; but it is my job to try to understand those problems.

The bulk of the criticism of Roosevelt came from those who could not or would not see the whole picture. He was particularly annoyed by some of his friends outside of government—cultivated, intelligent people. In a moment of quiet exasperation, in January, 1938, he stated to John Saltonstall, "Honestly, John, if educated people only knew more about national problems from the national point of view and not the local point of view, or the class point of view, or the rich point of view, or the poor point of view, these educated friends of mine would help me a great deal more than they have in the past five years." As a case in point, he went on to say that he had recently held a conference with four mature and successful businessmen. And after talking for an hour and a half, he related, they agreed upon one thing: "that they had never before realized the complexity of the problems before the nation." [27]

A president, in addition to general knowledge, must have adequate political experience. This requirement seemed so obvious to Roosevelt that he seldom elaborated upon it. In nominating Smith in 1928, however, he stressed the advantage of his candidate's mature experience:

"experience that does not guess, but knows from long practice the science of governing. . . ." He explained that he meant by this the comprehension resulting from years of study and dealings with taxation, social welfare, legislative procedures, constitutional law, and the other concerns of the State. The most important job in the government and in the nation should not be entrusted to a political amateur; it called for the best *professional* in the game.

A man's personality should be measured for the office, too. Roosevelt made capital of this in the campaign of 1928; for his candidate, "Al," had a warmer appeal than Hoover. As he told the Houston Convention, a man with the required preparation might become a reasonably efficient president, but one thing more was needed to make him a great president: "It is that quality of soul . . . which makes him a strong help to all those in sorrow and trouble, that quality which makes him not merely admired, but loved by all the people—the quality of sympathetic understanding of the human heart, a real interest in one's fellow men."

The importance of this trait may be seen in Roosevelt's own career. When he first entered politics, he appeared somewhat cold and aloof, but he soon developed an easy and understanding way with people. This was to bring him the support of millions who had never met him, but had seen, heard, and followed him. At closer range it won for him the dedicated loyalty of thousands (within government and without) who helped him to effectuate his program. Samuel Rosenman, who joined forces with Roosevelt as a campaign aide in 1928, has stated that he had anticipated a somewhat indifferent, businesslike relationship. "As the weeks went on, however, Roosevelt's warm, genial personality, his friendliness and cordial informality, drew me close to him. Nearly everyone who worked intimately with him had the same experience. Roosevelt loved people, and they learned quickly to return that affection." [28]

Without the binding force of mutual trust and confidence, the "Roosevelt team" could not have functioned. Roosevelt's aims were accomplished through a far-flung group of sympathetic friends and associates, who were his legs, arms, hands, and eyes. One cannot help being impressed, in reading through his personal correspondence, by the reciprocal expressions of support, encouragement, and devotion. This spirit invigorated his Administration; it was the foundation for active support of his policies in every part of the land. It is hard to see how a president could carry through a significant national program without that kind of unbought, personal assistance.

Roosevelt knew that loyalty was a two-way street, and that a president

must give to others what he expects from them. Edward J. Flynn, who
worked closely with him for years, has testified that he was exceedingly
loyal to his friends. A few, like Al Smith and Jim Farley, have cast
doubt upon this, but Flynn insists that he was always loyal to him and
to most of the White House circle. In addition, Flynn knew "numberless people" beyond that circle to whom Roosevelt was ever a "loyal and
sincere friend." [29]

Occasions arose when it proved impossible to maintain the desired
principles of friendship. When he decided upon a change in policies,
someone was usually offended; and if the individual was high in government service, the "break" was widely publicized. Roosevelt had an
almost hopeless reluctance to fire anyone, but sometimes he had to (or
the individual quit). Situations of this kind pained him, and he looked
upon them as a matter of unhappy duty.

Patience, perseverance, and tolerance he considered as necessary vir-
tues in a Chief Executive. Referring to the long and hard struggle for
the Constitution, he said, "Leadership toward the thought of a united
Nation had to be patient, and it was. Perseverance of leadership combined with patience has always won." [30] Roosevelt himself demonstrated imperturbable calm, under severe criticism, during the sit-down
strikes of 1937; he likewise played a waiting game during the "great
debate" over foreign policy in the late thirties. Rosenman states that he
was "most tolerant" in matters of race, religion, nationality, social status,
and general differences of opinion. When he became irritated or em-
bittered, it was usually because of personal attacks which he considered
unfair and untruthful.[31]

Fundamental to any president's composure is a proper sense of humor.
Roosevelt's advisers were initially shocked, but grew to appreciate, his
ability to laugh in the gravest situations. He had learned, as had Lincoln,
that humor is an antidote to fear and tension. "For hope and courage
always go with a light heart," he said in dedicating the Will Rogers
Memorial at Claremore. He was a good friend of Will's and believed
that his example was wholesome for the nation. "In a time grown too
solemn and sombre," he observed, Rogers "had brought his countrymen
back to a sense of proportion."

While he was playful, even adolescent, in some of his fun-making
efforts, he preferred this to the sardonic jibes that sometimes pass for
humor. He underlined this view in referring to the unique character of
Rogers' wit:

With it all his humor and his comments were always kind. His was no biting sarcasm that hurt the highest or the lowest of his fellow citizens. When he wanted people to laugh out loud he used the methods of pure fun. And when he wanted to make a point for the good of all mankind, he used the kind of gentle irony that left no scars behind it. That was an accomplishment well worthy of consideration by all of us.[32]

Roosevelt's humor, like that of his friend, was not dipped in gall. His well-known "Fala Story," told in the rousing Teamsters' address of 1944, brought laughter to millions and scored a political bull's-eye. Yet it wounded the feelings or reputation of no individual.

He believed that a president should inspire steadiness and good cheer, but he knew that the people looked for more than warmth and humor. Their Chief Executive must have the quality of idealism. Here was Roosevelt's conception, as quoted by *The New York Times* in 1932: "The Presidency is not merely an administrative office. That is the least of it. It is pre-eminently a place of moral leadership. All of our greatest Presidents were leaders of thought at times when certain historic ideas in the life of the nation had to be clarified. . . . That is what the office is— a superb opportunity for reapplying, applying to new conditions, the simple rules of human conduct to which we always go back. . . ."[33]

The three "strong" presidents whom Roosevelt had known possessed in high degree this desired quality. Cleveland, coming to office after a period of widespread corruption, typified "rugged honesty." Theodore Roosevelt and Wilson were both moral leaders, "each in his own way and for his own time," who used the presidency "as a pulpit." Roosevelt, in a letter to Wilson's biographer, Ray Stannard Baker, made this discerning comment upon the strength and limitation of his two predecessors: "Theodore Roosevelt lacked Woodrow Wilson's appeal to the fundamental and failed to stir, as Wilson did, the truly profound moral and social convictions. Wilson, on the other hand, failed where Theodore Roosevelt succeeded in stirring people to enthusiasm over specific individual events, even though these specific events may have been superficial in comparison with the fundamentals."[34] It is easy to see that he endeavored, in his own career, to combine the strong qualities of both men, who were heroes to him.

Of the two, he felt the closer affinity to Wilson, in whose official family he had served as a young man. Shortly after assuming the presidency in 1933, he wrote to Wilson's former secretary, Joseph P. Tumulty, "I wonder if you realize how often I think of your old Chief when I go about my daily tasks. Perhaps what we are doing will go a little way towards the fulfillment of his ideals."[35] The fact that Wilson's goals had not been reached did not dim his luster in Roosevelt's eyes. On dedicating his birthplace in Staunton, Virginia, he stated in 1941: "Of Woodrow Wilson this can be said, that in a time when world councils were dominated by material considerations of greed and of gain and of revenge he beheld the vision splendid. That selfish men could not share this vision of a world emancipated from the shackles of force and the arbitrament of the sword in no way detracts from its splendor." [36]

Roosevelt's intimate associate, Harry Hopkins, felt that his true character was in the tradition of Wilson. As he told Sherwood in 1941:

> You and I are for Roosevelt because he's a great spiritual figure, because he's an idealist, like Wilson, and he's got the guts to drive through any opposition to realize those ideals. Oh—he sometimes tries to appear tough and cynical and flippant, but that's an act he likes to put on, especially at press conferences. He wants to make the boys think he's hard-boiled. Maybe he fools some of them, now and then—but don't ever let him fool you, or you won't be any use to him. You can see the real Roosevelt when he comes out for something like the Four Freedoms. And don't get the idea that those are any catch phrases. He believes them. He believes they can be practically attained. That's what you and I have to remember in everything we may be able to do for him. . . .[37]

Relations with Congress

Roosevelt believed that a man with the essential qualities of leadership had the potential of a great president. But the potential could be realized only through effective relationships and associations. Most important in the long pull were relations with the legislative branch and with the voters. He became exceedingly skillful in these and left some guidelines for his successors—especially those who would be "strong" presidents.

"The relationship between an executive and a legislature is, in many ways, the criterion of success, whether it be in the Governorship or the Presidency," he wrote in 1928. "Theodore Roosevelt, especially during his earlier years as President, succeeded in passing great constructive measures, often against the personal desires of an unsympathetic Congress. President Taft did not have the temperament either to dominate Congress or to work with his Congress. The first six years of President Wilson brought out again the qualities of constructive leadership. It is difficult to characterize the administrations of President Harding and President Coolidge in the same way." [38]

Later, in a campaign speech of 1932, he gave his conception of the desired relationship. He thought that a co-operative approach, keeping partisanship in the background, was correct and feasible in most situations. Referring to his experience in Albany, he stated that he occasionally had clear-cut differences with the lawmakers; sometimes they had won, sometimes he had won. But on all matters affecting human welfare, even when a "knock-down and drag-out" fight had developed, "the Legislature and I have always ended by sitting around a table and getting something practical done." [39]

When he came to Washington in 1933, he had, for the first time in his executive career, a legislative body controlled by his own party. There was, moreover, an atmosphere of urgency; during his first year in office, an abnormal relationship therefore prevailed. Backed by the public desire for action, his recommendations to Congress were almost irresistible. The ordinary procedures of bill drafting by legislators, of protracted committee hearings, of haggling and compromises, gave way to ready-made bills, drawn up in the Executive branch. "It was an emergency," the President later explained, "We had to put them through. . . . it was a convenience to the Government and a convenience to the Congress." [40]

After 1933 he held looser reins over Congress. He showed willingness to compromise with the legislators and to turn aside from obstacles that he could not surmount. For a while it appeared that the reins were, indeed, too loose. In 1934, by leaving the framing of specific legislation to Congress, he opened the door to serious disagreements between the two Houses and within the Party organization. The President at last felt obliged to resolve the confusion; he brought the Party leaders together in the White House, where they plotted a joint course under his guidance. These conferences included the Speaker and Majority Leader of the House and the most important Democratic members of the Senate. "Orders could be issued to the lower chamber," Professor E. Pendleton Herring observed, "but the President saw the wisdom of cooperating with the chairmen of important Senate committees who could endanger his program."

A close liaison henceforth existed between the Executive Office and Capitol Hill. Roosevelt, according to Herring, evolved a kind of "master-ministry" of Congressional leaders, Cabinet officers, and executive officials working through the White House.[41] After Pearl Harbor he extended his consultation to include the minority leaders (Republicans) in both houses and on key Senate committees. This was part of his "bipartisan" policy on foreign affairs, in which Senator Arthur Vandenberg played a leading role.[42]

Matters did not always proceed smoothly for him in Congress. The Democrats had large majorities in both houses, but their organization lacked cohesion. A frank analysis of the problem in the Senate was sent to the President by Key Pittman, Chairman of the Committee on Foreign Relations. After the start of the Seventy-fourth Congress (1935), he painted this discouraging picture:

> I have, time and again, postponed burdening you with the political situation on the Hill. I might be unreasonably uneasy, but I am worried with regard to the situation and feel it my duty to communicate the situation to you as I see it. . . .
> It is apparent that there is no Democratic Party in the United States Senate. We have nearly two-thirds of the Members of the Senate elected and registered as Democrats. What's the matter with the situation and what can we do about it? Well, of course, the fault is that there is a lack of confidence in the success of the Administration. There is cowardice. There is discontent with regard to patronage. There is complaint that the Administration is responsible for the lack of Democratic solidarity; that the Democrats win a victory after twelve long years, and the Republicans hold office; that the Congress is not considered a part of the Administration; that they are supposed to pass bills and not be interested in the result of the administration of the acts; that strange and peculiar persons have become advisors; that there is no leadership; that thinking is farmed out; that defeat is inevitable; and every man must take care of himself. . . .
> May I beg of you to lay all administrative matters aside until you have your legislative matters straightened out.[43]

Communications of that sort, from a trusted lieutenant like Pittman, served to remind Roosevelt that national and party leadership was not a path of roses. After 1933, his program in Congress had to be ground out, step by step, in the rough arena of politics and power. He was not a novice at the game. He knew that legislation did not always proceed from high motives and honest persuasion. Because he understood this he did not become disheartened, but pushed on with the means of influence at his command.

One of the principal levers of control was the patronage available to a spending Administration. But, as Pittman's letter suggested, there is never enough to satisfy everyone. Throughout his years in the White House, Roosevelt also made full use of maneuver, at which he was most adept. As "quarterback" of the New Deal team, he sent countless memoranda of instructions to his loyal friends in Congress. These contained advice to compromise, delay, push hard, or whatever the legislative situation might call for. The President's confidential file of correspondence with Senate leaders offers a good sampling of letters of this kind, as well as many reports to Roosevelt from committee chairmen and other Senators.[44] Records were seldom kept of telephone messages and private conversations, but it can be assumed that these were even more important than the flow of memoranda.

In the relations between a President and Congress there is a border-land in which executive and legislative prerogatives clash. An unre-solved issue in that domain is the Congressional right to investigate and the President's responsibility to administer. This question has been a persistent source of friction between the two branches, and the Roose-velt Administration was no exception.

Soon after entering the White House, Roosevelt told reporters that he hoped for a new approach in this matter. He suggested that Con-gress keep in touch with administrative procedure from "day to day and week to week," straight through the year. This would be preferable, he thought, to the custom of investigating, every so often, administrative affairs of years gone by. If something is going wrong in the operations of the administrative branch, it should be made known right away. "So," explained the President, "I have been trying to work out some practical method of keeping the Congress in touch, day in and day out, with what the Administration is doing, so that there won't be an accumulation of things which may result after a long period of years in scandal or investi-gation. At the same time we would keep perfectly clear the separation of functions." [45]

His unrealistic suggestion did not, of course, materialize, and the issue of Congressional inquiries came up on several occasions. It was most dramatically raised during the Executive's bout with the un-American Activities Committee of the House—the "Dies Committee." The Dies group, searching out subversives in government, had intruded itself into several government departments and agencies, including the F.B.I. In October, 1940, the President declined to permit assignment of F.B.I. personnel to the committee, as Representative Dies had requested. He gave as reason the fact that the Department of Justice had hardly enough investigators for carrying on its essential functions. He added, pointedly, that the purposes of a Congressional committee were entirely different from those of an executive agency. One seeks information for determin-ing whether further legislation is needed; the other is charged with en-forcement of existing law. "This is a duty which cannot be shared with a Congressional Committee, since the responsibility for enforcement lies with the Executive branch of the Government." [46]

Roosevelt, nevertheless, believed that some form of accommodation could be worked out with Dies. He told reporters in November that the House Committee had "every right in the world" to make any kind of investigation—although it could not, under the Constitution, conduct *administrative* operations. "Somewhere in there," he said, "lies a line of demarcation where cooperation is undoubtedly needed. I think we shall get it." [47] A few days later he held a private conference with Dies, the only record of which is in the papers at Hyde Park. According to the record (nineteen typewritten pages), the President held consistently to the position that the basic aims of the Un-American Activities Committee were proper; he insisted, however, that there be no "investigative interference" with the Constitutional prerogatives of the Executive. He asked Dies to turn over to the F.B.I. any information he uncovered that appeared to require action. When Dies objected that the F.B.I. often did nothing with such information, Roosevelt replied that this matter must remain within the discretion of the Executive.[48]

Entirely aside from the issue of interference, Roosevelt had other reservations concerning legislative inquiries. As early as January, 1931, he stated publicly that two "often-forgotten" principles must be considered. First, the investigation must spring from a desire to promote the general welfare, and not from the political ambitions of any person or party. Second, it must be so conducted that "all persons, unless or until formally charged with crime, shall be shielded from suspicion and innuendo through publicity, lest the mere fact of their appearance in the investigation destroy their reputation or impair their standing among their neighbors." Recent violations of these principles, he added, had impaired the value of the inquiries themselves and had "impressed upon the public mind the need for their future observance." [49] The alert reader, recalling the rash of investigations after World War II, may wonder if the public, even yet, is sufficiently impressed.

Relations with the People

Co-operation of the Chief Executive with Congress, important though it may be, is secondary to his relations with the voters. For, in Roosevelt's words, "Congress is but a responsive legislative agency of the people. As the people think and speak the Congress acts." [50] He was not the first to state this truth. Lord Bryce had declared, half a century before, that public opinion was the ultimate force in American political life: "No one openly ventures to resist it." [51]

All "strong" presidents have understood this. Roosevelt considered that it was his duty to sense and carry out the popular will; at the same time he sought to guide that will according to his own lights. He saw his greatest single task as that of *teacher:* "Leadership must educate the public, if it expects to get the public response necessary for effective action." [52]

He demonstrated, in his own techniques, the necessary gifts of teaching. Above all was his ability to simplify and dramatize. Early in his career, Roosevelt discerned that the jargon of economists and financiers was incomprehensible to the average voter. He learned, too, that abstractions and statistics were often meaningless—and lacked the personal touch. Increasingly, he began to interpret problems in terms of their impact upon individual human beings. In a Fireside Chat of 1934 he told his listeners that he could cite figures and indices on prices, employment, bank deposits, and so on, to prove that economic gains were being made. "But the simplest way for each of you to judge recovery lies in the plain facts of your own individual economic situation. Are you better off than you were last year? Are your debts less burdensome? Is your bank account more secure? Are your working conditions better? Is your faith in your own individual future more firmly grounded?" [53]

Perhaps his most remarkable feat was in making his own aims and personality clear to the people. All who knew Roosevelt have agreed that he was an immensely complicated human being. "His character," Sherwood observed, "was not only multiplex, it was contradictory to a bewildering degree." But the supreme contradiction, he goes on to state, was the fact that, with all his complexity, Roosevelt achieved a grand simplicity. He "wrote himself by word and deed in large plain letters which all can read and in terms which all can understand." [54]

The radio had been available to Coolidge and Hoover, but Roosevelt was the first president to make effective use of it. He quickly sensed its power and liked the medium because it brought him into personal contact with the individual listener. He began the practice of radio reports in Albany—"not only to appeal directly to the people, but also to describe fully the facts about legislation which were not always given by many press reports." [55] He discussed frankly with his listeners social and personal problems which had never before been so widely considered. As Charles and Mary Beard have written, he "stirred the thought of the nation to the uttermost borders of the land." [56]

Conscious of the power of his voice, the President placed great importance upon the preparation of his speeches. Rosenman, Sherwood, and other advisers have described the numberless drafts, corrections, deletions, and "happy thoughts" that went into his major addresses. During the war his words were even more significant—for they were weapons of democratic survival. Roosevelt's speeches were sometimes criticized as lacking in "style," in the grand manner of Churchill. But the style was, perhaps, the most effective for his purposes that could have been devised—simple, clear, intimate, and persuasive.

He chose wisely not to overdo his use of the radio. He averaged only two or three Fireside Chats per year; these were in addition to his major

addresses and to political speeches carried on the air. His relations with
the people were, of course, not limited to the radio. The older means of
communication, especially newspapers, were effectively employed as
well. His chief instrument was the press conference, which he developed
into an unofficial agency of democratic government. Here, twice weekly,
reporters were free to fire any question at the President. He reserved
the right, of course, to refrain from answering; but his intent, as well as
practice, was to answer the bulk of legitimate queries. Equally important, he provided "background" and "off-the-record" information
for the correspondents, which permitted them to give their readers an
intelligible picture of what was going on in Washington. Where his
predecessors had looked upon the press conference as an unpleasant
chore, Roosevelt seized upon it as an enjoyable and helpful method of
enlightening and guiding public opinion. During his twelve years as
Chief Executive, he held more than one thousand regular and special
conferences.

He believed that the element of *timing* was of prime importance in
connection with public opinion. As Felix Frankfurter, his trusted coun-
selor, has written: "Politics in a democracy means a continuous process
of education. But education does not always mean exposition, and certainly not shouting. It involves much incubation. Not least of the arts of
statesmanship is that of correct timing, of knowing what to say and
when." [57]

Professor A. M. Schlesinger, Sr., suggested to Roosevelt in 1935 that
he make more frequent reports to the voters by radio. In reply, the
President wrote that he agreed about the value of regular reporting, but
had temporarily stayed off the radio because of a "strange and weird
sense known as 'public psychology.'" He stated that he had wanted to
go on the air the preceding winter but had a feeling that the public
might "hook me up with the Coughlins, Longs and Hugh Johnsons," who
were having a three-cornered fracas during that season.[58]

A year later his friend and adviser, Frank Walker, suggested that he
give another Fireside Chat in order to build strength with the voters.
Roosevelt replied that Walker was "absolutely right about the heart-to-
heart talks." But he thought it advisable to wait until after the adjourn-
ment of Congress. "As you know, every Administration slips during a
Congressional session and generally comes back after Congress ad-
journs. Congress, while in session, is a sounding board—when it is away
the President is a sounding board." [59]

He knew the importance of pushing his program while public psychology was "right." In the second year of the New Deal he told Colonel

House that "We must keep the sheer momentum from slacking up too much and I have no intention of relinquishing the offensive in favor of defensive tactics." [60] He also knew when *not* to act. He told Anne O'Hare McCormick in 1934 that his social security proposals had been drafted for more than a year, but would not be introduced until 1935. "The people aren't ready." This was a phrase heard often during White House press conferences.[61]

On one critical occasion he burned his fingers and never forgot it. In his "quarantine" speech of 1937, Roosevelt warned of the Axis threat and asked peace-loving nations everywhere to co-operate against aggression. But the people were not prepared for this bold suggestion, and their reaction was negative. This came as a shock to him. "It's a terrible thing," he later confided to Rosenman, "to look over your shoulder when you are trying to lead—and to find no one there." [62]

He did not again make a serious error of this sort. During the trying days of 1940 and 1941 he moved with a deliberation that exasperated many of those who saw America's stake in British survival. But by cautious pacing, he avoided the pitfalls of a disastrous popular rebuff, or "too little and too late." There are years and days when the safety of a nation depends upon the timing of its leadership.

6

The Great Game of Politics

IT IS A COMMON AMERICAN NOTION that government is a good and necessary thing, but that politics is a sorry business. Roosevelt was aware of
this widespread opinion and sought continually to refute it. Far from
apologizing for his choice of a career, he insisted that politicians were
indispensable to the American way of life. Danger to the republic arose
not from the practice of politics, but from the reluctance of able men
to seek office. Politics was the instrument for achieving government,
and neither one could be of higher grade than the politicians themselves.[1]

The Party System

As politicians give life to constitutions, party organizations provide a
mechanism for the democratic process. "It is well to remember," he
wrote in 1932, "that without some form of political organization, little
can be accomplished. Theodore Roosevelt, for example, believed in
organization and used its support, even though it had a poor record in
many of its previous actions. He got results for his state and nation
which could have been accomplished in no other way."[2] The need for
parties, he explained, arose with the beginning of our national government—as soon as it became clear that there were two divergent views

concerning American political affairs. It was inevitable, he thought, that the conduct of government would require "a proper presentation of these schools of thought to the electorate itself." The Jeffersonians, finding the established machinery of publicity almost wholly in the hands of their opponents, organized their own campaign of political education. They attempted to persuade their fellow citizens by improvised means: pamphlets, chain letters, and by sending out speakers on horseback—"Thus came into being the Democratic Party." The chief work of the party continued to be that of placing Democratic principles before every voter.[3]

When Roosevelt entered his first race for public office (1910), he had the backing of the Democratic organization in Dutchess County. Upon going to Albany as State senator, however, he became a leading antagonist of the State Democratic organization, controlled by Tammany Hall. This seemingly contradictory position could be explained as political opportunism, or as discrimination on the part of the youthful senator. Though he believed generally in the party system, he was not committed to *every* party organization. Whatever the explanation, after his initial tilt with "Boss" Charles F. Murphy, he moved gradually toward an understanding with Tammany.

A decisive turning point was Roosevelt's experience in the New York Democratic primary of 1914. While serving as a Wilson appointee in Washington, he decided to test his vote appeal at home. He filed for U. S. senator against Tammany-backed James Gerard (Wilson's Ambassador to Germany). Roosevelt campaigned vigorously as the "anti-Boss" candidate, but he was decisively beaten in the primary. Although stung by the setback, he learned his lesson well. He never again defied the Tammany organization in an election campaign.

While he did not entirely outgrow his distaste for the city leaders, he no longer made an open issue of his antibossism. He saw that the party organization was essential to a candidate's success and that he must make peace with it to gain its support. The Tammany leaders, for their part, learned a complementary lesson when Gerard was beaten by his Republican opponent in the general election of 1914. The organization could not deliver the votes upstate, while Roosevelt demonstrated surprising strength there. As the years went by, there was increasing realization that the fortunes of Roosevelt and the party organization were, for better or worse, bound up together.

He came to be known as a "party man." He appreciated and ultilized the Democratic organizations in county, state, and nation and took a personal interest in their problems. He also gave weight to political advice on appointments and policies. When he went to Albany in 1929, he named Edward J. Flynn, long-time "boss" of the Bronx, as his Secretary of State. Flynn has stated that Roosevelt's first term was a major test of his relations with the party. By and large, he concludes, the Governor conducted a "political" administration, and in his judgment the results were good.[4]

Patronage is the daily bread of parties. Flynn estimates that ninety percent of Roosevelt's Albany appointees were active Democrats. The Governor agreed to accept party recommendations (including those of Tammany) for the general run of positions. At the same time, he made it clear that he reserved the right of independent selection whenever he felt it vital to his policies. Some of his advisers, like Henry Morgenthau, urged him to exercise greater freedom of choice. But the Governor agreed with his Secretary of State that the "political" approach was essentially the correct one.

Roosevelt used his patronage to strengthen the party up-state. Before 1929 the New York City leaders held a firm grip on Democratic appointments to state offices, and the organization elsewhere was virtually starved of rewards. Seeing that Democratic hopes (and his own) rested upon a larger share of out-state votes, the Governor made it his business to rebuild the county organizations. During the "easy months" in Albany, he traveled by auto and canal boat to every part of the hinterland. In addition to spreading his charm and making friends, he gave nourishment to the local organizations by granting them larger portions of patronage than they had before. The results of this work were soon to be harvested. While Roosevelt had squeaked to victory by a handful of votes in 1928, he was re-elected governor in 1930 by an unprecedented margin of 725,000.[5]

His concept of the role of parties and of patronage remained consistent after he went to the White House. Harold Gosnell, who has made a close study of political organizations and Roosevelt's relation to them, has stated that the new President used his vast appointive power "to reward his political friends and build up strength among the voters." American politics, Gosnell observes, is run that way, and Roosevelt did not choose to combat that tradition. Cabinet appointments, as customary, were determined mainly by political considerations. General patronage clearance was assigned to the Democratic National Chairman, James Farley, who was named Postmaster-General. Farley, in turn, insisted that seekers of federal jobs (outside of the classified service) have "clearance slips" from their local Democratic committeemen. In this manner the President sustained the party organizations that were to bring him, over the years, successive Democratic majorities.[6]

After the election of 1936, he showed greater independence in his use of patronage. This led to increasing dissatisfaction among the organization chieftains and was in part responsible for the growing irritation and bitterness of Farley. In the main, however, the President continued to pay attention to party needs, and the organization continued to support him. His critics charged, meanwhile, that the Administration was unduly partisan—that the public spending program was primarily a means of buying votes for the Democratic Party. He replied indignantly to accusations of "politics in relief" or "politics with human misery." While not denying that *administrative* posts were filled according to usual political practice, he stated that he had issued strict orders against political considerations in connection with persons applying for relief.

He believed that some politics would creep into relief, no matter what his general policy might be. But, for perspective, he found it enlightening to make a comparison with politics in *local* relief administration. While relaxing with newsmen in a press conference at Hyde Park in 1938, the President spread before him a copy of the Poughkeepsie *Eagle*. He referred to a story in the paper regarding the Board of Supervisors' debate on how to handle the relief problem in Dutchess County. The article concluded by stating that the problem before the Board would be settled by its Republican caucus before the next meeting of the Supervisors. "I think that is one of the most beautiful object lessons on the handling of local relief in most places in the United States that I know of," said Roosevelt with a grin. It would apply to every part of the country—"relief policies will be determined by the dominant political organization." [7]

Ed Flynn stated that the President always gave preference in patronage matters to recommendations from the large city organizations. He thus engineered an alliance which insured a heavy portion of the swelling urban vote. His relations with the city "bosses" and their "machines" formed a subject of special interest to political observers and provided ground for attack by his opponents. Roosevelt took the position that practical politics required day-in and day-out attention by party workers; a "machine" was simply a well-knit, well-managed organization. As such, a machine contained all kinds of individuals and, like any other type of organization, was subject to abuses. Nevertheless, a party leader generally must work with the organization as he finds it.

Boss Frank Hague of Jersey City caused Roosevelt considerable embarrassment among his own followers. Hague's high-handed methods led many to wonder whether the processes of democracy were being subverted in Jersey City. Many letters of complaint were sent by Democrats and "liberals" to the White House. One of these was from Jerry J. O'Connell (Representative from Montana), who wrote to the President in May, 1938. He urged him, "as the head of our Democratic Party," to demand Hague's resignation as Vice-Chairman of the National Committee. O'Connell charged that he had been threatened with violence should he attempt to speak in Jersey City, and he concluded that it was time that "something definite" be done about Hague's "fascist regime." Roosevelt, aware of the ugly situation, and disturbed by such communications, referred the Congressman's letter to his Attorney General for draft of a reply. But Homer Cummings doubted that it would be "desirable" for the President to answer this letter; he suggested a simple acknowledgment, accompanied by an invitation to O'Connell to "discuss the matter" at the White House. Roosevelt evidently took this advice and passed it on to his secretary, Marvin McIntyre. McIntyre accordingly wrote to the Congressman, over his own signature: "I just want to drop you a little line acknowledging your letter to the President of May ninth. Some time when it is convenient, I wish you would drop in and have a little talk with me about this." [8] The "brush-off" was complete.

Another enemy of Hague's and a friend of Roosevelt's was Frank Kingdon. As a student and practitioner of politics, he recorded a telling illustration of the President's attitude toward machines and bosses. On one occasion a group of civic-minded citizens, including Kingdon, went to see Roosevelt about Hague. They asked for his aid, through manipulation of federal patronage, in weakening the machine in Jersey City. After the request had been voiced, the President turned to the group and said, "So you think I ought to take a stand against Hague?" When the men answered that they did, he paused, then went on without a smile: "If there were a completely free election in Jersey City tomorrow, without any undue pressure, so that the people could elect for mayor anybody they wished, who would get it?"

Kingdon reports that he and his friends could only answer, "Frank Hague would."

"Then," said Roosevelt, "I suggest that you go back there and educate the people of Jersey City to get rid of him." [9]

Both knew that the issue was not that simple, but the rationalization satisfied the President's conscience. Frank Hague's Democratic vote in Hudson County had often turned the tide of victory against the outstate Republican majority in New Jersey. Roosevelt was loathe to weaken an apparatus that helped give him the power to achieve his broader, national objectives. So he tolerated Hague (and the other bosses), leaving to local leaders the responsibility for local reform.

However, he did not always remain aloof from state and local affairs. But his intervention was rarely related to the issue of "bossism"; it was generally connected with national policies. Even on these grounds, it was his policy to avoid any public show of favor with respect to candidates or factions. He was often urged by political friends to take sides. In 1934 George Creel sought his endorsement for the Democratic "regulars" against Upton Sinclair's "EPIC" campaign in the California primary. But he was told that the President adhered to a "hands-off" policy in such contests. In the same year Senator Key Pittman, a faithful supporter, was being hard pressed in the Nevada primary. Roosevelt felt constrained to answer Pittman's request for aid in these words: "I wish to goodness I could speak out loud in meeting and tell Nevada that I am one thousand percent for you! An imposed silence in things like primaries is one of the many penalties of the job." [10] Even in general elections, he believed that the President and the members of his Cabinet should confine their active interest to campaigns in their home states.[11]

Only once did he make a major deviation from the "hands-off" policy. That was in 1938—the year of the "purge"—when he intervened in several primary campaigns against "reactionary" Democrats. At this time he took a different view of intraparty contests from that previously expressed. Stunned by reversals in Congress (after his overwhelming re-election two years before), he had come to feel that there must be a showdown between the "liberal" and "conservative" forces in the country. He was particularly put out by legislators of his own party who had voted consistently against major reform measures. They ran for office, he said, as New Dealers; but once elected, they obstructed his program. It was one thing to campaign as a conservative and vote like one; it was quite another to pose as a liberal and then act the reverse in office.

As leader of the Democratic Party, Roosevelt decided that he had the responsibility to try to keep it liberal—and therefore to identify and support *liberal* Democratic candidates. While he avowed this duty as a matter of principle, he actually took the stump in only a few places. In New York, where he opposed Congressman John J. O'Connor, he gave as special justification the fact that this was his home state. In Georgia, where he struck hard against Senator Walter George, he explained that he was doing so in his "adopted" state. Roosevelt claimed no ties of residence in Maryland (though it *was* close to the White House), but he spoke there against Senator Millard Tydings for "masquerading" as a liberal.

O'Connor lost to James Fay in the New York contest, but public attention over the issue of presidential interference was focused upon Georgia and Maryland. Here, Senators George and Tydings were re-elected. How much the President's influence helped or hindered them cannot be assessed. But the "purge" as a whole was judged a failure, and Roosevelt wrote it off as a mistake.

He did not give up the idea that he had a right, as party leader, to speak out as he did in the Democratic primaries. But he no longer regarded this as a *duty* after 1938. His action was a means rather than an end; when it proved ineffectual, he abandoned it. Two years later he chose to forget that he had ever strayed from strict neutrality. When Senator Harry Truman was opposed for re-election in the Missouri primary of 1940, the President declined a request to speak out in his favor. The White House Secretary, Stephen Early, explained that while Truman was an "old and trusted friend," it was Roosevelt's "invariable practice" to take no part in primary campaigns. "The President must stand aloof," said Early, "regardless of any personal preference he might have." [12]

Hitler's aggressions in Europe served to remind Roosevelt that party unity was now more vital than the issue of domestic liberalism. This was another reason (if one were needed) for his switch respecting intraparty contests. In 1939 the President could see that decisions critical to America's survival lay immediately ahead. It was urgent that he reconcile the various party factions, strengthen the Democratic organization, and turn it to the support of his foreign policies.

When students of government praise the functioning of our two-party system, they sometimes lose sight of the fact that it can be effective only when the majority party remains unified. This problem has existed for both Republicans and Democrats, but it has been generally greater for the latter. William Allen White shrewdly discerned the relation between party factions and Roosevelt's legislative program. Writing to James Farley in December, 1937, he observed that the President, in his attempts to push additional reforms, "can go no faster and no further than he can persuade Carter Glass and Pat Harrison and their kind to go along with him." He went on to say, "I note that our good friend in the White House is trying to cement together the various blocks which made your monolithic Democratic majority in November 1936. A monolithic party can only be held together by the steel reinforcements of consultation and compromise with all the various elements which comprise the monolith."

Impatient reformers often failed to appreciate these political facts of life. From a practical point of view, Roosevelt's skill in holding together the Democratic coalition was as important to the New Deal accomplishments as was his "progressive" idealism. And the compromises he accepted for the sake of party unity made for sounder reform action, because effective changes must be accompanied by evolution in public thinking. As White concluded in his letter to Farley, "When action comes faster than thought, as it came in N.R.A., nothing much really happens." [13]

Roosevelt accepted party unity and loyalty as necessary to the American democratic process. At the same time he saw definite limits upon both. Starting out in New York State politics as something of a party rebel, he never entirely lost his "mugwump" tendency. He advised voters in 1932 to be loyal to their party so long as its leaders stood for right ideals and practices in government. But, "If the party leaders are found wanting, the true loyalty of the citizen is to his community." [14] Although a lifelong Democrat (as was his father), he was always proud to say that he cast his first vote for president for a Republican—his distant relative, Theodore Roosevelt. This vote may hardly be regarded as a fair test, but he insisted that he "often" voted Republican in Dutchess County elections, "where I thought that cleaning house was a good thing or that the Republican was a better man." [15]

Members of party organizations, he conceded, were more bound than ordinary citizens to support their party candidates and policies. Still, in addressing the Democratic State Committee in Albany, in January, 1929, Roosevelt urged these leaders to support "all wise and just legislation," regardless of whether it originated in one party or the other. This, he thought, was not only good citizenship, but good politics. For the voters of the state appreciated and remembered the willingness of a party to aid good legislation, even when sponsored by its political opponents. He asserted that this broad-minded policy largely explained the steady increase in Democratic votes upstate (where registration was normally Republican).[16]

How much independence may a legislator exercise when voting upon specific measures? To what degree is he bound by the committee of his home district, the state organization, or the legislative caucus? Roosevelt faced this issue immediately after taking office as State senator. He did not wish to vote in the legislature for William Sheehan, the Tammany-approved nominee for United States sentator. Could he, as a party member, defy the Democratic organization? Confessing ignorance of procedure, the young politician sought the advice of the majority leader of the Assembly, Alfred E. Smith. Smith, a Tammany man, spoke to Roosevelt and several of his Senatorial colleagues: "Boys, I want you to go into the caucus, and if you go in, you're bound by the action of the majority. That's party law. But if you're serious about this fight, keep your hands clean and stay out. Then you're free agents." Roosevelt, relating this account, finished it by saying that the mavericks stayed out and "won the fight." [17]

He approved both Smith's stand for the party and his own irregular action on that occasion. He felt that the individual politician should reserve freedom of judgment and make his decision according to the issue at stake. More than a year before the National Convention of 1940 he wrote to Josephus Daniels that he was "sufficiently honest to decline to support any conservative Democrat" who might be nominated for the presidency.[18] As it turned out, he became the nominee himself, but he nearly balked when a drive was made to name a conservative as his running mate. He actually prepared a statement declining the presidential nomination, and he was ready to use it should the conservatives succeed. Henry Wallace was nominated (by a slim margin), so Roosevelt's resolve was not put to a test. It seems clear, however, that in his way of thinking, there were conditions which could justify "taking a walk" from the party. And while he expected party loyalty from Democratic leaders and workers, he extended the same right to others. The most notable illustration was the defection of Al Smith after the Democratic Convention of 1932. Roosevelt never questioned Smith's *right* to withdraw his support.

Party organization and regularity, up to a point, he considered essential to representative government. He was also a strong believer in the "two-party system," which had prevailed since the time of Jefferson. "There is room," he wrote to Democratic leaders in 1924, "for but two parties." [19] The idea of a party in power and a party in opposition seemed to Roosevelt the most effective means of carrying out the public will and of protecting the public interest. This system, he stated during the campaign of 1932, involved the alternation in office of the major parties. Apparently, Republicans and Democrats could concur in this principle, at least; for Roosevelt made use of a statement by Calvin Coolidge (first delivered in 1920):

> For one reason or another even a wisely led political party, given a long enough tenure of office, finally fails to express any longer the will of the people, and when it does so fail to express the will of the people it ceases to be

an effective instrument of government. It is far better for such a political party—and certainly better for the State—that it should be relegated to the role of critic and that the opposing political party should assume the reins of government.

To this Roosevelt added, "With every word of it I heartily agree." [20] The principle of alternation was attractive to Roosevelt in 1932, when his party (like Coolidge's in 1920) comprised the "outs." But after the Democrats were entrenched in office, he put away his view. When his 1932 speech was published among the *Public Papers and Addresses* in 1938, the quotation from Coolidge, with Roosevelt's endorsement, was missing. (Only an ellipsis indicated the omission.[21]) As a practical politician, the President thought that his earlier observation was best forgotten.

The "two-party" system, in his judgment, was useful only so long as the parties really stood for something, and for something different. It was Roosevelt's lifelong feeling that one of the great parties should be consistently "liberal," and the other, "conservative." From a historical point of view, he thought that the Democrats best represented the former tradition, and the Republicans the latter. The main differences that he saw between liberal and conservative philosophies of government were two: the liberals trusted in the wisdom of the majority, while the conservatives believed in the superiority of an elite (of education or wealth); liberals wanted government to do something about evolving social problems, while conservatives relied upon private initiative. And, he held, "There can, of course, be no quarrel by anybody with anyone who sincerely subscribes to the principles of liberalism or conservatism." Both points of view were legitimate and within the American way; the voters should have periodic opportunities to decide between them.[22]

Roosevelt was disturbed when the two parties failed to offer such a clear-cut choice. One reason why he plugged so hard for a liberal program in the Democratic Party was that he felt this alone justified its existence. He was faced, of course, with the fact that there was a powerful conservative element in the Democratic organization that always threatened to undermine the liberal position. This element, primarily from the Southern states, existed because of the "peculiar institution" of one-party government in Dixie. While Roosevelt did not actually make the break, he always had in mind the formation of a truly liberal party freed of the conservative element. It would take the shape of a coalition between liberals in both of the old-line parties—thus forcing the conservatives in those organizations to merge.

Ernest Lindley has written that Roosevelt, long before 1932, hoped
to make a liberalized Democratic Party the core of a new grouping.[23]
In 1937, according to Stanley High, he wanted to make the Democratic
organization the party of the New Deal.[24] That effort died in the
"purge" of 1938, but the underlying objective lived on as long as he
did. As late as June, 1944, he planned to build a liberal party with
Wendell Willkie. The time had come, thought Roosevelt, for the Democratic Party to "get rid of the reactionary elements of the South, and
to attract to it the liberals in the Republican Party." Willkie, leader of
the Republican liberals, was interested in the idea. It could not be put
into effect at once, but Roosevelt believed that steps could be started
after the 1944 election, aiming toward an effective regrouping by 1948.[25]
Willkie, however, died in October, 1944, and six months later Roosevelt,
too, was dead. Without their forceful personalities, the chance for a
political realignment collapsed. Traditional party bonds are not easily
broken; Roosevelt himself never thought the time quite ripe to launch
an all-out effort.

Pressure Groups: The Labor Lobby

The voters, by support of one or another of the major parties, determined broad policies at the polls. But Roosevelt's experience taught
him that the voice of "the people" was often muffled between elections.
The big noise in legislative corridors and executive anterooms was
that of "pressure groups." Roosevelt seldom referred to individual
lobbyists or their organizations though he was aware of their influence.
He realized that they could serve a useful purpose in public affairs,
but he never thought of them as "necessary" (like political parties).
His remarks about them were generally derogatory in tone.

One objection to lobbyists and publicists was that they often misrepresented the very people they purported to speak for. In New York
State, he had found that the legislative agents for chambers of commerce and manufacturers associations were almost invariably opposed
to social laws, like factory inspection and workmen's compensation.
Yet, in his opinion, such measures were actually favored by a majority
of bankers, manufacturers, and businessmen.[26] Accordingly, Roosevelt
looked with a suspicious eye upon most of the agents of special-interest
groups. Many of these "thousands of organizations for almost every
conceivable objective," were kept going, he thought, so that "some
executive secretary, legislative agent, or other officer may find so-called
useful employment." [27]

He also objected to the careless passing of group resolutions—usually upon subjects of the utmost complexity. Decisions on matters of this kind, he advised the American Youth Congress in 1940, should not be influenced "by any gathering of old people or young people, or anybody else, local or national, who get a smattering of the subject from two or three speakers, who have but a smattering of the subject themselves." But ignorance was only part of the indictment. The special-interest group posed a threat to Roosevelt's idea of a *community* of interests. He earnestly hoped that the country could more and more get away from pressure organizations—"groups coming down here with great vociferation, and often putting through legislation which is beneficial only to one particular group." [28]

One lobby that he seldom criticized was that of organized labor. The unions, of course, functioned primarily in the economic sphere, but they also had political objectives—and salaried publicists and legislative agents. He may have condoned them on the ground that they represented very large numbers of people. But his attitude was due mainly to his unique relation to the labor movement.

His association with union leaders traced back to the days when he was Assistant Secretary of the Navy. Through direct and sympathetic dealings, the young administrator gained the friendship of labor in the shipyards. He referred proudly to the Navy's "labor record" in World War I and rightfully assumed much of the credit. During his term as governor he strengthened his position with labor in New York. But it was the impact of the Depression, coinciding with his broadening interest in national politics, that drew him and the union leaders together. After his election to the presidency, their sense of mutual need and purpose evolved into a durable political alliance.

Alliance is the proper word, for Roosevelt never identified himself with labor. He did not live, think, or act as a worker or an employee; nevertheless, he was deeply sympathetic toward their problems and aspirations. The union leaders, for their part, did not regard the President as one of them—but rather, as their protector and champion. A study of his correspondence with Daniel Tobin, William Green, Philip Murray, and Sidney Hillman reveals the nature of this feeling. The letters are marked by an unmistakable tone of camaraderie and mutual fealty—different from that in messages to other friends, such as Hyde Park neighbors or Harvard classmates. It is the spirit of a crusading captain and his liege lieutenants. Roosevelt was, in a real sense, not only President and head of the Democratic Party, but the advocate of a large and rising social movement. This relationship had potent political implications, and he made the most of them.

While in the White House, he kept in constant touch with the principal labor chieftains. This was done by direct communication and personal talks, but more generally through "go-betweens" designated by the President. Anna Rosenberg, Marvin McIntyre, Rosenman, and other aides were variously assigned to this role. By these means, Roosevelt kept abreast of the views of labor leaders, while in turn advising them on policies and tactics. Assured of his good-will, they usually accepted his counsel of caution and patience. In a characteristic letter to James B. Carey (C.I.O.) in 1942, the President urged compromise in labor's demands. He stated that he and Phil Murray (President of the C.I.O.) managed to agree "nearly all the time." When specific differences arose in industrial relations, "a little give and take on both sides will still save us from the unthinking or political efforts of people on the Hill who really do not understand what is happening all over the world." [29] During World War II, labor's "no-strike" pledge was in large measure a personal pledge to the Commander-in-chief.

The co-operation of the workers helped Roosevelt maintain unity in the Arsenal of Democracy and thus paved the way for Allied victory. His alliance with the unions was also an indispensable foundation of his political strength. He knew, as a practical matter that the "community of business and wealth," with its interlocking power, was aligned against him. Labor was a counterweight, an ally that *must* be held if he were to retain power. It was chiefly for this reason that he generally took the side of the workers in the industrial and legislative field. He believed that the cause of labor was basically just, and that it conformed with the larger objective of national welfare. But he realized, too, that it was politically necessary for him to be "labor's friend" in the White House.

The Art of Politics

Politics, declared Aristotle, most of all deserves the name of *master-art*. For the true aim of politics is the good life, not merely for some individuals, but for a whole people. The determination of what is good and just, he added, will ever be "various and uncertain." Politics is by nature an art of "probable" reckonings—subject not to immutable laws, but only to experience and judgment.[30] The soundness of this ancient view is sustained by a contemporary legal philosopher, Justice Felix Frankfurter. It is a tragic misconception, he wrote in 1946, to think of government as "after all a very simple thing." It is, on the contrary, an exceedingly complicated enterprise, and democratic government is the most difficult of all.[31]

Roosevelt appreciated both the difficulty and the importance of the art. He deplored the low state to which it had fallen during the twenties; it was distressing to him, in the campaign of 1928, to see prohibition become the engrossing issue. He wrote to Josephus Daniels, "Frankly, I am more and more disgusted and bored with the thought that in this great nation, the principal issue may be drawn into what we do or do not put in our stomachs. Are there no great fundamentals to the science and practice of government left?" [32]

Four years later he had the opportunity to express his own views on the fundamentals. In a major speech to the Commonwealth Club of San Francisco, he observed, "Nothing is more striking than the simple innocence of men who insist, whenever an objective is present, on the prompt production of a patent scheme guaranteed to produce a result. Human endeavor is not so simple as that. Government includes the art of formulating a policy, and using the political technique to attain so much of that policy as will receive general support; persuading, leading, sacrificing, teaching always, because the greatest duty of a statesman is to educate."

He saw that statesmanship and politics were *one*. He felt, too, that the "practical politician" was sadly misunderstood by citizens at large. "It is a pity," he wrote in 1932, "that there is a distinction in the public mind between the statesman and the politician. Practically all of our statesmen have been politicians, and many of both qualifications have, by political methods, achieved ends worthy of the admiration of the people. . . ." [33]

Admittedly, there were good and bad politicians, as there were good and bad everything else. The main criterion for judging a politician was how well he performed his duty for good government. Preparation and qualification for office were, of course, important to doing an efficient job. But, thought Roosevelt, "motive in the long run is what counts—motive accompanied by good manners." Speaking to a Jackson Day gathering in 1940, he added an explanation of what he meant by good manners. He referred to his own spirit of friendship toward sincere leaders of the opposition, and to the common good humor which prevailed in Congressional cloakrooms. There were, of course, a few exceptions—men who stretched political disagreements into personal invective. "But," said the President, "why bring up unpleasant subjects at this dinner at which we are all having such a good time? I am genuinely sorry for those exceptions to the rule. They must find it mighty hard to live with themselves—and with their families and their friends as well."

Political Morality: Principles and Compromise

The practical aspect of the art of politics was bluntly put by Roosevelt in a White House conversation with Rosenman. "You know the first thing a President has to do in order to put through good legislation? He has to get elected! If I were now back on the porch at Hyde Park as a private citizen, there is very little I could do about any of the things that I have worked on. . . . You have to get the votes first— then you can do the good work." [34] He proved himself a master of this phase of statesmanship—of getting elected, again and again.

But he was more than a canny and talented campaigner. He understood the dynamics of power in America and knew that no candidate, however skilled, could win the presidency unless certain conditions existed. During the twenties he scanned the political horizon for signs of conditions which could bring his party (and himself) to power. He told Daniels in 1927 that he doubted if *any* Democrat could win the presidency so long as the "undoubted general prosperity" continued. The depression in agriculture was not enough to upset ingrained political habits. "You and I may recognize the serious hardship which the farmers in the South and West are laboring under, but the farmers in the South will vote the Democratic ticket anyway and I do not believe that the farmers of the West will vote the Democratic ticket in sufficient numbers even if they are starving." [35]

His forecast proved correct when Smith lost to Hoover in the flood tide of prosperity. The outcome neither surprised nor discouraged Roosevelt; soon after the election he sensed that an economic change was in the making. In January, 1929, he wrote to his Hyde Park neighbor, Herbert Pell:

> You are right that the business community is not much interested in good government and it wants the present Republican control to continue just so long as the stock market soars and the new combinations of capital are left undisturbed. The trouble before Republican leaders is that prevailing conditions are bound to come to an end sometime. When that time comes, I want to see the Democratic party sanely radical enough to have most of the disgruntled ones turn to it to put us in power again.[36]

The stock market collapsed later that year, the economy fell into a tailspin, and the Democrats came to power in 1932.

Once in power, a holder of high office must make trying moral judgments. As Roosevelt expressed it, "Politics is a series of decisions; they must be made for the long-range benefit of the public." [37] Many citizens, and even some political theorists, take a naïve view of the nature of these decisions. In a given situation, they suggest, the officeholder decides to follow either principle or expediency (his own immediate interest). Actually, the conflict between principle and expediency is a relatively minor problem of statesmanship. It is but one of many considerations that influence a decision. The paramount problem before the statesman is not principle versus expediency, but principle versus *principle*. He must choose from among a number of principles (or objectives), each of which may call for a different course of action. To illustrate: when Roosevelt proposed to borrow money to feed the unemployed in 1933, he chose the principle of "caring for human needs" over the principle of a "balanced budget." (Political expediency, too, was involved, but it was not the dominant consideration.)

What is really required of the statesman is the utmost discrimination and judgment in each situation. There can be no "pat" formula, no easy way of decision. And as conditions change, the leader may have to alter or reverse decisions. To illustrate again: while Roosevelt in 1933 favored feeding the hungry before balancing the budget, he would not have done so had such action impaired government credit (and thereby undermined the safety of all). The value of pursuing a given aim could be judged only in light of its probable results in a particular time and place. Thus, Roosevelt could often be accused of "inconsistency" or of "no principles at all." He *had* principles, but he did not follow them with a foolish consistency. A statesman must pursue the harder task of appraisal and reappraisal, must decide when and where to push for one principle and yield on another—thus subordinating his various principles to the larger end of the general welfare.

After deciding upon a principle, the politician has still to reckon with the aims and interests of others (both his collaborators and his opponents). He may use all his persuasive talents to win them to his view, but the stubborn fact remains that men of equal good will and intelligence often arrive at different conclusions. This situation, arising from contending interests and values (and the uniqueness of human personality), is the central dilemma of statesmanship. When such a difference appears, it is not a "problem" in the ordinary sense of the word—soluble by adequate "knowledge" and "reason." It is, rather, an irreducible fact requiring *adjustment*.

Opposing views in modern society usually take the form of group differences. And this, thought Roosevelt, placed a crucial responsibility upon statesmen. He told students at Rollins College in 1936: "It is the problem of Government to harmonize the interests of these groups which are often divergent and opposing, to harmonize them in order to guarantee security and good for as many of their individual members as may be possible. The science of politics, indeed, may properly be said to be in large part the science of adjustment of conflicting group interests."

So politics rests upon adjustment, which means compromise. It might mean a compromise between principles, between interests, or both. But in any event, it was patent that no statesman could have things all his own way. Furthermore, if he sought too much, if he reached too far too fast, he might fail altogether. Thus, Roosevelt emphasized that politics was pre-eminently the *art of the possible.* He considered that Al Smith, as progressive governor of New York, had proved a model politician. "He knew enough of the practical side of life," Roosevelt wrote in 1928, "to waste little time in seeking the impossible, or in scattering his energies in behalf of causes in which general public interest could not be aroused." He linked Smith with his own dynamic Uncle Ted: "Utterly different in so many ways, yet there is between Theodore Roosevelt and Alfred E. Smith an extraordinary similarity of political method. To get what one can, fight for it, but not jeopardize it by asking for the moon, brought concrete results to both of them." [38] Theodore, he recalled on a later occasion (1932), always expected to have to compromise. He was sometimes forced to accept "one-tenth of what he wanted," but he did so because one-tenth was better than nothing.[39]

Roosevelt was sometimes taken to task for not pushing hard enough for certain reforms. But his answer was, "First things, first!" His wife explained that he frequently withheld active support of causes he believed in because of political realities. She wrote, specifically, of her efforts to persuade him to put Administration pressure behind anti-lynch and anti-poll tax legislation, but neither of these became "must" bills. He told her, "First things come first, and I can't alienate certain votes I need for measures that are more important at the moment by pushing any measure that would entail a fight." [40] He knew that it was poor tactics to attempt to bring about reforms on all fronts at the same time.

He explained this philosophy in 1940, during a talk at the White House with representatives of the Youth Congress. The young men and women had been badgering the President, asking him why he had not assumed more vigorous leadership against this or that evil, which they fancied they saw on the American scene. To one of his more persistent questioners, he said, "Young man, I think you are very sincere.

Have you read Carl Sandburg's 'Lincoln'?" When he heard the answer, "No," he continued:

I think the impression was that Lincoln was a pretty sad man because he could not do all he wanted to do at one time, and I think you will find examples where Lincoln had to compromise to gain a little something. He had to compromise to make a few gains. Lincoln was one of those unfortunate people called a "politician," but he was a politician who was practical enough to get a great many things done for his country. He was a sad man because he couldn't get it all at once. And nobody can. Maybe you would make a much better President than I have. Maybe you will, some day. If you ever sit here, you will learn that you cannot, just by shouting from the housetops, get what you want all the time.[41]

Political compromises, part and parcel of the democratic process, did not require the breach of moral standards. They did not excuse or justify dishonesty of any kind—or extravagance and inefficiency in government. Roosevelt believed that the ethics of officeholders was on the rise in America, and that they should be lifted still higher. In 1932, as governor, he came to grips with the perennial question of the use of public office for private gain. Thomas M. Farley, Sheriff of the County of New York, had been charged with incompetence and misuse of his position. Roosevelt received a demand for Farley's removal and held a private hearing in the case. Chiefly on the grounds that Farley (a Tammany man) had not given satisfactory explanation of his accumulation of wealth while in office, Roosevelt ordered his removal as sheriff. In doing so, he laid down this basic rule:

As a matter of sound general policy, I am very certain that there is a requirement that where a public official is under inquiry or investigation, especially an elected public official, and it appears that his scale of living, or the total of his bank deposits far exceeds the public salary which he is known to receive, he, the elected official, owes a positive public duty to the community to give a reasonable or credible explanation of the sources of the deposits, or the source which enables him to maintain a scale of living beyond the amount of his salary. . . .

The stewardship of public officers is a serious and sacred trust. They are so close to the means of private gain that in a sense not at all true of private persons their personal possessions are invested with a public importance in the event that their stewardship is questioned. . . .

Public office means serving the public and nobody else.[42]

He was aware that officeholders could make unwarranted private gains not only directly, but by means of "outside interests." It was understood by the members of his Administration that he would not countenance such connections. He believed that high party officials were subject to similar restraints; he told newsmen in 1934 that members of the Democratic National Committee should not practice law before the federal departments. There was the danger, he explained, that they might hold themselves out to clients, "as having access to the back door of the Administration. It just 'is not done.'" [43]

A few days later the President had occasion to expand on the touchy issue of political ethics, of proper and improper rewards to office-holders. He was asked by a reporter for his view of a bill pending in Congress which would place statutory limits upon legal practice by men in government positions. Roosevelt expressed the belief that the basic situation could not be dealt with effectively by legislation—the problem was too broad and subtle for that. It was more a matter of general ethics. Placing his remarks strictly "off the record," he stated, "You and I know there are an awful lot of Senators and Congressmen who are getting paid for political influence. I am just saying that in the broad and what has hitherto been accepted as the proper sense with respect to the use of the words 'political influence.'"

"You mean they are practicing law while still serving in Congress?"

"Yes. As the Vice President [Garner] suggestively remarked a little while ago; he said it is perfectly proper for any Congressman or Senator to do political favors which would result in a political reward as long as it is not a financial reward. There is all the difference in the world between these two. Naturally, every member of the legislative body, and I have been one myself, will go out of his way to do favors for people in the hope that that is going to re-elect him. It is perfectly all right. That is an inherent part of our Government political system. But, when he does political favors for pay, that is a horse of a different color, and I think that is where the distinction should be drawn." [44]

Public officials had another moral obligation: to tell the truth. Ed Flynn, who was close to Roosevelt both in Albany and Washington, has written that Roosevelt had a good record in this respect. If Roosevelt gave a false statement or implication, it was usually to avoid hurting someone's feelings; he never did so for a "vicious end." Flynn goes on to state that the public interest often requires a leader to change his mind, to go back on a promise, or to "shade the truth." [45]

Roosevelt would have agreed with this. In addition, he would have pointed to the fact that the truth does not look the same to all men. ("What *is* truth?" asked Pilate.) Moreover, the "rules of the game" have established relative standards for various callings. In a political campaign, the candidate who sticks to literal truths—without selection, coloring, or exaggeration—imposes on himself a severe handicap. For the nature of the business gives rise to "viewing with alarm," excessive generosity of promises, and overzealous estimates of one's party. An appropriate standard can be set only within the context of politics. It is, however, reasonable and fair to judge a politician's "truthfulness" according to that standard.

Roosevelt's speeches against Hoover and the Republicans in 1932 are a case in point. They are in startling contrast with his solid, measured addresses as governor (and later, as president). Some of them, at least, involve distortions of the opposing aims and record to suit the Democratic claims. But Hoover's speeches were, if anything, less accurate ("Grass will grow in the streets!"). The situation was a typical American political scrap for high stakes; winning office was the overwhelming concern on both sides. The voters have long since become familiar with the standards of truth in election campaigns, and they apply the "usual discount" to what they read and hear.

For all that, Roosevelt believed in the principle of truth (as he understood it) and applied it rigorously as president. There were times, of course, when he felt that even this principle must yield to the higher one of national survival. After the blow at Pearl Harbor, he could not reveal the "whole truth" about damage to our forces there. In addition to information "classified" by the military, there were many other facts that could not be told without rendering aid and comfort to the enemy.

The giving or withholding of information is one of the most persistent problems in the presidency (and high office everywhere). Hoover misrepresented financial conditions during most of his term of office, in the hope of maintaining public "confidence." Wilson, Truman, Eisenhower—all the Chief Executives in times of crisis—have felt justified in holding back (or coloring) certain facts. The most trying ordeal for Roosevelt was in connection with his foreign policy from the time of Munich to Pearl Harbor. During those years, as Charles Beard pointed out, there was a considerable difference between "appearances" and "realities." [46] The President represented certain conditions and acts to the public in a way which did not reflect his own judgment of them.

He believed that this course was necessary in order to preserve the nation. Even before Munich, he had been disturbed by the threat of Hitler, but he knew that there was deep-seated isolationist feeling at home and a strong distaste for war. It would take time to educate the people to their peril before they could decide upon measures for their safety. He missed no opportunity to clarify the nature of the Axis menace; but action was imperative, meanwhile, to sustain those already fighting the aggressors. By 1940 Britain was sinking fast, and only American aid could save her. He was faced with a choice of principles: national independence (which depended heavily upon continued British resistance) or strict legality and frankness.

Had he pursued strict neutrality, Britain would in all probability have gone under. Had he, in frankness, gone to Congress for a war declaration, he would have split the country and might have lost the issue. By either course, he would have placed his nation's independence in grave jeopardy. He did not flinch from choosing the harder, more devious way—the only one that promised effective help for Britain without dividing the nation.

Some individuals, of course, will always search for faults, even if the total result be good. Nothing is easier than to sit back (when one does not hold the office) and moralize upon the words and deeds of others. But there is a vast difference between the position of such a critic and that of the responsible statesman. The former is not accountable for the consequences of official action (or inaction); the latter is. Every course has its flaws and dangers; but statesmanship is measured by over-all consequences—as compared with the (estimated) total effects of alternative courses. Roosevelt believed profoundly in this proposition.

Statesmen and Demagogues: Huey Long

Although he believed that a statesman must be a politician, Roosevelt had little use for the demagogue. The demagogue is a politician, too; but his ultimate goal is *self* advancement and profit, rather than the public good. He is willing, in full knowledge, to support socially destructive measures if by so doing he may promote his personal interest. Some of Roosevelt's critics marked him as a demagogue by this definition. The evidence, however, gives little support to the view. Many of his proposals appeared fallacious to orthodox observers; but he rarely sanctioned any plan which he did not consider sound. When one recalls the innumerable "crackpot" schemes that were offered to him while he was in the White House, it becomes clear that Roosevelt would not play the demagogue.

A good illustration was his opposition to the various "old-age pension" plans that mushroomed across the country during the thirties. These schemes, such as the "Townsend Plan," counted many millions of supporters; had Roosevelt been a demagogue he could have put forward a pension plan of his own which would have brought many of these voters to his standard. Instead, he stated openly that the "give-away" proposals were of dubious morality and economics. Writing to George Creel in California, he stated in October, 1938: "As for the '$30.00 every Thursday' plan I have never concealed the fact that I am against it. I hope it will not be tried—because on the one hand I feel quite sure it won't work and because on the other hand I feel quite sure that we can evolve from the present Social Security statute methods of obtaining security for old age which will work better and better each year." [47]

On another, even more critical issue, he again put statesmanship before popularity. The Administration, considering the need for trained military manpower as imperative, supported a Selective Service Act in the summer of 1940. Many Democrats considered this unprecedented move for peacetime conscription as ill-advised in a presidential election year. A partisan editor, L. B. Sheley of Pinckneyville, Illinois, wrote to Roosevelt that support of the bill would cost the Democrats many votes in November. The President answered,

I fully share your doubt as to whether a limited form of selective draft will be popular. In fact, it may very easily defeat the Democratic National ticket —Wallace and myself.

Nevertheless, the situation demands it. Boys need training and toughening and equipment. Voluntary enlistments are for too short a period.

You may be right from the point of view of votes this Fall but if you were in my place you would realize that in the light of world conditions it is, for the sake of national safety, necessary for us to prepare against attack just as fast and just as sensibly as we can.

There are some occasions in the nation's history where leaders have to move for the preservation of American liberties and not just drift with what may or may not be a political doubt of the moment.

I know you will appreciate the spirit in which this personal and confidential letter is written to you but I do hope you will think this thing through in terms of national safety and not just in terms of votes.[48]

Roosevelt would not be a demagogue himself, but he knew their ways and had to reckon with them. The most successful (and most dangerous) was the "Kingfish" of Louisiana—the irrepressible Huey Long. During the campaign of 1932 Roosevelt accepted his support as a Democrat, but he had serious misgivings about him. Rexford Tugwell relates the occasion of a dinner at the Hyde Park estate. A telephone call came through for Roosevelt, interrupting the table conversation. It was Senator Long on the line; and as Roosevelt held out the receiver, the dinner guests (political advisers) could hear the torrent of language from the Kingfish. Among other things, Long warned Roosevelt not to consort with Democratic Party conservatives—men like Owen Young and Newton Baker.

After bidding the Senator good night and hanging up the receiver, Roosevelt turned toward his advisers. "It has its funny side," he said gravely, "but actually Huey is one of the two most dangerous men in the United States today. We shall have to do something about him." [49]

What, if anything, he would have done about Long if the hand of the assassin had not intervened, no man can tell. There were times when he acted swiftly, and there were times when he procrastinated. In his relations with Huey, he played a "waiting game," and it succeeded. He did this from intuition and because he had learned from experience that a "bad actor" might destroy himself, given enough time and leeway. He was also reluctant to part with Long's political support. Long had backed him in the Democratic Convention and in the presidential campaign, and had helped to put New Deal legislation through the Senate. While perceiving Long's true character, Roosevelt was willing to cooperate with him to some extent, as a practical matter. He often said to his secretary, Grace Tully, "You cross a bridge with the Devil—until you reach the other side!" [50]

Meanwhile, he kept the Kingfish under close surveillance. He had two chief concerns about Huey: one was the constitutional question of maintaining a "republican form of government" in the state of Louisiana; the other was the question of Huey as a national political force. Hundreds of letters came to the White House, protesting against the Long regime in Louisiana as tyrannical and un-American. At the same time, reports came to both Roosevelt and Farley, regarding the extent of Long's following in the country and its impact on the President's leadership. The official and unofficial files show that Long was taken very seriously by the Democratic chieftains.

From a legal point of view, Roosevelt could find no substantial basis for intervention in Louisiana. Asked particularly about alleged violations of the state's primary laws in 1934, he told newsmen that he could do nothing regarding the situation. Federal laws, he explained, did not cover state primary elections "in any shape, manner, or form. We are all tied up and, of course, Huey Long knows it." [51] However, he did ask Homer Cummings, the Attorney General, for an opinion as to whether there had been any breach of the Constitution in Louisiana. A reply prepared in the Attorney General's office by Alexander Holtzoff, reached the President in April, 1935. It concluded that the definition of a "republican form of government" was very broad, and that there had been no clear violation in Louisiana. Roosevelt sent this report to Vice-President Garner and to Senator Joseph Robinson, the Majority Leader, for their "study and return." [52]

Huey Long, with his colorful oratory and rabble-rousing instinct, was a man to watch during the critical Depression years. He could promise the moon, and his "Share-the-Wealth" clubs were springing up by the thousands across the land. The title of his autobiography, *Every Man a King,* suggests the demagogic nature of his appeal, which found strong response in certain regions of the country. Huey was not restrained by any false sense of humility; his confidence was reflected in a subsequent book title—*My First Days in the White House.* Ironically, this book did not appear until after his death, for Long was shot down in September, 1935, in the marble halls of the state capitol which he had built as his monument.

Confidential surveys had revealed to Farley and Roosevelt that Long could be a potent threat to the President's re-election in 1936. The Kingfish had no chance to gain the Democratic nomination and could not have won on a third-party ticket. If he chose to run on such a ticket, however, he might easily receive three or four million votes, most of which would otherwise be cast for the Democratic candidate. This simple fact was the basis of Long's bargaining power in the party during 1934 and 1935; it explains why Roosevelt was loathe to break with him and handled him with extreme caution. Long, pursuing a policy of "rule or ruin," might well have determined to bring about Roosevelt's defeat in 1936 should the President refuse his bidding. The issue was never put to a test because of Huey's death; but Roosevelt was aware of the threat and its relation to Republican plans. In February, 1935, he summed up the situation in a letter to Colonel Edward House. The document is a revelation of Roosevelt's political sensitivity and insight, as well as his precision of thought:

Here are the schools of thought of our opponents at the present time:

1. Regular Republicans who want to stand by the Old Guard organization and nominate Vandenberg or someone even more conservative, even though this might mean defeat.

2. More liberal Republicans who think in terms of Glenn Frank and think they could win with such a candidate.

3. Progressive Republicans like LaFollette, Cutting, Nye, etc., who are flirting with the idea of a third ticket anyway with the knowledge that such a third ticket would be beaten but that it would defeat us, elect a conservative Republican and cause a complete swing far to the left before 1940.

All of these Republican elements are flirting with Huey Long and probably financing him. A third Progressive Republican ticket and a fourth "Share the Wealth" ticket they believe would crush us and that then a free for all would result in which case anything might happen.

There is no question that it is all a dangerous situation but when it comes to a showdown these fellows cannot all lie in the same bed and will fight among themselves with almost absolute certainty. They represent every shade.

There is no question that the rest of this Session will be more or less of a madhouse—every Senator a law unto himself and everyone seeking the spotlight. Out of it all I am inclined to think that there will be such disgust on the part of the average voter that some well-timed, common sense campaigning on my part this spring or summer will bring people to their senses. Incidentally, the general economic situation is getting distinctly better, as you know, and as this goes on, there will be added cries of "don't rock the boat."

This "rumor factory" called Washington almost gets under my skin—but as long as it does not actually do so, we are all right.

Do let me know any new thing you hear.[53]

The threat of demagogues and of substantial third-party movements diminished after Long's death. There remained other men of smaller size—propagandists like Gerald L. K. Smith and Father Charles Coughlin. Although Roosevelt paid attention to them, he never regarded them as having significant power—either to upset his program of reforms or his position as national leader.

Objectives and Methods: The Pragmatic Approach

The demagogue, seeking power for his own purposes, is little concerned with the problems of constructive statesmanship. The civic-minded officeholder, on the other hand, feels a responsibility for getting things done. This consideration was ever-present in Roosevelt's mind as he set about to fashion effective methods of achieving objectives. For the statesman must do more than establish goals; he must find ways of moving toward them.

Roosevelt, smashing historic precedent, flew to Chicago in 1932 to accept the presidential nomination from an excited Convention. His act was more than a clever turn of campaigning; it was the sign of a bold, new approach to the way of doing things. "I have started out on the tasks that lie ahead by breaking absurd traditions"—these were his first words as Democratic nominee. He considered it essential to breach the barrier (with respect to methods), so that a sensible policy of experimentation could be applied to modern problems. A year before his acceptance speech he had told students at Van Hornesville School (New York) that the "rules and remedies" of the past did not provide answers for existing economic ills. "Every one of the new factors in our lives is the result of experimentation, and it is therefore only logical and not radical to insist that through experimentation also we must solve the social and economic difficulties of the present." [54]

But the difference between methods and objectives must ever be kept in mind, warned Roosevelt. Broad objectives, such as economic well-being, or world peace, were constant; the course toward those goals must be changed as conditions changed. After going to the White House, he often reiterated this idea at his press conferences. On March 4, 1938, an anniversary of his First Inauguration, he was asked for a "message" by one of the correspondents. The President chose this theme for his informal reply: "I think it is worth while to draw the distinction between objectives . . . on one side, and what we may call methods on the other side." He went on, by way of illustration, to discuss government fiscal policy after 1933. The aim, all along, he said, was "stabilization of the price level, or values." When inflationary forces appeared to threaten that aim, counteracting fiscal measures were initiated by the government; when deflation became the stronger threat, government action was reversed. Hence the means was changed, but the objective remained firm. Yet many persons, he observed, mistook the changes in tack for changes in destination. "Most of you good people are guilty of it, and a lot of other people are, too," he chided. "You do not see the big thing. You see the thing of the moment. This is not a complaint, because it is a perfectly natural, human thing to do. It makes a story."

On the occasion of New Year's Day, 1943, the first anniversary of the United Nations Declaration, he was again in a broadly philosophic mood. A reporter at his news conference asked for his thoughts about the postwar world. He answered that there were many objectives that the nations should continue to seek, but the most important was a lasting peace. "Almost all other things we hope to get out of the war are more or less dependent on the maintenance of peace." Quickly, another query was put forward: would the President care to say how the peace could be upheld? "No, no," he replied. "That's a different thing. In other words, you are talking about details. I am talking about objectives. I think we have got to keep that very firmly in mind on everything we do from now on. The details are not the important thing. The issue is: the objective."

Because he refused to be doctrinaire as to method, he has sometimes been thought a mere improviser. This was the interpretation of those journalists referred to by him in his news conference; it has also been the opinion of some historians. Richard Hofstadter suggested that he lacked a "positive program of ideas," that he relied upon "personal benevolence, personal arrangements, and improvisation." Hofstadter stated that this approach would not do; what is needed is a more inclusive and systematic conception of "what is happening in the world." [55] All this sounds very well, but one may ask if such a conception is really possible. Roosevelt did not think it was, and he did not deceive himself (and others) by embracing a package doctrine which purported to have all the answers.

He did have intelligible and consistent broad objectives. Looking back over his first Administration, he wrote these words in 1938 for the General Introduction to his *Public Papers and Addresses:* "In these volumes those who seek inconsistencies will find them. There were inconsistencies of method, inconsistencies caused by ceaseless efforts to find ways to solve problems for the future as well as for the present. There were inconsistencies born of insufficient knowledge. There were inconsistencies springing from the need for experimentation. But through them all, I trust that there will be found a consistency and continuity of broad purpose." [56] Roosevelt did not fear the inevitable mistakes that such a course (or any course!) must bring. He once consoled the conscientious Tugwell with this advice: "You'll have to learn that public life takes a lot of sweat; but it doesn't need to worry you. You won't always be right, but you mustn't suffer from being wrong. That's what kills people like us." [57]

The consistency of his objectives was confirmed by those who knew him well. Anne O'Hare McCormack, writing for *The New York Times* in August, 1937, emphasized this fact. She had first talked with him in the spring of 1932, and had interviewed him about once a year since that time. During his first Administration, she wrote, the President achieved some of his aims and failed in others—"But the basic ideas remained unchanged." [58] Similar views were expressed later by Rosenman, Hopkins, and Sherwood. But perhaps the point was best stated by Justice Frankfurter. After Roosevelt's death, he wrote: "Undoubtedly there were surface deviations and inevitable tacking from time to time in the course Roosevelt pursued. But . . . during the thirty-five years of his public life he steered a true course—the course of his dominant impulses." [59]

In his methods of action and standards of judgment, Roosevelt was decidedly a pragmatist. He had high ideals and values, but he did not measure human achievements directly by these. His test was both practical and relative: did a given project accomplish its purpose, and was the result an improvement over what had been? He thus saw his own program within the perspective of an evolutionary concept of history.

If such a method in politics sounds vague or planless, it can perhaps be better understood as the work of a creative artist. Frances Perkins was for many years a collaborator in certain phases of Roosevelt's thought and planning. The New Deal, she explains, was not a preconceived theory or plot in existence before 1933. Roosevelt started with central objectives, but his plans for moving toward them were "burgeoning" plans—growing out of events—something to do "next week or next year." He acted this way, says Madame Perkins, because of his feeling that nothing of human judgment is final: one may take the step that seems right today because it can be modified tomorrow if it does not work well. As the artist begins to paint, the picture takes form.[60]

Roosevelt described his own method in a tribute to George Washington in April, 1932. This is what he told the Conference of Governors about the First President:

He met his problems by patient and informed planning, enlightened by a lively imagination but restrained by practical prudence. This practical and prudential manner of working has made him seem to many historians ultra-conservative, but careful examination of his policies shows that they were far-reaching and liberal for the time and circumstances under which he was working. . . .

Washington would have us test his policies by present needs, not by a blind and unreasoning devotion to mere tradition, just so long as the fundamental is sound. Certainly he did not permit himself to be bound by the past. He met one great critical challenge after another by a calm appraisal of the facts and ever-refreshed knowledge of the social and economic conditions of the people of his country—all the people, high, middle, and low. . . .

7

Truth and Citizenship

A PHILOSOPHY OF ACTION based upon empirical knowledge requires a free flow of ideas. Roosevelt not only had the deepest instinct for free inquiry and expression, but he regarded them as indispensable to progress and democracy. He said in 1939 that men needed, more than ever before, the emancipation from error promised by the words, "Ye shall know the truth and the truth shall make you free." [1]

He placed intellectual freedom above every other in importance. "The truth is found," he declared, "when men are free to pursue it. It is this belief in freedom of the mind, written into our fundamental law, and observed in our everyday dealings with the problems of life, that distinguishes us as a nation. . . ." [2] He agreed with Jefferson that all truths were the product of a continual refining process: the unending combat of ideas. Institutions which could not withstand the force of free inquiry were doomed. The untrammeled exchange of ideas, moreover, was the mainspring of creativity.

Roosevelt was witness to the shackles placed on thought in other lands. He deplored every form of tyranny over the mind; yet he was confident that in the end the shackles would be broken. "We all know that books burn," he wrote in 1942, "yet we have the greater knowledge that books cannot be killed by fire. . . . No man and no force can put

142

thought in a concentration camp forever." [3] He was equally sure that nations could not isolate themselves from ideas, for ideas knew no boundaries. To him, the Iron Curtain was as futile as it was foolish.

Education in American Democracy

First responsibility for preserving and extending knowledge rested with the schools and colleges. In a democracy this responsibility included a special task: preparing individuals for intelligent citizenship. Roosevelt, like Jefferson, held that successful popular rule depended upon a sound system of public education. "Government," he said, "could be no more effective than the collective wisdom of its citizens." [4] As he applied the principle of education to democracy, he applied the principle of democracy to education. "We cannot afford to overlook any source of human raw material," he asserted. "Genius flowers in most unexpected places; 'it is the impetus of the undistinguished host that hurls forth a Diomed or a Hector.'" [5]

As he looked about him during the thirties, he saw that equality of educational opportunity was more a theory than a fact. Many sections were deficient in teachers and facilities, chiefly because local communities could not afford them. This meant that young people did not have the same opportunity to develop in all regions. He turned for illustration to his native state of New York and his adopted state of Georgia. He told correspondents in 1934 that the contrast in rural areas of those states was particularly striking. In the South one could not get away from the impression of real poverty. The "human stock" there was equal to that of any section, but economic conditions retarded the schools. "We have got to raise the standards of education; they are perfectly terrible." [6]

How could more equal opportunity be brought about? He thought that the question, in the main, was financial: "It is the problem of dollars and cents." He was opposed, in principle, to the idea of federal subsidies to education—and in no case did he approve of "interference" in the administration and control of schools. However, in areas where adequate services could not be supported by the residents, he came to believe that the federal government could properly supplement local resources. Such aid should be confined to "lifting the level at the bottom rather than giving assistance at the top." [7]

He was reluctant at first to give federal assistance to college students. In August, 1933, Robert M. Hutchins had a conference with him and suggested that some way be devised to give young people a chance to go to college at government expense. Roosevelt told newsmen that he balked at this proposition. "Frankly, the objections are pretty serious, because it would start the Government on a policy of paying for education, which has always been a state and local matter. The chances are ten-to-one that we won't do anything in the way of sending boys and girls to college. It is just one of many thoughts to be considered." [8] But as the unemployment of youth steadily mounted, he changed his mind. In December, 1933, work-aid to students was started by the Federal Emergency Relief Administration, and in 1935 the program of the National Youth Administration was established. Within a year, some 400,000 students were receiving benefits.[9]

World War II opened the door to a far larger program of support. Roosevelt actively promoted the "G. I. Bill of Rights," under which the government offered to pay educational costs for veterans attending public or private schools. According to Samuel Rosenman, the President saw the G. I. Bill not only as a just reward for servicemen, but as an "entering wedge" for federal aid to education. In Rosenman's opinion, the administration of that program reduced opposition to such aid, for it demonstrated that financial help does not necessarily result in loss of local control.[10]

Though Roosevelt believed that all Americans should have equal chance for education, he did not think that everyone ought to go to college. The aptitude and purpose of the individual, as well as the needs of society, should be considered. He knew a number of young people, he said, who were better advised to attend a business or trade school than a college or university. Reflecting his view of economic conditions in the thirties, he felt that there might be too many in the professions already. He did not foresee the enormous demand for educated manpower which was to develop in the forties and fifties.

Roosevelt was not a career educator, like Wilson, and his thoughts on higher learning were not original or profound. But he had a broader view than some of the professionals. He saw the colleges and universities, not through the eyes of teachers, scholars, or administrators, but from the standpoint of society as a whole. As he was often invited to speak at academic exercises, he had frequent opportunity to express his thoughts.

He stepped warily between the lines of antagonistic educational philosophies. He saw good in each camp; both the "traditionalists" and the "functionalists" were partly right. He respected classical learning, the foundation of his boyhood training, but he felt that it was not sufficient to modern needs. The colleges should, indeed, pass on to each generation "the best of our culture that has been tested in the fire of history." But the eternal ideals of truth and justice must be applied in terms of the *present*. Growth and change, he thought, were the law of life. Yesterday's answers are inadequate for today's problems—just as the solutions of today will not fill the needs of tomorrow. Roosevelt presented this challenge to the classicists: "Eternal truths will be neither true nor eternal unless they have fresh meaning for every new social situation." [11]

The problem of keeping up with knowledge was overwhelming, he knew. He frankly sympathized with young people, who needed to know "twice as much as their fathers did." And he gave credit to the educators who recognized and tried to make provision for the new learning. It was no easy task, and those who tried it were often rewarded by jibes from complacent colleagues. But Roosevelt pointed out that continual broadening of the curriculum was the true tradition of education in America. From the beginnings at Harvard and at William and Mary, there had been a steady expansion and accretion— in spite of insistence by older departments that the new-fangled courses were ill-suited and unsound.

Just as Roosevelt urged a balance between traditional and "new" learning, he favored compromise between specialized and general education. Society needed its technicians, experts, and professional men, but these men must be more than just specialists. He put the argument most strongly in his address at the Harvard Tercentenary celebration (September, 1936): "Here are to be trained not lawyers and doctors merely, not teachers and business men and scientists merely; here is to be trained in the fullest sense—man."

He did not pretend to know what form of organization or pattern of courses would best achieve the desired goals. He was sure of only one thing: the plans should be flexible and open to change. He was suspicious of any monistic approach to such a varied and perplexing problem, and he welcomed the multiple forms of higher education in America. All played a useful role: the privately endowed and the tax-supported institution, the small college and the great university, the liberal arts school and the technical institute.

He once told the Regents of the University of the State of New York what every shrewd administrator has sooner or later learned: one of the chief ways to advance an educational program is to call attention to "what other states are doing." Competitive striving, the result of America's pluralistic system, was the best means of finding answers to educational problems. "We have made possible," he explained to the Regents, "the free use of experiments, some of which have been rightly discarded, others of which have been accepted as desirable." [12]

Experiments in methods of teaching and learning were viewed as beneficial for the same reason. In this, Roosevelt applied his general pragmatic philosophy to education. He admired the man of imagination and boldness, who constantly sought something better. His view of education and life was summed up in remarks to Rollins College students in 1936. Without passing judgment on the merits of a new program undertaken there, he praised the effort. The fact that it was in some ways a break from "old academic moorings" should not condemn it, he declared. "In education, as in politics, and in economic and social relationships, we hold fast to the old ideals, and all we change is our method of approach to the attainment of those ideals. I have often thought that stagnation always follows standing still. Continued growth is the only evidence that we have of life."

Roosevelt did not believe that learning should be confined to libraries and classrooms; practical experiences of various kinds should be part of a liberal education. Similarly, he did not consider that a college degree, of itself, gave the holder an adequate view of public affairs. One of his pet subjects was the importance of travel and firsthand observation. While on a trip himself, stimulated by new sights and faces, he became particularly expansive on this theme. He once told the story of an acquaintance who had a Bachelor's degree and several advanced degrees. "When I knew him he was forty-five years old and had been at college for more than a quarter of a century. He was a walking encyclopedia but had never been outside his home town, and he was the most bigoted, narrow-minded, unsophisticated and generally impossible person I have ever met." He urged educated citizens to make special efforts to know their country better. He offered this travel advice:

Take a second-hand car, put on a flannel shirt, drive out to the Coast by the northern route and come back by the southern route. Don't stop anywhere where you have to pay more than $2.00 for your room and bath. Don't talk to your Chamber of Commerce friends, but specialize on the gasoline station man, the small restaurant keeper and farmers you meet by the wayside and your fellow automobile travelers.[13]

Seeing the country in a down-to-earth way was valuable for an honest view of national conditions. Roosevelt thought of it as a phase of continuing education, which he believed should go on for everyone after formal training was ended. He had a lively interest in popular learning and supported every means which seemed effective. What the people needed most was regular access to reliable sources of information—plus the opportunity to discuss public issues freely. Roosevelt's experience in talking to thousands of citizens in all walks of life taught him that this need was greatest in rural areas. He wrote to his neighbor, Henry Morgenthau, in 1929: "What hits me most is the very high percentage of ignorance. I am not concerned about prejudice, personal stupidity or wrong thinking as much as by the sheer, utter and complete ignorance displayed by such a large number of farmers [in New York]. . . . I am inclined to think that someday we will not stop compulsory education at the age of fourteen but will compel every citizen throughout life to attend a school of information once a week." [14]

He never pressed seriously for an extended school requirement, but on every possible occasion he encouraged voluntary adult education. He thought that civic knowledge could be furthered by study groups and public forums, and he sent hundreds of communications to people active in this kind of work. In a characteristic message, he wrote this to Dr. John W. Studebaker, Commissioner of Education: "It is of great importance to the future of our democracy that ways and means be devised to engage the maximum number of young people and adults in a continuous, fearless and free discussion and study of public affairs. This should be the natural post-graduate program of all citizens whether they leave the full-time school early or late." [15]

He did not overlook the role of books and magazines in popular education. The possibilities of these had not been realized, he thought —chiefly because able writers put their efforts into specialized studies, rather than works for the general public. In a letter to his friend, H. G. Wells, Roosevelt sent good wishes on the project of a new "World Encyclopedia." He could not, however, refrain from telling Wells that "you are more good to the world in writing books, which hundreds of thousands of people read and discuss, than in catering to the intelligentsia—there are so few of them. Give us more books that will teach people who can read but have never thought, more about the past and more about the possibilities of the future. Thus you will greatly sustain democracy." [16]

The printed word could be effective not only for civic education, but for cultural growth as well. Willem Hendrik Van Loon wrote to Roosevelt in 1938 concerning the astonishing response to his popular songbooks and to his major work, *The Arts*. With considerable feeling, Van Loon told of the mail he had received from back-country people everywhere, asking for more books of the same character. "We wanted something in our lives outside bread and butter, but we never knew

how to go about getting it," they wrote. Van Loon declared that these
letters had inspired him with a sense of mission: "I have found my
job—to preach the gospel in the name of Bach, Rembrandt, and Bee-
thoven." The President replied that he was exceedingly pleased with
Van Loon's success in a difficult field, and he wished him good speed
in his further endeavors. Then he expressed his own hopes regarding
the cultural experience of ordinary men and women:

> I, too, have a dream—to show these people in the out of the way places,
> some of whom are not only in small villages but in corners of New York
> City—something they cannot get from between the covers of books—some
> real paintings and prints and etchings and some real music. But it is neces-
> sary for them to know what it all means beforehand, and that is what you
> are accomplishing.[17]

During his Administration in Washington, he often called attention
to the possibilities of radio and motion pictures. He congratulated the
directors of broadcasts such as the "University of the Air" and "Town
Meeting," and called for further use of radio to meet the informational
needs of the public. But education by this means made little progress
as measured by its potential. The public was not very enthusiastic,
broadcasters were cool, and critics conjured up the bugbear of "government propaganda." This was also used to check development of
educational films, which Roosevelt once looked to hopefully. In December, 1933, Senator Royal S. Copeland (New York) wrote a glow-
ing letter to the President, outlining the value and feasibility of a series
of one-reel films explaining government operations to taxpayers. These
could be produced by private companies, thought Copeland, without
cost to the government. The Bureau of Mines already possessed a fine
library of such films, which were in "amazing" demand by schools and
civic organizations. Roosevelt thanked the Senator for his suggestion
and agreed that such films could be made the basis of a "very effective
educational campaign."[18]

A few documentary films were produced for the government during
the thirties, and they appeared promising. Roosevelt could write to
Clarence Cannon (Representative from Missouri) in 1939: "You
doubtless know of the real success of those two films which the government got out—one on dust storms on the plains and the other on
soil erosion and floods. The educational value of these films was en-
hanced by the fact that they were both human interest stories and,
therefore, popular with young and old alike."[19] Despite the fact that
they had artistic merit as well as usefulness, these pictures did not form

a pattern of things to come. The new "mass" instruments are yet to be harnessed effectively for popular education.

The Role and Responsibility of the Press

While recognizing the potential of films, radio, and television, Roosevelt saw that the chief source of public information remained what it was in the days of the Founders—the newspaper. The average citizen depended upon the press for most of what he knew about his government and about local, national, and world events. He attended no classes or forums in current affairs; he rarely read a book or listened to an educational broadcast; he went to the movies for entertainment. But he saw the headlines almost every day and usually scanned his paper for "news" and "features." For better or worse, adult education was largely in the hands of the press.

There is probably no single matter upon which Roosevelt's views are so fully set forth as the subject of newspapers. He regarded himself as an expert in this field, and his press conferences often turned into seminars as he lectured reporters on the nature and techniques of their business. He had, without doubt, a lively feeling for journalism; his proudest memories of Harvard were associated with the *Crimson*. Some newsmen grumbled that he made too much of his college adventures in writing. But the excellent rapport between Roosevelt and the press corps rested, in considerable measure, upon the feeling that he was a spiritual colleague. He had a fine sense for news; he could look at public business from the standpoint of the reporters' stories; and in countless ways he helped them do a better job for their readers.

Long before he went to the White House, he perceived the vital role of the press in public education. In his First Inaugural as governor, he took pains to address himself to the newspapers of New York State. He urged them to devote more space to legislative matters in Albany. Most citizens were willing to support progressive government, he stated, but only through the press could they "learn and understand what is going on."

Some time later he sent a special message to the National Editorial Association. He asserted that inefficiency and corruption in government were due mainly to lack of public knowledge. The states were spending millions of dollars for schools, but most citizens were out of school by the time they were old enough to vote. It was up to the newspapers to bring them the facts. In large cities, people usually had access to an informative press (although local government was not well reported), but there was a serious deficiency in rural areas. He believed that state governments should give thought to bolstering rural journals by using them as a medium of adult education.[20]

No man had stronger faith than he in the principle of a free press. He often chided reporters and objected to the inaccuracy and unfairness of some papers, but he never suggested any kind of censorship or control. In this, too, he shared the sentiments of Jefferson. "It is so difficult," the Virginian wrote in 1803, "to draw a clear line of separation between the abuse and the wholesome use of the press, that as yet we have found it better to trust the public judgment, rather than the magistrate, with the discrimination between truth and falsehood." Roosevelt agreed, believing with Jefferson that "Where the press is free, and every man able to read, all is safe." [21]

He was opposed not only to outright control, but to government subsidies to papers or news services.[22] He believed that editors should have a sense of responsibility and patriotism, but he did not want to see them become agents of the government. In his opinion, much of the European press failed to demonstrate true independence. He and Cordell Hull were acutely aware of this at the time of the London Economic Conference (1933). British and French papers combined to build up certain expectations regarding the Conference—then raised a clamor when Roosevelt, in the course of the proceedings, balked on currency stabilization. Blamed in American papers, too, for having "torpedoed" the Conference, he was unusually bitter about the situation the British and French press had created. He let off steam afterward in the company of White House newsmen:

> Well, there is one thing I can tell you literally and strictly and entirely in the family and off the record. The Secretary [Hull] confirmed that one of the contributing factors to the fact that the Conference broke down . . . was the Continental and London press. It was rotten, absolutely rotten, and they gave us a dirty deal from the time we left until we got home.
>
> I would like to say a lot more on it. The whole press just ganged up on us from the start to the finish. And their press was told what to say by their governments, and of course the French press is owned by anybody that will buy it, and there you are.

When he finished, his charges were corroborated by Hull. "I have never been accustomed to a really bad press," he told the correspondents, "but I did get a good dose of it over there. . . . It was an impossible situation." Referring to the foreign papers, Hull concluded, "They are pretty well organized. A large cross-section keeps in close touch with their governments." [23]

When Roosevelt spoke of a "free" press, he meant one free of any kind of government connection. He realized, of course, that the American press was controlled—by its owners—and he never lost sight of the enormous power this placed in relatively few hands. As a practical politician, he accepted newspaper support whenever he could obtain it. Although he disliked William Randolph Hearst, he appreciated the weight of influence of his chain of papers, and preferred to have it on his side. Hearst endorsed his candidacy in 1932, and Roosevelt, by way of response, sent the most polite overtures to him. After the election, while relaxing at Warm Springs, he invited Hearst to visit him there. The magnate of San Simeon sent his regrets, giving reasons of health; but he added that his editors across the country had been directed to support the new Administration.[24] Roosevelt might have gasped a little as he observed how easily the Hearst machine was shifted into gear.

It was not long before the gears were reversed, and the power of Hearst was thrown full force against the New Deal. Roosevelt really felt more comfortable after this happened, for he was accustomed to having the bulk of the newspapers against him. He and his party had won elections in spite of this, but these results did not obscure in his mind the political value of newspaper support. In an address to the Democratic State Committee of New York, in January, 1929, he placed leading emphasis upon the need for more party newspapers. The Democrats, he contended, faced serious difficulty in getting their message to voters who lived outside of the large cities—because of a "pitiful lack" of a party press. He asked for a thorough study of means of solving this problem; it was crucial to the building of solid political strength.

"Support your nearest Democratic paper," he urged members of the Committee. He declared that they had a duty, by placing their subscriptions and their advertising, to help the publishers who backed Democrats for office. In too many localities, he thought, the existing papers, even when labeled "Independent," were mere organs of the Republican organization. In such situations, Democrats should dig down in their pockets and help start their own journals. If this proved impracticable, Party workers should at least undertake protest campaigns, to insure that local papers gave fair treatment to both sides. He was confident, though, that if Democrats would aid party papers in every way possible, a surprising number could be published, "through which we could educate the voters." [25]

His proposals received but feeble response, and no means has since been developed to correct the situation of a one-sided press. Throughout his career, Roosevelt faced a press (outside the South) which was predominantly unfriendly or hostile. Though he considered this a heavy handicap to a candidate and a party, he became more or less resigned to it. What gave him much greater concern, and what he struck out against repeatedly, was dishonesty and falsehood in the reporting of facts. He believed that newspapers, in return for freedom, had a high responsibility: to present news stories truthfully and in fair proportion, and to keep them separate from editorial opinion.

Distortions in news columns took many forms, some subtle and some brazen. In one respect, the subtle devices were the more dangerous, because they were less likely to be detected by readers. During the early days of the New Deal, the President complained that opposition papers gave unwarranted space to "petty" news and stories of differences among Administration leaders; they neglected the broad program and progress of national recovery. There was a tendency, too, to "play up" items that would tend to stir fears and doubts in the minds of the voters. Since most readers had no way of checking upon the actual national scene, they tended to accept the image drawn in the press as true.

Headlines and leads were used to give one party an unfair advantage. By selection of reports from the news services, editors could fill their pages with items reflecting credit on one side and discredit on the other. Individual wire stories were sometimes cut or rearranged to suit partisan purposes. Roosevelt offered examples of these practices during a meeting with members of the American Society of Newspaper Editors in April, 1938. He pointed to the way in which minority speeches in Congress were played up and those of the majority played down. He spoke of stories in which only one side of an argument was carried while the other side was dropped out. "If you people think that is fair newspaper editing, I do not." None of the editors took issue with him on the examples he presented.

The "coloring" or "slanting" of stories by correspondents was most often due, he thought, to directions from their home offices. He made this statement to newsmen frequently, adding that he believed most of them were for him, but had to please their bosses. This notion did not go without challenge; some reporters protested that they had never received orders on how to write a story. He insisted that it was largely true, however, and that he had received letters from men who had resigned their jobs because they could not conscientiously follow such orders. This raised a question which he occasionally threw out to the press corps: "How long should a man stay on a paper and, in order to retain his job, write things, under orders, he doesn't believe are true or that he thinks are unfair?" He conceded that this question was not peculiar to journalism, that it applied to all professions. But it was becoming increasingly serious, and he just didn't know the answer.[26]

He rarely placed blame on the reporters themselves, but on one occasion he "cut loose" with bitterness. It was during the year 1937, after his Supreme Court rebuff, when he was sensitive to attacks by the press. He was particularly annoyed by what he considered "made-up" stories, which were being carried as news.

In a press conference in his Hyde Park study, on a sticky August afternoon, he had his most unpleasant session with correspondents. He took several of them to task for stories about a meeting between himself and Ed Flynn, which resulted, allegedly, in his decision to intervene in the New York City mayoralty race. The issue itself was not particularly important, but his nerves were on edge, and this breach was to him the climax of a series of fallacious reports. He singled out Ernest Lindley for his account of the meeting and insisted that he retract the "lies" in his newspaper. Lindley, squirming under the charge, nevertheless refused to make any admission of his error, if error it was. Roosevelt declared that he was tired of "denying" stories which newsmen wrote and which proved untrue; he pointed out that such denials never caught up with the original falsehood. "What is going to be done about it?" he insistently asked the reporters, who were somewhat aghast at his unaccustomed severity. His resentment was due partly to his feeling that the stories represented ingratitude (as well as untruth)—after the many privileges and confidences he had granted his friends of the press. He reminded them sharply that he could always "close the gate" on anyone who did not play squarely with him.

The reporters looked sheepish, but offered no retractions and no promises. For his part, Roosevelt took no steps and made no further threats after this session; "cracking down" was not his way. This had been a time when he simply got something "off his chest" which was hurting him. At his next meeting with the press, he resumed his normal, easy manner; and there was never again that kind of "hair-down" session. But it is probable that Lindley and the others were a bit more careful in their news stories—at least for a time.

Roosevelt's main attack on newspaper unfairness was directed at the owners. During 1940, in the heat of his "third-term" campaign, he wrote to Josephus Daniels, "I know you will not mind if I say to you that the more I see of American newspapers, the more I am convinced that they represent, in nine cases out of ten, the personal slant or point of view not of the publisher, not of the editor, not of the public, not even of the advertiser, but of the fellow who owns the paper!" He offered a second observation that when the owner reaches a certain position of affluence, he begins to associate with other people in the upper income brackets. At the same time he decreases his association with the "little fellow" and begins to embrace the Hamiltonian theory of society and government. "Soon the check book and the securities market supplant the old patriotism and the old desire to purvey straight news to the public." [27]

One of the serious shortcomings of the new race of owners was the fact that very few of them were true newspaper men. Quoting Grover C. Hall, editor of the Montgomery *Advertiser*, Roosevelt explained that most of them came "not from news room desks but from the counting room, otherwise they would not have the money necessary to buy even a country daily." Some were lawyers, bankers, manufacturers, or advertising managers—few were reporters at heart. "Most of them do not know the difference between an objective news story and a free reader for a furniture store." It was the President's conviction that such men could not edit papers in the interest of the general public.[28] He did not, however, offer a solution to this problem, which lies at the heart of modern journalism.

While Roosevelt thought that the problem was a general one, he singled out certain papers and individuals for criticism. His favorite target during press conferences was "Old Man" Hearst. He often quipped to reporters that if something appeared in a Hearst paper "you know it must be false." In a moment of particular bitterness he wrote to Robert Hutchins, "I sometimes think that Hearst has done more harm to the cause of Democracy and civilization in America than any three other contemporaries put together." [29] His view of Robert R. McCormick, a fellow alumnus of Groton, was not much higher. Bob Hope once cracked, at a White House performance, that the President's dog, Fala, was the "only dog in the country that was housebroken on the Chicago *Tribune*."

There were other, more "respectable" publishers and papers, that were also slanted and unfair—though in a genteel manner. Roosevelt sometimes referred to these as the "fat-cat" or "Tory" press; on the request of reporters he once listed ten of these papers by name. *The New York Times* and the *Herald Tribune* were included. While appreciating the outstanding position of the *Times* in American journalism, he believed that it often handled news in a biased fashion. He resented, too, the superior attitude of its top staff. In 1940 he recalled his attendance at a luncheon (many years earlier) in the "French mahogany carved sanctum" of the *Times*. He wrote to Daniels: "In that rarefied atmosphere of self-anointed scholars, I had the feeling of an uneducated worm under the microscope. But the America of the satisfied professors will not survive, and the America of you and me will." [30]

As for the slick news magazines, he believed that Henry Luce's *Time* could not be trusted for accurate reporting. Hutchins wrote to Roosevelt in 1935, expressing concern about a misleading article in *Time*, involving himself and the President. Roosevelt answered: "Beginning with the first number of *Time*, I discovered that one secret of their financial success is a deliberate policy of either exaggeration or distortion. Pay no attention to them—I don't." [31]

He thought that columnists and commentators were the peculiar bane of modern journalism. It was not the expression of their opinions that bothered him, but the "false statements of fact, which is not their right." [32] He had some experience himself in turning out a regular column; he wrote in 1925 for the Macon (Ga.) *Telegraph,* and again in 1928 for the Beacon (N.Y.) *Standard.*[33] He found it difficult to have an "honest" topic at hand as each deadline came up, and he believed that this was part of the trouble with men who earned their living as columnists. He put his view in strong terms in a note to Stephen Early: "I am convinced that no person alive can write a column that is more than a diary every day, or even two or three times a week—and that that is what we are suffering from most greatly in the United States today." [34]

In his opinion, the columnists not only had to "make up" stories, but had to slant them to suit their clients, the newspaper publishers. He once stated that a well-known commentator had told him that he was not personally opposed to the New Deal reforms, but that he had to criticize them in his column in order to sell it. "I can sell my column to sixty papers, and if I commented the way I really feel I would not have any clients left."

When Roosevelt criticized unfairness or dishonesty in the press, newsmen usually looked pained, or just shrugged. Some felt that he was being querulous or developing a persecution complex. During a conference with editors in 1938, he got this comment from William Allen White, who had been listening to his complaints: "I think I have a little comfort for you," said White. "Seven years ago I was down here on another visit, and . . . here in this hall, walking up and down, was the President [Hoover]. And he was talking about conditions and grumbling with his hands behind his back." Hoover had made the same protests about unfair journalism. The President should "forget" about newspaper abuse: "That is the way they make their money and that is the way they want to run their paper. It cannot hurt you, and it gives them some comfort."

Everybody laughed, but Roosevelt remained serious. He pointed out that the unfair attacks upon Hoover were no more justified than those upon himself; abuses were not to be condoned because they had existed in the past. He then went to the heart of the matter: the newspapers were not injuring the President alone; they were hurting the nation and themselves.

They won't hurt me. Oh, no! It is a much bigger thing than any individual. But they may hurt about 125,000,000 people. They have a very great responsibility. The responsibility is based on a very simple effort that I hope the Press will make, and that is to tell the whole story, both sides, evenly, equally and fairly, without recrimination, without the kind of petty stuff that we have been so accustomed to. . . .

People like to read the Walter Winchells and the Paul Mallons and the other columns; they like to read the amusing stories, the Pearson and Allen stuff, and so forth and so on. But, in the long run, they are getting to the point of saying, "Oh, hell, it is funny, it is grand; I love to read it every morning, but what can I believe? I have read so much of this sort of stuff for years and years."

And I want to tell you, with due solemnity, that we are beginning to get a phrase in this country that is not good for this country; it is bad for this country and it is bad for the newspapers: "Oh, that is one of those newspaper stories."

One reason why Roosevelt broadcast over the radio was because he thought the press had fallen so low. In June, 1940, he explained this in an acid letter to Helen Rogers Reid of the New York *Herald Tribune*. He called her attention to a series of false statements and charges that had been circulated in the newspapers during the months just past. Referring to his Administration, he said, "One of our most difficult tasks has been to get news in factual form to the people of the United States." The newspapers had been more of a hindrance than a help:

I did not speak on the radio the other night because I wanted to. I spoke in order to give a report to the people of the United States—to give them facts about the international situation and our situation at home—facts they needed because so many fanciful and confusing statements had been made regarding our national defense, our Army and Navy, and the government itself. You probably read printed assertions that the government in the past eight years had poured some seven billion dollars down a rat hole.

When a section of the press can bring itself to such extravagant falsification it becomes necessary to resort to other media in order to give the people of the country the facts they are entitled to have concerning what their government is doing.[35]

But resort to the radio was only an expedient; it was not a substitute for newspapers. Moreover, news presentations on the air had become almost entirely dependent upon the same wire services that supplied the press—while the syndicated columnists were finding in radio a larger outlet for the same worn goods. What, in truth, was the remedy? The problem, like many of the other big ones that Roosevelt dealt with, had no apparent solution. He met it, wrestled with it, and left it pretty much as he found it. The crux of the dilemma was how to have a press that was free and yet fair. As control of the press fell into fewer hands, this question became more and more acute.

Roosevelt was not prepared to suggest a cutting of the Gordian knot. He urged, he cajoled, he pleaded for responsible journalism. As in other fundamental matters, he put his hopes in the idea that freedom, somehow, would provide its own corrective. But he saw that in his time the press as a whole was not fulfilling its principal mission. It had lost the confidence of the people; it presented a distorted picture of reality; it failed to supply the facts and ideas essential to sound education and citizenship.

8

The Good Neighbor

THE SENSE OF LOSS when Roosevelt died was global. He was the only statesman of his time (indeed, of history) who was, literally, a *world* leader. Ordinary people, whether European, Asiatic, African, or American, felt that he understood their problems and sympathized with them.

American Policy in the World of Nations

What was the philosophy and policy that made him a world leader? Some of his appeal was due to temperament and personality—his light touch, optimism, and courage. But to millions around the world, he represented more than a gay smile and cheering words. He stood for ideas and practices which promised a better, more decent life for all peoples. In his First Inaugural he declared, "In the field of world policy I would dedicate this nation to the policy of the good neighbor—the neighbor who resolutely respects himself and, because he does so, respects the rights of others—the neighbor who respects his obligations and respects the sanctity of his agreements in and with a world of neighbors." He hoped that, by example, America could lead the way for other nations—to make mutual trust and aid the core of international relations.

He believed in first things first, and after becoming president he gave chief attention to domestic recovery and reform. He was aware, however, that the nation was part of the world, and he set out to secure friendly relations with other countries. Though his policy of the Good Neighbor was universal in aim, he was able to apply it most fully in the Western Hemisphere. For this reason it has generally been identified with inter-American relations.

By no means was he the first or only national leader to favor more enlightened dealings with countries "South of the Border." The earlier interventions by Theodore Roosevelt, Taft, and Wilson had been fiercely resented throughout the hemisphere. Recognizing this, the Coolidge and Hoover administrations took steps toward "normalizing" relations with the Latin republics. It fell to Franklin Roosevelt to follow this lead and complete the foundations of friendship and solidarity.

He came to the task after considerable experience in hemisphere affairs. As Assistant Secretary of the Navy, he had a personal hand in the interventions in Santo Domingo and Haiti. While he did not at the time criticize the policy, he later took the view that such actions were unfortunate and unwise. In a speech before the Woodrow Wilson Foundation in December, 1933, he declared that intervention, for whatever reason, was bound to result in enmity toward the United States:

> I do not hesitate to say that if I had, for example, been engaged in a political campaign of some other American Republic I might have been strongly tempted to play upon the fears of my compatriots of that Republic, by charging the United States of North America with some form of imperialistic desire for selfish aggrandizement. As a citizen of some other Republic I might have found it difficult to believe fully in the altruism of the richest American Republic. In particular, as a citizen of some other Republic, I might have found it hard to approve of the occupation of other Republics, even as a temporary measure.

He felt the time had come to supplement the "Mobile Doctrine" (enunciated by Wilson in 1913)—that the United States did not seek "one additional foot of territory by conquest." He accomplished this by declaring that the nation also would refrain from armed intervention. No one country, he said, bore the responsibility for the internal affairs of the American republics: "The maintenance of law and of the orderly processes of government in this hemisphere is the concern of each individual nation within its own borders first of all. It is only if and when the failure of orderly processes affects the other nations of the continent that it becomes their concern; and the point to stress is that in such an event it becomes the joint concern of a whole continent in which we are all neighbors."

His conviction was put to test during his first months in the White House. General Gerardo Machado, President of Cuba, was overthrown in August, 1933, and several months of political confusion ensued. Rather than make any move toward intervention in the island republic, Roosevelt issued a statement of American policy. This nation would not extend recognition, he explained, to any government which did not clearly possess the support of the people of Cuba. "We feel that no official action of the United States should at any time operate as an obstacle to the free and untrammeled determination by the Cuban people of their own destinies." He expressed friendly concern over the situation and hoped that the Cubans would soon reach a common and peaceful agreement in support of a government. When Colonel Carlos Mendieta succeeded in gaining such support, in January, 1934, his regime was recognized by the United States.[1]

Further proof of the attitude of the President and his Secretary of State was given at the Conference of American States, which met at Montevideo in December, 1933. Secretary Hull put his signature to several important protocols, one of which declared that no nation had the right to interfere in the affairs of another. Roosevelt later remarked, "I believe that the signing of this convention, after the positive refusal by the United States to intervene in Cuba . . . , served to convince the other countries of this hemisphere of the absolute sincerity of this new nonintervention policy on the part of the United States." [2]

The culminating event in his Good Neighbor program was the Inter-American Conference for the Maintenance of Peace, held at Buenos Aires in December, 1936. Marking its importance, Roosevelt decided to attend the opening in person, an unprecedented act by a president of the United States. He made his trip the occasion for friendly visits to other major capitals of South America; everywhere he was received with enthusiasm. He sounded the new note at Rio de Janeiro:

We are showing in international relations what we have long known in private relations—that good neighbors make a good community. In that knowledge we meet today as neighbors. We can discard the dangerous language of rivalry; we can put aside the empty language of "diplomatic triumphs" or "shrewd bargains." We can forget all thought of domination, of selfish coalitions, or of balances of power. These false gods have no place among American neighbors.

After addressing the Conference at Buenos Aires, Roosevelt returned home. Secretary Hull stayed on and contributed much to the final results of the meeting. Pacific means for settlement of inter-American disputes were developed, with provisions for consultation and waiting periods prior to any use of force. Should the peace of the hemisphere be threatened from across the seas, the American nations agreed to consult with one another regarding common policies and actions. These accomplishments were proof to Roosevelt that governments of good will could move together in finding means of enduring peace. The Buenos Aires meeting, he thought, should be an inspiration to the peoples of the Americas and an example to the rest of the world.[3]

Though the Good Neighbor policy aimed to promote peace everywhere, it was conceived primarily in the national interest. Roosevelt was not a "visionary internationalist," as sometimes pictured. He recognized that in his day the basic units of world society were national states, and his first concern was for America. But he knew, as in domestic affairs, that the welfare of each individual or group is affected by the condition and acts of others. His nation would benefit from stability and friendship in the world; it could only be injured by wars and oppression abroad.

During the thirties he believed that the national interest could best be served if the United States retained broad freedom of action in world affairs. He regarded this policy as a matter of method, rather than objective; with the coming of the war he leaned toward collective action by the democratic nations. Until then, however, he avoided commitments which might tie his hands. It was an era in which the old diplomacy could not be trusted, and in which events were moving so fast that precise prediction was impossible. Roosevelt was persuaded that the greatest relative safety for the nation lay in the ability to change course at will.

It was consistent with this view that he changed his position on American membership in the League of Nations. Since he had been a leading proponent of the League after World War I, his reversal in 1932 shocked many of his followers. Some charged that he had abandoned ideals for the sake of political expediency; his move was seen as a surrender to Hearst, whose political support hinged on the issue. Roosevelt was prompted by the political angle to declare his new stand when he did, but the explanation he offered was logical and realistic and may be taken at face value. It is a clear illustration of his pragmatic and flexible mind. This is what he said to the New York State Grange in February, 1932:

> In common with millions of my countrymen, I worked and spoke, in 1920, in behalf of American participation in a League of Nations, conceived in the highest spirit of world friendship for the great object of preventing a return to world war. For that course I have no apology to make.

If today I believed that the same or even similar factors entered into the argument, I would still favor America's entry into the League; and I would go so far as to seek to win over the overwhelming opposition which exists in this country today.

But the League of Nations today is not the League conceived by Woodrow Wilson. It might have been, had the United States joined. Too often through these years its major function has been not the broad overwhelming purpose of world peace, but rather a mere meeting place for the political discussion of strictly European national difficulties. In these the United States should have no part.

The fact remains that we did not join the League. The League has not developed through these years along the course contemplated by its founders. . . . American participation in the League would not serve the highest purpose of the prevention of war and a settlement of international difficulties in accordance with fundamental American ideals. Because of these facts, therefore, I do not favor American participation.[4]

He did, however, support co-operation with League activities which coincided with American aims. He never assumed an attitude of indifference toward the rest of the world, but insisted, during the thirties, that the right of independent decision be reserved. He often found it necessary to underline this point during press conferences. Early in his Administration, reporters were asking him about a statement by Ramsay MacDonald, following conversations with Roosevelt. The Prime Minister had said that the United States had indicated willingness to take part in "consultative pacts," for the furthering of European security. The reporters wanted to know if decisions reached in "consultation" would be binding upon American action—a form of entanglement. The President explained that agreement to such a pact would mean simply an obligation to consult; it would not require this country to accept the verdict. "Therefore it does not tie the hands of the United States in any shape, manner or form and leaves our final action entirely up to us. . . . We in no way are limiting our right to determine our own action after the facts are brought out."[5] He was reluctant to agree even to consult unless progress in world disarmament was made first. Since this did not come about, the consultative pacts never materialized.

An effective independent foreign policy must rest upon realistic appraisal of each situation. This was the principal thought which underlay recognition of the Soviet Union in November, 1933. The President, in opening negotiations with Mikhail Kalinin a month earlier, wrote that he wished to end "the present abnormal relations between the hundred and twenty-five million people of the United States and the hundred and sixty million people of Russia." He believed that serious differences had created the anomalous situation, but that these could be removed by "frank, friendly conversations."[6] After a further exchange of letters and mutually satisfactory discussions, normal diplomatic intercourse was restored.

Roosevelt was pleased by the outcome of negotiations and put the matter in these words to an audience at Savannah: "For sixteen long years a nation, larger even than ours in population and extent of territory, has been unable to speak officially with the United States or to maintain normal relations."[7] His move was criticized as aiding the Red tyranny and facilitating Communist efforts in this country. But he regarded it as the ending of a futile gesture against the Soviet Union. It also had the positive effect of placing a check upon two potential antagonists of the United States. By strengthening Russia's international position, he put additional pressure upon the flanks of both Germany and Japan.

American policy, he believed, should be humanitarian as well as realistic. He upheld our tradition as a haven for the oppressed and favored liberal immigration rules. Branding the Chinese Exclusion Laws as a national mistake, he successfully urged their repeal in 1943. His deepest concern was for refugees from persecution—especially from the Nazi tyranny. During the early thirties there was a steady exodus from Germany of men and women who did not wish to live under Hitler—especially those minorities which faced discrimination and punishment. This was another dark chapter in the age-old story of political oppression. Far more shocking was the gradual realization that the Nazi program did not stop with that—it aimed at the extermination of the Jews as a people.

In 1938 Roosevelt took steps to speed up emigration for the hundreds of thousands of Jews that remained in Germany and Austria. The problem proved to be exceedingly involved and stubborn. Delicate negotiations had to be conducted with the Nazi government, financing and selection arrangements had to be worked out, and areas of resettlement had to be found. The outbreak of war in September, 1939, intensified the difficulties. Roosevelt appointed a War Refugee Board in 1943 and tried to check Nazi atrocities—by threats of punishment and by underground rescue operations. But the number saved was small compared to the millions persecuted and destroyed.

While Roosevelt sympathized with the yearning of Jews for a "National Home in Palestine," he did not regard Zionism as a major solution to the refugee problem.[8] He saw that the question of displaced persons would be greatly magnified after the war—would be more than a concern of Jews alone. In October, 1939, he stated, "Every war leaves behind it tens of thousands of families who for many different reasons are compelled to start life anew in other lands." He estimated that there would be ten or twenty millions of men, women, and children—"belonging to many races and many religions, living in many countries and possibly on several continents, who will enter into the wide picture— the problem of human refuge." He therefore urged that planning be on a broad scale, not for relocation of a few individual groups, but for major movements of world population.[9]

He was disappointed by the unwillingness of most governments to accept refugees. People of many nations showed considerable willingness to help minority families escape from tyranny, but they were singularly cold toward admitting them to their own countries. Roosevelt made no move to raise American immigration limits; he felt that existing quotas represented a fair share of the displaced persons. The numbers were too large to be absorbed by America alone. What he hoped and worked for was the opening of new lands in sparsely settled areas of the globe, where many millions could settle and build their own civilizations.

Unfortunately, no such land could be obtained. The President sought aid from numerous advisers and experts, statesmen and geographers, in looking for suitable areas. Africa and the Americas were studied, and many acres were found to be open. But major obstacles to settlement stood in the way. These usually involved water supply, communications, or policy of the controlling governments. Roosevelt's approach to the sorrowful problem of refugees was sound in theory, but it did not lead to a practical solution.

Legitimate Aspirations of Peoples: Repudiation of Colonialism

The hand of the Good Neighbor, thought Roosevelt, should be held out to all peoples who were seeking their just aims. He regarded self-determination as an inherent right of each nationality—the right to shape its own future. He emphasized this idea especially in connection with small nations, which were often deprived of their independence by force. After the Nazis overran Denmark and Norway in April, 1940, he declared, "If civilization is to survive, the rights of the smaller nations to independence, to their territorial integrity, and to the unimpeded opportunity for self-government must be respected by their more powerful neighbors."[10] He rejected the notion of overlordship based on alleged superiority of one group to another. "We believe," he told the White House Correspondents Association in March, 1941, "that the rallying cry of the dictators, their boasting about a master-race, will prove to be stuff and nonsense. There never has been, there isn't now, and there never will be, any race of people on the earth fit to serve as masters over their fellow men."

It was in keeping with this faith that Roosevelt joined Churchill in the framing of the historic Atlantic Charter, in August, 1941. The Charter stated that both the United States and the United Kingdom "desire to see no territorial changes that do not accord with the freely expressed wishes of the people concerned," and that they "respect the right of all peoples to choose the form of government under which they will live." These were *principles* which applied to every portion of the world; but it was patent that the facts of power, and conflict with other principles, would not always permit their immediate realization. In addition, there was the problem of practical application—of agreeing upon what grouping or area constituted a natural or logical *unit* for self-determination. These conflicts and difficulties, not mentioned in the Charter, were to cause serious disappointments later on.

Roosevelt made certain reservations concerning the principle of self-determination itself. In a Fireside Chat following the Teheran Conference, in December, 1943, he saluted the underground resistance groups and the armies of liberation in countries occupied by the enemy. He reminded them—and the American people—"that the right of each nation to freedom must be measured by the willingness of that nation to fight for freedom." It was likewise understood, he said on another occasion, that no nation had the right to create a Fascist or Nazi form of government. "For the right of self-determination included in the Atlantic Charter does not carry with it the right of any Government anywhere in the world to commit wholesale murder, or the right to make slaves of its own people, or of any other peoples in the world." No nation, by a truly free choice, would establish that kind of regime, he asserted—"For such forms are the offspring of seizure of power followed by the abridgment of freedom." [11] In this connection he discreetly avoided reference to the regime of his military ally, the Soviet Union.

Every independent nation was entitled, he thought, to reasonable security of frontiers. This could be achieved by a combination of military forces and defensible borders. Application of the principle leads, unfortunately, to the most vexing of international problems, because military security is a relative thing. Every increase or decrease in the power of a state, anywhere in the world, registers some effect upon the security of the others. Roosevelt was aware that reasonable military policy for a nation must depend upon judgment of the total situation. But the principle was clear enough. He stated to newsmen, with reference to naval disarmament conversations in 1934, that "Our whole position has been that every nation is entitled to relative security." [12] Arms and men comprised legitimate forces if geared to a sensible estimate of surrounding power.

The strategy of security clearly involved the approaches to each country, and this presented a particularly thorny question. The endless round of border wars and maneuverings for position in European history suggests that no final answer is possible. It has not always been easy for Americans to appreciate the European concern for this problem, but World War II brought the point home, in global terms, to strategists in the United States. In August, 1944, while on a tour of Pacific defenses, the Commander-in-chief made some informal remarks to naval officers and men at Adak, Alaska. He said that the armed services had learned some shocking lessons in the past few years:

> If back in 1940 or early 1941 I had said to the Chiefs of Staff of the Army and the Navy, "Our next war is going to be in the Aleutians and down in the Southwest Pacific," they would have laughed at me. They are the experts in that sort of thing. I am not an expert. I am just an ordinary American. We can see now that we Americans were caught unprepared, because we were ordinary human beings, following the best advice we had at the time. No one would have guessed in 1941 that we would be attacked in such an unsportsmanlike manner as we were. No one could have visualized Pearl Harbor, either out there or in Washington. But if we had known then what we know now, we would have expected an attack in 1941. . . .
>
> Live and learn. That is one thing we are all doing these days. In the days to come I won't trust the Japs around the corner. We have got to make it impossible for them—and we are doing a great deal to make it impossible for them—to repeat this particular route of access to the United States. . . . We are going to make it humanly possible to deny access to or aggressive attack by the Japanese of another generation against any part of the United States.[13]

These words had a similar ring to those of Marshal Stalin, spoken a few months later at Yalta. Russia, in Stalin's lifetime, had *twice* been invaded by the Germans, marching through Poland. The Soviet dictator asserted that Germany (which also committed a "sneak attack" in 1941) must never again have access by that historic route. Though Roosevelt sympathized with Polish aspirations for self-determination, he could also see Stalin's point. He (and Churchill) therefore concurred at Yalta in the view that Russia's security required a "friendly" Poland. But the difficulty of reconciling this idea with the principle of Polish independence was the rock upon which Allied unity foundered in 1945. It was easy for Americans to see the necessity of holding the Pacific Ocean and the land-steps between Tokyo and San Francisco. It was much harder for them to understand why the Russians should be concerned about the land-space between Berlin and Minsk.

Roosevelt believed that protection of a people involved more than border defenses and weapons; it required a sound economic life. This was recognized and made a cardinal point of the Atlantic Charter: the United States and Britain pledged themselves to work toward equal access by all nations to world trade and raw materials. They expressed their desire also to collaborate with other nations for general economic advancement.

It was Roosevelt's feeling that in his day the leading aspiration of most peoples of the earth was for a better standard of living. Even in dealing with aggressor nations, he recognized that their people had legitimate economic desires. He repeatedly urged Hitler to seek, through negotiation, favorable adjustments for trade, raw materials, and colonies. He thought it only fair that the so-called "have-not" powers should have greater opportunity in these respects. However, he was unwilling to lend his assistance to those countries unless they agreed not to attack their neighbors and took steps toward disarmament. He was interested in their economic well-being, but he had no wish to contribute, directly or indirectly, to the building of an aggressive military machine.

The peoples of Asia and Africa, generally speaking, had the most urgent economic needs and were therefore the most deserving of help. Countries which were better off—in resources and technology—should assist them to achieve decent standards of life and health. Wherever Roosevelt went in his travels, he took special note of economic conditions and possibilities.

On his first trip to confer with Stalin (at Teheran), he had an opportunity to see the countries of the Middle East. His sympathy and impulse to help were instantly aroused. Soon after returning to the United States, in December, 1943, he wrote to his old Headmaster, the Reverend Endicott Peabody: "I had the most interesting trip I have ever taken—and I am glad to get away from the poverty and disease and barrenness of North Africa and Egypt and Palestine and Iran. But we can help those countries in the days to come—and with the proper management get our money back—if only we do not revert to the ostrich policy of 1920." [14] He sent Patrick J. Hurley to study the possibilities of giving technical aid to areas of the Middle East, and he responded warmly to the suggestion that Iran be used as an example of what such aid could accomplish. "I am thrilled," he wrote to Hurley in March, 1944, "with the idea of using our efforts in Iran as an example of what can be

done by an unselfish American policy. If we can get the right kind of
American experts who will remain loyal to their ideals I feel certain that
our policy of aiding Iran will succeed." [15] Thus the seed was sown for
President Truman's "Point Four" program.

Roosevelt made it clear that American economic aid was not a device
for imposing control over foreign lands. He was singularly bitter about
European colonialism—and condemned it in the sharpest terms. Poverty
in many parts of the world, he judged, was the result of exploitation of
native peoples by intruders. The consequences were cruel not only to
the exploited but to the world at large. For a people so treated would
lack the will and power to resist attack (or ideological subversion),
and would fall easy prey to aggressors. In a conversation with his son
at Casablanca, in 1943, the President said with feeling: "Don't think for
a moment, Elliott, that Americans would be dying in the Pacific tonight,
if it hadn't been for the short-sighted greed of the French and the
British and the Dutch. . . . When we've won the war, I will work with
all my might and main to see to it that the United States is not wheedled
into the position of accepting any plan that will further France's imperialistic ambitions or that will aid or abet the British Empire in its
imperial ambitions." [16]

Turning specifically to the French, he took the view that they had no
right of restoration in the colonies lost during the war. "How do they
belong to France?" he asked. Writing to Hull in 1944, he predicted: "In
regard to Morocco something new is bound to happen in the next ten
years, and I do not think that a population, which is ninety percent
Moors, should be run permanently by France." [17] He was convinced,
even more deeply, on the question of Indo-China, and he expressed
his views frequently on the future of that country. His position was revealed most frankly in a press conference on board the *U.S.S. Quincy*,
during the return voyage from Yalta. The record of this discussion also
explains how the issue of colonialism opened a breach between Roosevelt and Churchill:

QUESTION. De Gaulle has announced that French Indo-China is to be
soon liberated. By whom, Mr. President?
PRESIDENT. For two whole years I have been terribly worried about Indo-
China. I talked to Chiang Kai-Shek in Cairo, Stalin in Teheran. They both
agreed with me. The French have been in there some hundred years. The
Indo-Chinese are not like the Chinese.
The first thing I asked Chiang was, "Do you want Indo-China?"
He said, "It's no help to us. We don't want it. They are not Chinese. They
would not assimilate into the Chinese people."

I said, "What are you going to advocate? It will take a long time to educate them for self-government."

He said they should not go back to the French, that they have been there over a hundred years and have done nothing about educating them, that for every dollar they have put in, they have taken out ten, and that the situation there is a good deal like the Philippines were in 1898.

With the Indo-Chinese, there is a feeling they ought to be independent but are not ready for it. I suggested at the time, to Chiang, that Indo-China be set up under a trusteeship—have a Frenchman, one or two Indo-Chinese, and a Chinese and a Russian because they are on the coast, and maybe a Filipino and an American—to educate them for self-government. It took fifty years for us to do it in the Philippines.

Stalin liked the idea. China liked the idea. The British don't like it. It might bust up their empire, because if the Indo-Chinese work together and eventually get their independence, the Burmese might do the same thing to England. . . .

QUESTION. Is that Churchill's idea on all territory out there, he wants them all back just the way they were?

PRESIDENT. Yes, he is mid-Victorian on all things like that. . . .

QUESTION. This idea of Churchill's seems inconsistent with the policy of self-determination?

PRESIDENT. Yes, that is true. . . .

QUESTION. Do you remember the speech the Prime Minister made about the fact that he was not made Prime Minister of Great Britain to see the empire fall apart?

PRESIDENT. Dear old Winston will never learn on that point. He has made his specialty on that point. This, of course, is off the record.[18]

Roosevelt heartily endorsed the announced program of Queen Wilhelmina for granting independence to the various peoples of the Dutch East Indies as quickly as they became capable of self-government. He believed that India should be granted commonwealth status during the war and the choice of complete freedom five or ten years afterward. The most galling suggestion, to old-line Britishers, was his proposal at Yalta that Hong Kong (as well as Dairen) be made into an international free port. His entire position seemed, in fact, naïve and wrongheaded from the British point of view. They felt that he misrepresented the aims and results of royal imperialism. More important, they warned that breakup of the Empire would weaken the West in a world of "power politics." It would leave dangerous areas of confusion and strife—"power vacuums" into which potential aggressors (the Reds) could move.

The President was familiar with these arguments, but regarded them as beating on a broken drum. He felt that his position reflected a more realistic appraisal of conditions and popular aspirations. His view seems to have been confirmed, since 1945, by the death-gasps of colonialism in North Africa and Indo-China. A fresh approach—through the principle of trusteeship—might have proved less tragic.

The Cause and Menace of War

The relation of colonialism to war was clearly discerned by the President, but he knew that it was only one of many contributing forces. Economic rivalries—efforts to secure markets and raw materials—were often at the bottom of conflicts among nations. Roosevelt met with Mackenzie King in March, 1937, to probe the causes of war and chart a course for preventing another struggle in Europe. The best chance, they agreed, lay in a co-operative effort to solve the social and economic problems "which lie at the root of national discontent, world unrest, and international strife—and which are the fundamental cause of war.[19]

National jealousies, the race of armaments, and waning confidence in treaties also made for war and fear of war. Danger was intensified by the spread of authoritarian government, which placed supreme power in one man. He was convinced that "ninety percent" of the world's population wanted to live at peace. The real threat came from the possibility that the other ten percent might follow the lead of powerful autocrats, who were seeking aggrandizement. He had no illusions about the nature of modern warfare. On Armistice Day, 1935, he warned the younger generation not to be lured by the false glamour of arms, or the opportunity to escape from the drabness of work to glory on the battlefield. The elation and prosperity which might come from a new conflict would only lead—for those who survived it—to "economic and social collapse more sweeping than anything we have experienced in the past." But stronger words were yet to come. In a speech at Chautauqua, N. Y., in August, 1936, the President expressed his feelings:

I have seen war. I have seen war on land and sea. I have seen blood running from the wounded. I have seen men coughing out their gassed lungs. I have seen the dead in the mud. I have seen cities destroyed. I have seen two hundred limping, exhausted men come out of line—the survivors of a regiment of one thousand that went forward forty-eight hours before. I have seen children starving. I have seen the agony of mothers and wives. I . . hate . . war.

And he knew that if a major clash began in Europe, the peace of the entire earth would be broken. In the countries immediately engaged, millions of lives would be lost "under circumstances of unspeakable horror." The economic and social structure of every nation involved would be wrecked, and no country, whatever its pacific intention, could escape some measure of the consequences.[20] After Hitler unleashed his *Panzers* in 1939, these dark predictions were fulfilled. As the struggle neared its climax, and the world approached a new threshold of atomic destructiveness, Roosevelt saw that all nations had become bound to either life or death. The issue of peace was uppermost in his mind as he prepared what was to be his last message to the American people. The Jefferson Day address, which he would have delivered on April 13, 1945, concluded with this challenging thought—the culmination of his life's philosophy:

> Today, science has brought all the different quarters of the globe so close together that it is impossible to isolate them one from another.
> Today we are faced with the preeminent fact that, if civilization is to survive, we must cultivate the science of human relationships—the ability of all peoples, of all kinds, to live together and work together, in the same world, at peace.
> Let me assure you that my hand is the steadier for the work that is to be done, that I move more firmly into the task, knowing that you—millions and millions of you—are joined in the resolve to make this work endure.
> The work, my friends, is peace. More than an end of this war—an end to the beginning of all wars. Yes, an end, forever, to this impractical, unrealistic settlement of the differences between governments by the mass killings of people.

The Vain Search for Peace

At the close of World War II, the President believed that a new era was at hand, in which peace could be achieved if the people worked for it. He hoped that this would not be another road to disappointment like the roads which had been traveled by preceding generations. He knew, indeed, the acrid taste of disillusionment and failure in the quest for peace. He had seen Wilson's vision sullied and shattered; he had seen his own efforts frustrated by stupidity and madness.

In his attempts to prevent war during the thirties, he shifted from one approach to another. Though his *objective* remained constant, he switched tactics as successive means failed to crack the problem. His work for peace is a foremost example of his dynamic method of thought and action. He followed no rigid course, but responded to facts and possibilities in the flow of events.

From 1933 on, he set forth the view that international differences could be adjusted through negotiation, without resort to arms. This was the policy of the Good Neighbor demonstrated in the successful Inter-American Conferences. All that was needed was good will—and willingness to sit down "around the table." Roosevelt used this approach in connection with the Sino-Japanese "incident," which opened the China War in July, 1937. In a Fireside Chat he announced that the United States had agreed to attend a conference of parties to the Nine-Power Treaty. They would seek a solution to the situation in China, thereby setting an example "of one of the possible paths to follow in our search for means toward peace throughout the world." [21]

It was a *possible* path, but one that was not followed (outside of the hemisphere) during the decade of forgotten promises and treaties. In April, 1939, Roosevelt made a last effort to check the drift toward war in Europe; he offered to act as an intermediary in arranging discussions by the powers on disarmament, trade, and political questions. But, in order to establish a "peaceful atmosphere" for such talks, he asked Hitler and Mussolini to promise to invade no territory for a period of "ten years at least." [22] As he received no answer to these appeals, it was again made clear that international disputes were to be settled not by talk, but by the sword.

His hopes for keeping the peace through negotiation were linked with efforts for disarmament. His most spectacular move in this direction was in May, 1933. He addressed an appeal to all nations of the world, urging them to support positive action to save the faltering Disarmament Conference in Geneva. "Petty obstacles must be swept away," he declared. The ultimate objective, which alone would bring a sense of security in the world, was the elimination of all offensive weapons. This could not be done at once, but a start should be made. He called upon heads of government to stop building additional bombing planes, heavy guns, tanks, and other weapons of attack—while proceeding, in a series of steps, to reduce existing weapons. In order to assure the peace of the world during this period of progressive disarmament, he proposed that all nations enter into a "solemn and definite pact of non-aggression." This would mean, in simple terms, that they would agree to send "no armed force whatsoever across their frontiers." [23] Heartening acknowledgments of his message came back from every nation, but no practical agreements or results were forthcoming.

The difficulty with his appeal (and with subsequent appeals) was succinctly analyzed by the President himself in the 1939 volume of his *Public Papers and Addresses.* Ninety percent of the world's people, content with their own territorial limits, welcomed the principle of discarding weapons of attack. They could not do so, however, so long as the possibility remained that the other ten percent might seek expansion by force. The refusal of that small "ten percent," on various pretexts, to stop their ambitious programs of rearming, killed any real hope of general reduction. "Obviously, unless every nation were willing to eliminate weapons of aggression and offensive warfare and to bind itself not to invade any foreign territory, it was useless to expect any other nation to disarm." [24]

From the beginning, Roosevelt saw the Nazis as the principal threat to the success of disarmament. Several days before sending his proposal to the world capitals, he had a frank discussion in the White House with Dr. Hjalmar Schacht. He emphasized that American policy would be to keep German arms at their existing strength, and to bring the weapons of other countries down to that level. Any other approach to the problem would prove disastrous, said the President, and he asked that Schacht convey this point of view to Hitler.[25]

His suspicions of Germany were so strong that he opposed any plan of disarmament that did not provide for international inspection. He did not wish France to disarm without assurance that Germany would not take advantage of her weakness and "seek revenge." He therefore lent support to the "French Plan" for continuous inspection. This meant, in general, that foreign military officers would be permitted to look at American shipyards and arsenals, while American officers would have like privileges abroad. The President was aware that his acceptance of the inspection idea would encounter "many objections" at home, but he felt that the "overwhelming majority" of Americans would support him if inspection were necessary to achieve disarmament. He was sure that it *was* necessary: "I would not disarm unless I had assurance that the other fellow is going to disarm." [26]

Hitler had no intention of stopping his build-up of arms, which was more or less an open secret. Actually, however, it was the British who balked at the suggestion of arms inspection. Roosevelt became uneasy when advised of this in 1933, but he hoped that their position would be modified. But their attitude remained firm. He was informed from Geneva, in March, 1935, that the British were unwilling to accept the principle because it would expose their "alleged armament weakness." They also declined to release detailed information on munitions orders placed in England, on the ground that such action might injure their arms trade. This was a blow to Roosevelt's hopes, for disarmament hinged upon inspection. He wrote to Hull, "I am much discouraged." [27]

Now, he saw that the military race was on, and he was powerless to stop it. The "armament disease," as he put it, would be fatal to Europe within a few years unless a major operation were performed. And though he continued to hope and pray, he knew that the patient would refuse an operation.

He strove to do what he could in the limited area of warship construction. When the Naval Conference of England, Japan, and the United States met in London in December, 1935, he praised the accomplishments of the Washington Conference (1922) and the first London Conference (1930); he urged that further reductions in tonnage (up to twenty percent) be agreed upon. He made it plain to the American delegate, Norman Davis, that he could not approve, or submit to the Senate for approval, any treaty calling for larger navies. "Governments impelled by common sense and the good of humanity ought to seek treaties reducing armaments; they have no right to seek treaties increasing armaments." [28] But the Japanese were not interested in smaller navies. When their demand for parity of tonnage with England and the United States was rejected, they withdrew from the conference. Since previous naval treaties were to expire in 1936, the race on the sea, as well as on land and in the air, was wide open.

Roosevelt did not cease to speak out for sanity and caution in international affairs. But he was now certain that the aggressors would not be restrained by mere words. This is the question which became uppermost in his mind: how could the United States best weather the coming storm abroad? His initial answer was that America would do best by avoiding any form of involvement in the struggles of Europe and Asia. There was no way of escaping the indirect effects of modern war, but a policy of nonintervention appeared to be a safer course than taking sides. His mood, in 1935, was almost one of "washing his hands." He had seen his repeated efforts to preserve the peace of the world—by negotiation, trade, and disarmament—all collapse. He witnessed the contempt for treaties and promises by the aggressors and the cynical "business-as-usual" attitude of the British and French. They were, all of them, beyond hope of rescue. Roosevelt continued to feel and show sympathy for their peoples, but his main concern now was to shield America from the blows about to fall.

It was at this time that his feeling came closest to that of the "isolationists" and pacifists in the country. There was powerful sentiment against "foreign entanglements"—and in favor of statutory restrictions to keep Americans from being drawn into struggles overseas. In response to this, Congress passed the "Neutrality Act" of 1935, and it was signed in August by Roosevelt.

The measure was the most far-reaching legislation of its type ever passed in the United States. It provided that when a state of war was proclaimed by the President, the export of arms, munitions, and implements of war to belligerents would be automatically prohibited. American ships were not to carry arms to countries at war, and American citizens were permitted to sail on belligerent vessels only at their own risk. A Munitions Control Board was authorized for supervision of the arms business, and licenses were required for export and import of weapons. When the law was renewed in the following year, a provision was added prohibiting loans or credits to nations at war.

Roosevelt had sought for some time to obtain government supervision of the traffic in arms, and he was generally sympathetic with most of the other features of the neutrality legislation. He pointed out later that the act was not really related to neutrality, as understood in international law. (Under international law, neutrals had much greater freedom of action.) Its purpose was to "decrease possible points of conflict with belligerents," and thus decrease the likelihood of involvement.[29] This aim he supported wholeheartedly. On Armistice Day, 1935, shortly after signing the Neutrality Act, he declared, "The primary purpose of the United States is to avoid being drawn into war."

He did object to the inflexible features of the act. In giving approval to it, he stated that the embargo section ought to be reconsidered. No Congress and no President could foresee all possible situations. "It is conceivable that situations may arise in which the wholly inflexible provisions of Section I of this Act might have exactly the opposite effect from that which was intended."[30] Once again, Roosevelt was stressing the need for national freedom of action in a world of danger. As he considered it unwise to be bound by foreign commitments, he also believed it unwise to be bound by domestic statute.

Though he favored repeal of the embargo provision, he remained generally satisfied with the law during the first two years of its operation. The United States, having taken the lead in trying to preserve peace—and having been rebuffed—would sit back, as far from the sparks as possible, and watch the flames leap up in the Old World. Roosevelt's mood, soon after he approved the Neutrality Act, was mirrored in a letter to Breckenridge Long, Ambassador to Italy, in September, 1935. Referring to the self-interested moves of Britain and France, and League indecision while Mussolini prepared to strike Ethiopia, he wrote: "What a commentary this whole situation is on what we like to think of as a modern and excellent civilization. You and Dodd [Ambassador to Germany] have been far more accurate in your pessimism than any of my other friends in Europe. In any event, I think our American position is unassailable—so much so that I really believe that even if hostilities start, I can still make my cruise . . . getting back to Washington inside of four weeks."[31]

When William E. Dodd protested from Berlin that the Neutrality Act was an "unmitigated evil," the President replied that he could not agree. He said that he favored an even stronger law, that would make it possible to forbid export of war materials, as well as arms and munitions. He hoped to obtain such legislation soon.[32]

After the Spanish Civil War began, he asked for extension of neutrality provisions to cover that conflict. When the authority was granted, in January, 1937, he imposed an embargo on arms to Spain. He was severely criticized for this by persons friendly to the Republican Government, and he admitted in 1939 that it might have been a mistake.[33] But the fact that he sought to extend the embargo is further proof of his faith in the neutrality idea at that time. Though Roman Catholics in the country favored General Franco and the embargo, there is no evidence that their influence on the President was decisive.

Looking back upon his action, in 1941, Roosevelt gave this explanation: the leading European powers had adopted a pact of nonintervention in Spain; it was hoped, by the democratic countries at least, to isolate the struggle and prevent it from spreading. From the view of subsequent events, it appeared that Spain should have been the place for the European democracies to stop the aggressors. But, whether or not that was true, "the people of the United States and their representatives were not prepared in 1937 to risk the slightest chance of becoming involved in a quarrel in Europe which had all the possibilities of developing into a general European conflict." In answer to his pro-Loyalist critics, he observed that the Rebel forces controlled more shipping than the Loyalists. Had he not imposed an embargo on Spain, the "overwhelming probability" was that the Rebel forces would have received the greater aid from American implements of war.[34]

As it became clear that the Italians and Germans were using Spain as a springboard to world power, he began to turn away from the policy adopted in 1935. His hope that the United States could best come through the period of foreign wars by means of aloofness and self-imposed restrictions was thoroughly shaken. He saw that the conflicts were not going to be merely local, or even continental, affairs. The Fascist triumphs in Europe and Africa, the rise of Japan in Asia, and development of "understandings" among the aggressors posed a threat of global domination. Roosevelt realized that he must change course— and quickly! Involvement now seemed a lesser risk for America than complete Axis victory. Henceforth, the United States must, in every feasible way, build its own strength and throw its influence against the world aggressors.

He knew that he could not move in this new direction without firm public support. In order to test the national mood and to try, at the same time, to enlighten his fellow citizens, he sent up a "trial balloon" in October, 1937. The "Quarantine" speech, delivered in Chicago, was a frank statement of his own reappraisal of the international scene. It reflected recent developments in Spain, as well as the Japanese offensive in China, which had started in July.

"Without a declaration of war," said Roosevelt, "and without warning or justification of any kind, civilians, including vast numbers of women and children, are being ruthlessly murdered with bombs from the air. . . . Nations are fomenting and taking sides in civil warfare in nations that have never done them any harm." He then gave his view of what this meant to the United States: "If those things come to pass in other parts of the world, let no one imagine that America will escape, that America may expect mercy, that this Western Hemisphere will not be attacked. . . . There is a solidarity and interdependence about the modern world, both technically and morally, which makes it impossible for any nation completely to isolate itself from economic and political upheavals in the rest of the world, especially when such upheavals appear to be spreading and not declining. . . . It is, therefore, a matter of vital interest and concern to the people of the United States that the sanctity of international treaties and the maintenance of international morality be restored."

He was making an historic switch from declarations about noninvolvement to a plea for collective action. The peace-loving nations, he said, must make a concerted effort against the growing international anarchy—"from which there is no escape through mere isolation or neutrality." The epidemic of world lawlessness was spreading; he suggested, therefore, that the community of nations join in a *quarantine* of the diseased patients. But he did not explain how this could be done. He said he would pursue a policy of peace—while seeking a means of checking war.

In spite of his vague assurances, the speech excited apprehension in the country. The isolationist press was up in arms, with charges of "warmongering." Liberals and conservatives alike were stirred, and only the small group of "confirmed internationalists" took cheer from his words. There was a disturbing mystery about the President's meaning. Why had he chosen this particular time to set forth his proposal? What motive lay behind it? Above all, what did he really mean by a "quarantine" of aggressors? On the day after his speech, reporters at his press conference had a frustrating experience. They tried, in every manner, to obtain amplification of his idea. But he parried all questions. He had made no moves, he said. "We are looking for some way to peace," but have advanced no further than the "speech itself." It represented an attitude, not a program—but he was searching for a program.

He was as shocked as anyone—by the general reaction to his address. And he was sobered by the demonstration that public opinion was far behind him, and decided that he must put on the brakes in public while doing what he could to educate the people to their peril.

Testing public opinion was not, however, the only purpose of the quarantine speech. He wished to encourage those already resisting aggressors. Too, he hoped that he might yet awaken a will for united action among the frightened and mesmerized peoples of Europe. He did not think it necessary to offer them a concrete plan of action; it was always his feeling that if agreement could be secured upon an objective, specific methods could be worked out. Privately, he considered the possibility of a general blockade (naval, military, and economic) against aggressors. This would place relations with those countries on a "non-intercourse" basis, thereby avoiding the discredited concepts of economic sanctions or boycotts.[35] But he wanted all avenues toward peace explored; his own probing, innovating mind was ever looking for new paths when the old failed. At the press conference following his Chicago address, he told the perplexed reporters, "There are a lot of methods in the world that have never been tried yet." [36]

Receiving little response, either at home or abroad, to his quarantine idea, he turned to a more practical level of affairs. He moved to modify existing laws in the United States so that the nation could more effectively employ its power, moral and material, against Axis aggression. He was now more than ever convinced that the automatic embargo provision of the Neutrality Act was a positive danger to the nation's security. He pointed out, time and again, that its application more often helped rather than hindered aggressors—and thus improved their chances of world domination.

Congress and the country, however, were loathe to depart from the neutrality provisions. It was not until after Hitler's invasion of Poland (September, 1939) that Roosevelt secured repeal of the arms embargo. The revised law applied "cash and carry" provisions to all trade with belligerents and prohibited American vessels from carrying arms to them. These provisions, while still under the name of "neutrality," had the effect of immediate aid to the British and French, who were now at war with Germany. They had the ships and the cash (for a while) to buy the arms they so desperately needed.

Repeal of the embargo was a significant step in the new direction he pursued after the summer of 1937. Casting off the cloak of aloofness, Roosevelt took the lead in seeking co-operative action against aggressors. He hoped that America's role could be limited to measures "short of war." But he did not shrink from the possibility, if it proved necessary to save our "outer defenses," of resort to arms. This feeling had crystallized at the time of Munich (September, 1938). He wrote to Ambassador William Phillips in Rome:

> Chamberlain's visit to Hitler today may bring things to a head or may result in a temporary postponement of what looks to me like an inevitable conflict within the next five years.
> Perhaps when it comes the United States will be in a position to pick up the pieces of European civilization and help them to save what remains of the wreck—not a cheerful prospect. . . .
> You are right in saying that we are an emotional people over here in the sense that we do not easily lose our heads, but if we get the idea that the future of our form of government is threatened by a coalition of European dictators, we might wade in with everything we have to give.[37]

The New Concept of Defense

For political reasons, he did not discuss the possibility of military action in public; he did not wish to frighten opinion into a retreat to isolation. But he moved as rapidly as he could to build up American strength. In 1938 he asked for a substantial sum for major warship construction. (He justified this request by pointing to burgeoning arms programs abroad, but this did not save him from the charge of naval chauvinism by die-hard pacifists and isolationists.) The Munich crisis taught him the new lesson of air power. He saw the spectacle of Britain (with the greatest navy in the world) and France (presumably with the greatest army) yielding to Hitler's threat of aerial bombardment.[38] At a White House conference with defense leaders he expressed his new appreciation of air weapons and ordered full speed ahead for production of heavy bombers. General "Hap" Arnold regarded this conference as the "Magna Carta" of the Air Corps.[39]

While urging more and better arms, the President linked the security of the United States with that of the hemisphere. This policy had several aims: marshaling the resources of the Americas for resistance to aggression, establishing bases beyond our territorial limits, and providing a justification for long-range military weapons. He tried to liberate strategic thinking from the obsolete notion of "defense of our coastlines." He explained to newsmen in November, 1938: "As a result of world events in the last few years, and as a result of scientific achievement in waging war, the whole orientation of this country in relation to the continent on which we live . . . from Canada to Tierra del Fuego . . . has had to be changed." He stated that the American republics were substantially unanimous in the belief that the continental solidarity established at Buenos Aires must be maintained. This meant that they were concerned about threats to that solidarity in any part of the hemisphere.[40]

Roosevelt knew that the safety of the Americas was related to resistance against aggression overseas. He considered it advisable at this time to avoid discussing the European conflict; there was a panicky feeling in this country about possible intervention on the continent. But in January, 1939, he decided the time had come to put the facts before the Military Affairs Committee of the Senate. The transcript of his secret meeting with the Committee gives a full account of his worldview after Munich.

All his efforts toward preserving European peace had failed, he told the Senators. The aggressors (Italy, Germany, Japan) had been permitted to push ahead, and in 1936 they were joined together by the signing of the Anti-Comintern Pact. In addition to the published portions of this treaty, said Roosevelt, there was a "gentlemen's agreement," whereby they pledged to co-ordinate their expansionist progams. This was strengthened in the following years by successful aggressions and by steadily closer "understanding"—what amounted to an offensive and defensive alliance.

How could the United States best meet this threat of world domination? He believed that the first line of defense in the Pacific was our island bases, from which our forces must prevent a Japanese advance. In the Atlantic, he declared, the first line of defense was the "continued independence of a very large group of nations. . . ." This was a frank and logical analysis, but it was misconstrued by some of the Senators. They reported, privately, that he had placed America's military frontier "on the Rhine."

Actually, he did not mention the Rhine or any other boundary. He named the countries of Europe, indicating those that were independent and those that were partially so. But those that were independent would not be so for long, he said, if the Germans and Italians continued on the move. He then turned to the possible directions that lay open to Hitler—"this wild man." If he went westward, as he had intimated on various occasions, he could overrun Holland. On the other hand, he might move eastward, down the Danube and over into the Ukraine. A third possibility was to move, in conjunction with Mussolini, both west and south—into the Netherlands and toward the Mediterranean. "It is anybody's guess." But whichever way Hitler moved, if Britain and France and the other independent nations decided to fight the Axis, what could they do about arms? In Roosevelt's opinion, the outcome of such a war would be a "fifty-fifty bet," with the supply of airplanes the determining factor. Without aid, he believed, Britain and France would be compelled to yield, and the Axis would gain military control of Europe. Smaller countries then would "drop into the basket," as it would be futile to resist. "Africa automatically falls. That is obvious, because Africa is ninety-five percent colonial."

Meanwhile, he said sarcastically, "We are peacefully out of it. Grand." But what effect would these Axis successes have upon the Americas— and the United States?

The next perfectly obvious step, which Brother Hitler suggested in the speech yesterday [January 30], would be Central and South America. Hitler would dominate Europe and would say to us in the Argentine, "Awfully sorry, but we won't buy your wheat, meat, or corn unless you sign this paper." And the paper that the Argentine is asked to sign says, "Number one, we will take your corn and pay for it in our goods and we will pay for your cattle in our goods and we will pay for your wheat in our goods and we will select the goods. Then, next, you have got to turn over all your military defenses and training to our officers. Oh, yes, you can keep the flag."

Well, if we were Argentine, we would sign because if we were forbidden to export our cattle, wheat and corn to Europe, we would go bust.

And then next would come Brazil. You have already a nucleus; there are 250,000 Germans in there. . . . We have definite knowledge today that in Brazil the Germans have an organization which, probably on pressing a button from Berlin, would be put into operation and would constitute, even today, a very serious threat to the Brazilian Government. You would have a new government in Brazil completely dominated by Germany and Italy and Japan. . . . The same thing, of course would be possible in other places. . . .

Central America? Properly equipped and with the knowledge of how to get the right people to do it for us, we could stage a revolution in any Central American government for between a million and four million dollars. In other words, it is a matter of price.

These are the things you ought to regard. How far is it from Yucatàn to New Orleans or Houston? How far from Tampico to St. Louis or Kansas City? How far?

Now, do not say it is chimerical; do not say it is just a pipe dream. Would any of you have said six years ago, when this man Hitler came into control of the German Government, Germany busted, Germany a complete and utter failure, a nation that owes everybody, disorganized, not worth considering as a force in this world, would any of you have said that in six years Germany would dominate Europe, completely and absolutely? That is why we cannot afford to sit here and say it is a pipe dream. . . . It is the gradual encirclement of the United States by the removal of first lines of defense. That is in Europe and the Mediterranean area.

He went on to speak of the British and French missions that were seeking arms in the United States. Since their continued independence was part of our line of defense abroad, he would give those countries every encouragement to place orders here. This would strengthen them and help put our factories on a mass production basis, which was required for our own growing military forces. He concluded his statement to the Senators by summarizing his position in forthright language:

> I think it was Arthur Krock [*N. Y. Times*] who said, "Isn't this unneutral?" Yes, it might be called that. But I will do everything I possibly can, as Chief of the Army and Navy and head of the Executive Department, to prevent any munitions from going to Germany or Italy or Japan. Why? Because self-protection is part of the American policy. And I will do everything I can to maintain the independence of these other nations by sending them all they can pay for on the barrelhead, to these about forty or fifty now independent nations of the world. Now, that is the foreign policy of the United States. (Applause) [41]

The way of the Good Neighbor, the search for peace, Roosevelt still believed in. But he now faced the fact of world-wide aggression. He focused his thought, therefore, upon means of checking the Axis—and insuring the survival of American independence.

9

Strategy for Survival

DESPISING WAR, Roosevelt hoped that American independence could be preserved by other means. In retrospect it may appear that military action became inevitable, once we placed our moral and economic strength on the side of nations resisting aggression. Roosevelt was aware that the policy of aid tended toward the ultimate use of arms; but as long as the possibility remained of avoiding war, he clung to the hope that we might keep out. It may be noted that it was the military weakness of the Western democracies, more than our support of them, which drew us ever closer to war in Europe. If, with our aid, they had turned back the Axis drives, it is unlikely that we would have become fighting partners. In Asia, where there was no modern power to resist Japan, the situation was different. Japan could have been prevented from dominating the Pacific only by armed action—and that had to come from the United States. This basic fact could not have been changed—whether we had sent help or had kept hands off.

Collective Action—"Short of War"

Roosevelt's principal fear was Germany. After the Munich crisis he moved in numerous ways to bolster the strength and will of the European countries. The means he used ranged from moral support, to supplies of arms, to actual shooting in the open Atlantic. Before Pearl Harbor, even though outside the war, he was looked to as the prime mover of resistance to the Axis. After Pearl Harbor, he became the military leader as well—the chief co-ordinator of the Grand Alliance.

For almost three years (1939–41) the American contribution to collective action took forms that were "short of war." It made sense to Roosevelt to join those who were already opposing the aggressors; they were keeping the war from America's shores. If, indeed, war at last came to the United States, the country was gaining precious time to prepare while others held the line.

There were some citizens, of course, who feared that any form of "taking sides" might drag us into armed clash with the Axis. After Hitler invaded Poland, and the European war was on, their fears grew sharper. Roosevelt found himself under considerable pressure to work for a "negotiated peace"—and to make friends with the Axis powers. But he wholly rejected these suggestions. In a Fireside Chat of December, 1940, he explained why: "The experience of the past two years has proven beyond doubt that no nation can appease the Nazis. No man can tame a tiger into a kitten by stroking it. There can be no appeasement with ruthlessness. There can be no reasoning with an incendiary bomb. We know that a nation can have peace with the Nazis only at the price of total surrender."

Instead, he chose to throw the weight of America's moral position on the side of those fighting aggression. This was the chief meaning of the Atlantic Conference with Churchill, in August, 1941. The Atlantic Charter—which was a declaration, not a treaty—made plain the kind of world the United States was working for; there could be no compromise between this and the program of the Axis. The British and their allies fought on, largely because they knew the President was on their side; he was rendering what material aid he could, and the resources of the United States stood behind his policy.

He made use of diplomacy, too, as a means of helping the democracies. This proved especially effective after the surrender of France; he kept pressure on Vichy to limit French concessions to the Nazis. Churchill acknowledged how much the free world owes to Roosevelt, and he was particularly appreciative during that period, so critical for the British. The President was less successful in dealing with Mussolini, whom he tried to keep out of the conflict. He used every approach—reason, cajolery, warning, and promises—but as France tottered, Mussolini decided for war. When he took that fatal step, in June, 1940, Roosevelt could not contain his bitterness and contempt. "The hand that held the dagger," he declared, "has struck it into the back of its neighbor." [1]

Mussolini's intervention and the fall of France brought a reaction in this country in favor of "all-out" arms production. But to achieve this would require many months, and in the meantime Britain had to be sustained. If that nation were to fall, the United States would have to face the Axis alone. The President put these facts to the people: "If Great Britain goes down, the Axis powers will control the continents of Europe, Asia, Africa, Australasia, and the high seas—and they will be in a position to bring enormous military and naval resources against this hemisphere. It is no exaggeration to say that all of us, in all the Americas, would be living at the point of a gun—a gun loaded with explosives bullets, economic as well as military." [2]

It was this conception which underlay his program of military assistance to Britain. During the thirties, he was certainly no Anglophile. His papers show a deep-seated suspicion of British diplomacy and finance, and he considered that the myopia of their statesmen was largely responsible for the rise of Hitler as a threat to European security. But he preferred the British, with their known faults and weaknesses, to the brutal, bullying Nazis. And he knew enough of the history of British sea power to appreciate its role as a shield for the Americas. Consequently, as the best practical means of defending the United States, he proposed to send large supplies of arms to the valiant defenders of England. "We must become," he said, "the great arsenal of democracy."

But arsenals cost money, and he explained in his Annual Message of 1941 that the British did not have sufficient resources to buy the weapons they needed. "The time is near when they will not be able to pay for them all in ready cash. We cannot, and we will not, tell them that they must surrender, merely because of present inability to pay for the weapons which we know they must have." He then proposed his "Lend-Lease" idea—that the United States send the British what they needed—to be repaid, after hostilities, in the same or similar materials.

Production of arms was the chief contribution of the United States—before declaring war—to collective defense against aggression. However, the arms had to be delivered, and the Commander-in-chief did not hesitate to expand American naval operations, to accomplish this. The Royal Navy, hard-pressed around the globe, could not do the job alone. There was intense opposition in Congress to providing American convoys, but the President side-stepped the issue by extending naval "patrols."

Though he parried questions about the operating instructions or locations of the patrols, he explained that their function was to report upon potentially aggressive ships which might be coming toward the hemisphere. He also stated that the patrols were on guard against Nazi seizure of bases in the Atlantic. In a radio address of May, 1941, he warned that occupation of Iceland or Greenland would bring the war close to our continental shores. Those islands were but steppingstones to Labrador and Newfoundland and to the industrial centers of the northern United States.

The possibility of seizure of bases was reduced when the President, by agreement with the authorities concerned, ordered construction forces to Greenland (June, 1941). A month later American troops relieved British defense forces in Iceland, so that they could be redeployed elsewhere. However, the toll at sea went on. By September Roosevelt was preparing the country for naval *war* in the Atlantic, as the only means of keeping supply lines open to Britain. In order to justify this move, he turned to the principle of "freedom of the seas."

In a militant Fireside talk of September, 1941, he referred to the centuries-old struggle for freedom of the seas. "It means," he said, "that no Nation has the right to make the broad oceans of the world at great distances from the actual theater of land war unsafe for the commerce of others. . . . Unrestricted submarine warfare in 1941 constitutes a defiance—an act of aggression—against that historic American policy." He carefully chose words that would justify in the public mind the *offensive* operations which he now considered necessary:

No act of violence, no act of intimidation will keep us from maintaining intact two bulwarks of American defense: First, our line of supply of material to the enemies of Hitler; and second, the freedom of our shipping on the high seas. No matter what it takes, no matter what it costs, we will keep open the line of legitimate commerce in these defensive waters. . . .

When you see a rattlesnake poised to strike, you do not wait until he has struck before you crush him. These Nazi submarines and raiders are the rattlesnakes of the Atlantic. . . . Their very presence in any waters which America deems vital to its defense constitutes an attack.

This was stretching language out of normal usage, but he had no qualms. "Do not let us split hairs," he said. He felt that the Nazis had declared war, in essence, upon all nations, including the United States. The situation in the Atlantic was desperate, and now called for positive action by the American Navy. Congress was not ready to declare war, but the situation would not wait. He therefore proposed to *make* war in the name of self-defense. "In the naval waters which we deem necessary for our defense," he announced, "American naval vessels and American planes will no longer wait until Axis submarines, lurking under the water, or Axis raiders on the surface of the sea, strike their deadly blow—first." The following month, on Navy Day, he used even blunter language. The order had been given, he said, to "shoot on sight."

By the fall of 1941 he was playing an active, concerted role, in the anti-Axis struggle. He gave hope to the victims of aggression, and he was sending vital munitions of war to England, Russia, and China. These were measures "short of war"—and in the Atlantic, poised on the brink of "all-out" conflict, the United States was engaged in actual fighting at sea. His moves were of questionable legality and propriety, but he thought them necessary for the safety of the United States. Referring to his orders to the Navy, he told the people: "I have no illusions about the gravity of this step. I have not taken it hurriedly or lightly. It is the result of months and months of constant thought and anxiety and prayer. In the protection of your nation and mine it cannot be avoided." [3]

Global Conflict: The Grand Alliance

The Japanese delivered the blow that released American forces from limited to total war. Thus America became the pivot in a global struggle on two major fronts, Europe and Asia. This was signified in January, 1942, when the representatives of twenty-six nations met in the White House to subscribe to the Declaration of the United Nations. Each government pledged to co-operate, with all its resources, for the defeat of the Axis. Each government also agreed to make no separate armistice or peace with its enemies.

It was evident, of course, that strategical direction would come from the three major military powers among the United Nations: Russia, Britain, and the United States. Actually, the latter two had agreed upon a general plan of strategy many months before Pearl Harbor. In March, 1941, a formal paper (ABC-1) was approved in Washington by representatives of the United States and British military staffs. It provided, in the event of American involvement in the war, for a broad plan of world-wide co-operation. Essentially, this called for defensive measures to protect the Western Hemisphere and the United Kingdom; maintenance of strong positions in the Near East, India, and Far East; and protection of sea communications. Offensive strategy was based on the belief that, since Germany was the most powerful member of the Axis, the Atlantic and the European areas were to be considered the decisive theater. The main effort was to be made there, and operations elsewhere were to be subordinated.[4] The Nazi attack on Russia (June,

1941) did not upset the premise of this Anglo-American conception; and after Japan forced America into the war, the plan was adopted by Roosevelt and Churchill. Its implementation was the subject of successive top-level conferences at Washington, Casablanca, and Quebec—and later (with the Russians) at Teheran and Yalta.

The "Germany first, Japan second" approach conformed to the President's own thinking. When he was asked, as early as April, 1938, how American forces could defend the hemisphere against possible attacks, he gave this answer: "Well, of course, if you have one enemy, we are all right. But suppose you have two enemies in two different places; then you have to be a bit shifty on your feet. You have to lick one of them first and then bring them [military forces] around and lick the other. That is about the only chance." [5]

From the inception of the Axis conspiracy in 1936, he saw the threat in global terms. Probably more than any other statesman, he kept in sight the interdependence of aggression and defense throughout the world. In 1941, when England stood alone against Hitler, he kept an anxious eye upon the Far East. He wrote to Joseph Grew, the Ambassador to Japan, that the conflict in Europe, Africa, and Asia must be seen as a *single* struggle. "Our strategy of self-defense," he said, "must be a global strategy which takes account of every front and takes advantage of every opportunity to contribute to our total security." [6] He believed that possible war with Japan must be considered from the point of view of its effect on the precarious British position. It might draw vital American materials from shipment to England; at the same time, he feared that Japanese seizure of Malaya and the Indies would greatly decrease England's chance of winning by cutting off strategic supplies.

This concern underlay his policy in the Pacific until the Japanese "day of infamy." He wrote to his wife in November, 1940, answering the question of why he did not try to stop American exports of war materials to Japan: "The real answer, which you cannot use, is that if we forbid oil shipments to Japan, Japan will increase her purchases of Mexican oil and, furthermore, may be driven by actual necessity to a descent on the Dutch East Indies." [7] By negotiation, by delay, by suggestion of an eventual "compromise" agreement, Roosevelt and Hull tried to hold back the Japanese advance in South Asia.

In the summer of 1941 Roosevelt tried a firmer line toward Japan. This was due partly to the deterioration of Chinese morale; he felt that something must be done to encourage China to stay in the war. The shift was also due to growing British fears of Japanese expansion toward

Malaya. Churchill advised that a tough attitude toward Japan would be more likely to restrain her than a lenient one, and that she was unwilling to fight Britain and America together.[8] In July Roosevelt froze Japanese credits and cut off shipments of gasoline and oil. This action added to the pressure on the Tokyo militarists, but it was a subordinate factor in their decision to make war on the United States. All the imperial plans were shaping up to a climax. When Nomura and Kurusu undertook their "final" effort to reach an agreement with this country, the high command set a secret deadline for its conclusion.

On November 26 Hull dispatched the note (termed an *ultimatum* by the Japanese) rejecting their last "compromise" proposal. Both he and the President knew that the militarists would react by pushing south. But Roosevelt could not have accepted the proffered settlement. It would have undermined Chinese resistance by stopping our aid to them while guaranteeing oil and credits to their enemy—thus permitting the Japanese to consolidate their gains in Asia.[9] His decision was arrived at, again, in light of its probable consequences in the *worldwide* struggle. The one consequence that he did not foresee—even though the United States had broken the Japanese code—was the sneak assault upon Oahu.

Far from setting up the fleet as a lure to entice attack (as charged by some writers), Roosevelt had sought to postpone a showdown in the Pacific. He was already engaged in naval action in the Atlantic, where he considered the battle crucial to British survival. He would have welcomed expansion of the war against Hitler, but in the Pacific he sought to avoid any act which might give the Japanese a pretext for striking. This policy explains, in part, the absence of more aggressive patrols and readiness in the Pacific. He wanted to avoid war there as long as possible; and if war came, he wanted no mistake about who started it.

The blow at Pearl Harbor was a terrible shock to him, although he was relieved to have the issue with the Axis formally joined. It turned out, in fact, to be the most serious strategical error committed by the aggressors, for it brought America into the war with a unity and will to victory that could not otherwise have been achieved. The isolationists who had insisted that the aggressors "would never attack *us*" were silenced. All Americans learned a lesson, after that fateful Sunday morning, which some were unable to grasp before. The President could say, truthfully, in asking Congress for the declaration of war, "But always will our whole nation remember the character of the onslaught upon us."

The Navy suffered severe damage in the Japanese assault, but the injury had no significant effect upon the over-all plan of operation against the aggressors. Roosevelt, already the leading spokesman of the anti-Axis world, now became the chief director of a unified strategy. Soon after America's entry into the war, he put his view in simple, "A B C" terms for his fellow citizens. In a Fireside Chat in February, he asked his listeners to look at their maps of the world. He pointed to the nations around the globe whose manpower and resources were opposing the enemy, and he suggested that the first requirement was to maintain communications, so that none of these be allowed to fall. American moves against Japan would follow the policy prepared many years before against the possibility of an attack on the Philippines. It called for delaying actions in the western Pacific while the war as a whole took the form of a process of attrition against Japan. "We knew all along that, with our greater resources, we could outbuild Japan and ultimately overwhelm her on sea, land, and in the air."

As the struggle went on, the President demonstrated time and again his remarkable grasp of military operations and their critical interrelation. In a message to Congress on the progress of the war, in September, 1943, he reiterated the governing strategic principles and applied them to the panorama of world action:

Every American is thrilled by the sledgehammer blows delivered against the Nazi aggressors by the Russian armies. . . . It is certain that the campaign in North Africa, the occupation of Sicily, the fighting in Italy, and the compelling of large numbers of German planes to go into combat in the skies over Holland, Belgium and France by reason of our air attacks, have given important help to the Russian armies. . . .

Similarly, the events in the Mediterranean have a direct bearing upon the war against Japan. When the American and British expeditionary forces first landed in North Africa last November, some people believed that we were neglecting our obligations to prosecute the war vigorously in the Pacific. Such people continually make the mistake of trying to divide the war into several water-tight compartments—the western European front—the Russian front—the Burma front—the New Guinea and Solomons front, and so forth—as though all these fronts were separate and unrelated to each other. You even hear talk of the "air war" as opposed to the "land war" or the "sea war."

Actually we cannot think of this as several wars. It is all one war, and it must be governed by one basic strategy.

He concluded his survey of battle fronts with a reminder of the parallel strategy of resources: "Since the beginning of our entrance into the war, nearly two years ago, the United Nations have continuously reduced enemy strength by a process of attrition. That means, cold-bloodedly, placing the ever-increasing resources of the Allies into deadly competition with the ever-decreasing resources of the Axis."

One final consideration was kept in mind by the President—the full power of the Allies should be kept in constant pressure against their enemies, in order to achieve victory in the shortest time feasible. He was aware that new instruments of destruction were constantly being created on both sides. Delay in delivering the winning blow might give the enemy time to produce a decisive weapon, which could turn the tide of victory.[10] That was why he pressed so hard for a direct smash into Germany from across the English Channel. A slower, circuitous approach from the Adriatic or the Aegean might have forestalled Russian occupation of the Balkans or Central Europe—as "Monday-morning" experts have since pointed out. But, even if successful, this alternate strategy would have meant a *longer* war—and the risk that the Germans, in the extra time given them, might perfect and produce new weapons. In all probability, the Channel invasion itself could not have been mounted if another year had been allowed to pass. All southern England would then have been under fire by "V-2" rockets, and against those deadly missiles there was no effective protection.

The need for global teamwork among the United Nations raised the question of co-operation with the Soviet Union. There were some in England and in the United States who thought that no help should be sent when the Nazis unleashed their *Panzers* against the Russians in June, 1941. There were some, after the war, who felt that it would have been better (for the West) if Russia had been allowed to fall into the clutch of the Nazis. Roosevelt and Churchill, who fully appreciated the Axis menace, thought otherwise; they pledged, without hesitation, moral and material aid to the reeling Reds. It was not a question of sentiment or ideology, but a simple matter of military advantage. As Churchill later expressed it in his memoirs, "If Hitler had invaded Hell, I would have had a good word to say for the Devil in the House of Commons!"

Roosevelt's attitude toward the Russians passed through several stages before 1941. In 1933 he had hopes that the Soviet system would gradually be liberalized and that its government would maintain decent relations with other countries of the world. He was disappointed when the Russians failed, in his judgment, to fulfill some of the pledges which they made at the time of recognition. But the event that turned him against them was the signing of the Russo-German Non-Aggression Pact in August, 1939. The Russians had their reasons, after failing to secure satisfactory assurances from the West, for reaching a temporary settlement with Hitler; but the Pact seemed to be the signal for the

Nazi assault on Poland. Since war followed in a matter of days, and the Russians occupied a portion of Poland's eastern territory, they appeared to the West as accessories to the crime.

When, in November, 1939, the giant Soviet Union attacked little, democratic Finland, Roosevelt's sympathy (along with that of almost all Americans) was entirely on the side of the brave Finns. What he and others in the West were even more concerned about was the possibility that Russia and Germany had come to an agreement concerning division and control of Europe, the Middle East, and Africa. Such a combination of power by the two totalitarian states would have been almost irresistible.[11] It now became the fashion in the United States, in speaking or writing, to lump Stalin with Hitler and Mussolini—as the unswerving enemy of liberty and decency.

These new developments opened the question of whether we should continue relations with the Russians. Although they had what they considered legitimate defensive reasons for their war with Finland (which later proved justified), they appeared in the light of 1939 as barbaric and ominous. Roosevelt, at that time, held even the aggressive Japanese in higher regard than the Russians. He wrote to Ambassador Grew in Tokyo that the entire United States was not only horrified but thoroughly angry. He went on, "People are asking why one should have anything to do with the present Soviet leaders, because their idea of civilization and human happiness is so totally different from ours. We have not yet that feeling about Japan, but things might develop into such a feeling if the Japanese government were to fail to speak as civilized Twentieth Century human beings." [12]

Right after the attack on Finland, he issued a statement urging aeronautical manufacturers to refrain from selling articles to nations that engaged in bombing open cities.[13] This "moral embargo" was applied to the Soviet Union until, at the State Department's suggestion, it was lifted in January, 1941. The Russians were thenceforth able to purchase aircraft in this country—which would be sorely needed when the Nazis struck six months later. Roosevelt, however, remained stony toward the Russians and their system. He wrote to Winthrop Aldrich in June that it was his conviction that the American people would "tolerate no compromise with totalitarianism or dictatorship." [14]

Thirteen days after his letter to Aldrich, the *Panzers* stormed into the Ukraine, and Roosevelt shortly announced that America would send aid to Russia under Lend-Lease. Had he changed his views about the Russians? He tried to make it plain that he had *not*—that he still considered Stalin's regime to be an intolerable dictatorship. But he could not help being cheered by what the Russians were doing. He wrote to Ambassador William Leahy in Vichy: "Now comes this Russian diversion. If it is more than just that it will mean the liberation of Europe from Nazi domination." He was convinced that Hitler's armies were the only real danger to the West. "I do not think we need worry," he said, "about any possibility of Russian domination." [15]

In a letter to Pope Pius XII, he explained why he considered the Russians to be a lesser threat than the Nazis:

> The only weapon which the Russian dictatorship uses outside of its own borders is communist propaganda which I, of course, recognize has in the past been utilized for the purpose of breaking down the form of government in other countries, religious belief, et cetera. Germany, however, not only has utilized, but is utilizing this kind of propaganda as well, and has also undertaken the employment of every form of military aggression outside of its borders for the purpose of world conquest by force of arms and by force of propaganda. I believe that the survival of Russia is less dangerous to religion, to the church as such, and to humanity in general than would be the survival of the German form of dictatorship.[16]

He believed that Russia's military effort must become a part of the world-wide fight against the Axis, and he determined therefore to co-operate with it in every effective way. He saw that the maintenance of unbreakable unity among the Big Three was essential to final victory; and he was responsible, more than any other statesman, for preserving it. There was never any serious question about fundamental understanding between the Americans and the British; Roosevelt and Churchill were a "natural" team (in spite of certain differences) right from the start. The only real question involved the Russians. How could positive co-operation, in war or peace, be assured from a nation so unlike the democracies in form of government, religion, economy, and cultural tradition?

Mutual need, in the struggle against the Axis, was the main force holding the opposite poles together. The heroic defense by the Russians won the President's admiration; their terrible losses stirred his sympathy. The Russians, for their part, were greatly encouraged by the massive aid which came from the United States. But aid alone was not enough. Unless mutual confidence developed, the alliance could never be secure.

Roosevelt understood this fully, and he tried, therefore, to look at problems from the Russian point of view as well as from his own and Britain's. He knew that the Soviet leaders were suspicious of the West; after all, the Allies in 1918 had sent troops into Russia to crush the

Revolution—and during the thirties some Western leaders were hoping out loud for a Nazi push into Russia. He went to special pains to remove possible ground for continued suspicions. In this connection, he was especially concerned that the United States make good on its Lend-Lease promises. He once observed, that had he been Stalin, the delays in deliveries would have looked to him like a "run-around" by America and England. Roosevelt was also conscious that his frequent bilateral conferences with Churchill might produce a mistaken impression in Moscow. Early in 1943 he proposed a meeting between himself and Stalin (near the Bering Strait) as a move to counter this. The meeting could not be arranged, however, until December, when the Big Three met together for the first time at Teheran.

Particularly as the ring was tightened around Germany, the danger of splitting the Big Three and of bids for a separate peace was recognized by the President. After the failure of Von Rundstedt's desperate offensive in January, 1945—the Battle of the Bulge—Roosevelt told Congress that "The wedge that the Germans attempted to drive in Western Europe was less dangerous in actual terms of winning the war than the wedges which they are continually attempting to drive between ourselves and our allies. Every little rumor which is intended to weaken our faith in our allies is like an actual enemy agent in our midst. . . . We must resist this divisive propaganda—we must destroy it. . . ." [17] One reason for his insistence upon the principle of "unconditional surrender" was that he wished to prevent the enemy from bargaining with individual allies for a separate, "easier" peace. Relaxation of that principle by the Big Three would have opened the door to unpredictable consequences.

Churchill was less concerned than Roosevelt about the psychological response of the Soviet leaders, but he agreed fully upon the need for unity during the war. He was prepared at Yalta to make further concessions in some respects than was Roosevelt. He told Anthony Eden and Edward Stettinius that he was inclined to yield to Russian insistence upon the "veto" principle, even with reference to procedural matters in the projected Security Council. Everything, he declared, depended upon unity of the Big Three; without it, the world would be subject to catastrophe. Whatever would preserve unity would therefore have his vote.[18] Churchill applied this principle to the wider range of political decisions; in his memoirs, he met the postwar criticisms of Yalta with this justification:

It is easy, after the Germans are beaten, to condemn those who did their best to hearten the Russian military effort and to keep in harmonious contact with our great Ally, who had suffered so frightfully. What would have happened if we had quarreled with Russia while the Germans still had three or four hundred divisions on the fighting front? Our hopeful assumptions were soon to be falsified. Still they were the only ones possible at the time.[19]

Major strategical decisions of the Grand Alliance were made in the famous top-level conferences, such as Yalta. The moves of the war rested upon detailed staff work by hundreds of professional experts, but final judgment on plans for their respective military forces was reserved to Roosevelt, Churchill, and Stalin. This was due, as Roosevelt explained, to the fact that the "Generals and Admirals do not always agree"; it was often necessary for the President to choose among divergent plans of the army, navy, and air experts. On combined strategy, likewise, there was frequently a difference between the American, British, or Russian staffs. These differences were settled, at first, in conferences headed by Roosevelt and Churchill—later, in meetings of the Big Three.[20]

Roosevelt saw these meetings as the principal keys to conduct of the Alliance. They involved not only military co-ordination, but the making of related political decisions and the building of mutual confidence. He viewed the latter meetings as important also for laying the foundations of international organization and a lasting peace. Yalta, which represented the high tide of allied co-operation (February, 1945), may be seen in these various aspects. The Big Three agreed there upon final plans for the defeat and occupation of Germany, entrance of the Soviet Union into the war against Japan, and organization of the United Nations. Many other perplexing matters were dealt with, and solutions to some problems had to be postponed. But the participants rightly judged their work, on the whole, as a signal accomplishment.[21] The cleavage between Russia and the West came *after* Yalta and the death of Roosevelt. He had not expected the Big Three conferences to create an order of automatic harmony; he regarded them as steps in a developing process.

The United Nations

Roosevelt had hopes of seeing a working mechanism for co-operation before the end of his days. His lifetime experience, which included two world wars, strengthened his conviction that the old political order was obsolete. It was not really an order at all, but an anarchy of nations.

His views on international organization had a clearly defined evolution. As a follower of Wilson, he was one of the leading spokesmen for the League of Nations in 1920. He grew disillusioned with it after America failed to join, but he continued to believe that Wilson's *idea* was sound—and that somehow it must be realized if world chaos were to be averted. The League, even with its limitations, was a step in the right direction. Roosevelt understood that a great new concept could not be realized, full-blown, upon the first attempt. It is achieved only after the failure of numerous trials—called "premature" because they do not immediately succeed.

During his illness in the twenties he gave much thought to an improved form of international organization. His ideas were formalized in a definite plan, which he prepared for submission for the Edward Bok Peace Award in 1923.[22] While preserving the "best features" of the League, this proposal added strength to its peace-keeping functions— and included modifications aimed at securing American adherence. Referring to the plan, many years later, Roosevelt observed that it was similar to the draft of the United Nations organization, discussed at Dumbarton Oaks in 1944.[23] The principal sanction it proposed was the severing of *all* relations with any country resorting to war; this was to occur automatically as member nations were notified of the hostile act. It seems clear that this idea was what he had in mind in 1937 when he suggested a "quarantine" of aggressors.

He saw the interdependence of nations drawing them, inevitably, into closer association. "Every trend of modern science," he declared in 1926, "is toward the greater unification of mankind." The nations had found collaboration essential in their efforts to control disease, expand their economies, and extend scientific knowledge. The common man had become especially aware of the nearness of other peoples, both friend and foe. Now, he said, "Wars and armaments are the concern of more than kings." [24]

After becoming president, he believed that steps could be taken to reduce the likelihood of war. But he was convinced that the basic problem could not be solved by old-fashioned diplomacy or occasional international conferences. He stated his view in December, 1933: "I say that the old policies, the old alliances, the old combinations and balances of power have proved themselves inadequate for the preservation of world peace." [25]

Roosevelt considered World War II as a last opportunity for creating a climate of opinion favorable to a new approach. The chance had been tragically lost in 1919–20; it must not be missed again. When he met with Churchill in August, 1941, he insisted that the aim of establishing a "wider and permanent system of general security" be written into the

Atlantic Charter. A few months later he coined the name, "United Nations," just before the historic Declaration was issued.[26] At the time, the term referred only to the united will of the nations fighting the Axis, but Roosevelt looked forward to linking it with a lasting association for peace.

Right after signing the Declaration of the United Nations, he moved toward accomplishment of his goal. He appointed Sumner Welles to head a commission for drawing up plans for a world organization. Welles had accompanied him to the Atlantic meeting with Churchill, and their conversations formed the basis of a draft proposal. Roosevelt approved this in the late summer of 1942 and took it with him to Teheran the following year. He was impatient to push forward more quickly but was restrained by his Secretary of State. Hull was sympathetic with the idea and, next to Roosevelt, was the most influential person in carrying it through. However, he feared that early announcement of the plan would be politically unwise.[27] In public, therefore, the President spoke only in general terms before 1944; but what he had in mind in 1941 (and even as far back as 1923) was essentially the plan which became the United Nations.

His desire for speedier consideration was not just a matter of impulse. He understood the dynamics of public opinion and knew that the impact of war was critical to the overcoming of "normal" prejudices and indifference. Necessary compromises and adjustments could best be worked out with allies while in the comradeship of common struggle. Some leaders and observers feared that negotiations for a postwar organization might lead to differences that would weaken the alliance; Churchill would have preferred to put them off until military victory had been won. But Roosevelt knew that the risk must be taken. He reminded Congress, in his Annual Message of 1944:

> In the last war such discussions, such meetings, did not even begin until the shooting had stopped and the delegates began to assemble at the peace table. There had been no previous opportunities for man-to-man discussions which lead to meetings of minds. The result was a peace which was not a peace. That was a mistake which we are not repeating in this war.

The main difference between the new plan and the old League of Nations was the provision for a body in continuous session (the Security Council) which could act quickly to preserve peace. When aggression starts, explained the President, there is not time to "send out notices" about a meeting to be held on the question "next month." Next month might be too late. Action must be quick and must be effective. The new plan also differed from the League in providing for a number of auxiliary agencies, such as a food organization and a financial organization, which could alleviate economic troubles—and thereby cut down the causes of war.[28]

The new organization, it was clear, must have a military force at its disposal. This did not mean the creation of a "superstate" with its own police forces and other means of "coercive power." It meant that agreements must be worked out, whereby the various nations would maintain, "according to their capacities," adequate armed forces. These must be subject to call by the world body whenever it deemed "joint action" necessary to prevent war.[29]

Roosevelt stressed that the conception of the United Nations was not that of an *ultimate* organization. It was in no sense a world government, but only a steppingstone to greater security. He was certain that at some distant time a world federation would evolve. National armies, navies, and air forces would then disappear except for small security units. Public opinion would become the main force in world affairs; "Big Power" vetoes would be eliminated; and the federation would be governed by democratic procedures.[30]

But the "interim" organization to be formed at the end of the war would be a compromise in many respects. Roosevelt knew that as a practical matter the plan would not be acceptable to the Senate unless the United States representative had the right of veto over enforcement actions. Britain and Russia were equally insistent upon the same prerogative. Stalin took the view that even items of *discussion* in the Security Council should be subject to veto. His point was that the rules should be designed to prevent the possibility of public quarrels among the great nations—since the only real threat to world peace was dissension among the Big Three. There was some logic in this argument, but Roosevelt answered that differences among the great nations would become known anyway. Open discussion would demonstrate to the world the mutual confidence among the powers. Reluctantly, Stalin yielded on this point.[31]

The President, too, made minor concessions. He recognized that the organization could not fulfill its purpose unless all the major countries participated. He made special efforts to induce the Russians to join, for they were understandably wary. Their experience in international associations had been disappointing, to say the least. They had suffered the final indignity of expulsion from the League in 1939 on account of their war with Finland (which they regarded as defensive). The Russians knew, moreover, that the Western nations would have a preponderance of votes in the UN. In light of this experience and prospect, they were fearful and suspicious. They preferred to rely for security upon their own strength and influence.

Roosevelt sought to overcome this attitude. He tried to persuade the Russians that they must gain world confidence in order to become truly secure, and that they would forfeit that confidence by refusing to cooperate. It appears that his argument and assurances had a positive effect. At any rate, the United Nations could hardly have come into being without his planning, leadership, and negotiation. Some will say, "So much the better!" But formation of the UN at least held open the *hope* of lasting peace. Any other course would have been, essentially, a reversion to international anarchy—which could lead only to another world war.

Security in the Postwar World: Russia and the West

The United Nations was a central part of Roosevelt's thinking about the postwar world. He realized, of course, that there were other vital matters to be dealt with and settlements to be made. As usual, he looked for sound *objectives*, believing that method and details could be shaped by experience.

In his planning for the future, he wished to avoid the false hopes of 1919. The tragic failure of Wilson had burned itself into his mind. In April, 1940, looking toward the end of the European conflict, he reminded a group of editors of Wilson's error—"he was looking too far ahead; he was looking toward the permanent ending of war. Well, because of hindsight, because we have seen what happened in the last twenty years, we have all learned a lesson, and I cannot look any further ahead to a world that has ended war than a limited period, twenty or twenty-five years." [32]

Roosevelt stressed that building the peace would require compromises among the allies and among various principles. No one nation or group of nations was likely to secure all the objectives it wanted. In replying to a congratulatory message from Walter Lippmann, after the Moscow Conference of 1943, he struck this moderating note: "Moscow was a real success. Sometimes, however, I feel that the world will be mighty lucky if it gets fifty percent of what it seeks out of the war as a permanent success. That might be a high average." [33] He carried this warning to the public. In the Annual Message of 1945, he said, "Perfectionism, no less than isolationism or imperialism or power politics, may obstruct the paths to international peace." The people should not be discouraged by partial results, but should keep on working for better things.

He began, while hostilities were still in progress, to discuss the broad outlines of the immediate postwar settlement. Reporting on the Teheran and Cairo conferences late in 1943, he set forth initial guides. "Those principles," he stated, "are as simple as they are fundamental. They involve the restoration of stolen property to its rightful owners." At the same time, the means and the will to war must be rooted out of the aggressor nations. In the Pacific, the empire of Japan must be permanently eliminated as a potential force of conquest; in Europe, Germany must be stripped of her military might and given "no opportunity within the foreseeable future to regain that might." [34]

After World War I, he recalled, the peacemakers had *talked* along similar lines. But when the talking was over, and contrary to the terms of the treaty, Germany succeeded in rearming. This must not happen again. The only sure way of safeguarding against it, he believed, was to place temporary policing power in the hands of the victors (the Big Three) when hostilities ceased. They would see to it, by force if necessary, that world order was preserved and the aggressors kept disarmed. This plan would apply during the "transition period," the President explained, but it might work out so well that the United Nations would want to continue it indefinitely." [35] He spoke often of the idea of a transition, or "cooling off" period. The world, reeling from the shocks of war, would hardly be ready to form a durable peace as soon as the last shot was fired. He therefore considered that the great powers had a kind of "super-obligation" to take it upon themselves to act as "sheriffs"— for a period of from two to four years. In the meantime, sound objectives and plans for the postwar world could be evolved. [36]

Roosevelt carried this idea with him to Yalta and found both agreement and willingness on the part of Stalin and Churchill. Stalin took the strongest position of the three. He stated that the three great powers should have the exclusive right to preserve the peace, and that while he would protect the rights of small nations, he would not agree to submitting the action of the Big Three to the judgment of lesser powers. Roosevelt agreed that the peace should be written by the United States, Britain, and Russia. Churchill demurred somewhat, protesting that more regard should be given to the voice of the small nations. He did not, however, propose how this could be done in conformity with the great power principle. [37]

An outstanding merit of the "policing plan," in Roosevelt's mind, was the fact that it would relieve small countries from the burden of armaments. The curse of centuries would thereby be lifted, and economic recovery and reconstruction could proceed more rapidly. It was largely with this thought that he proposed that France should not rebuild her army at the end of the war. At Churchill's insistence, however, he reconsidered and changed his position about France. Churchill firmly believed that a strong Western army was needed on the continent for "European stability" (counterbalance to Russia).[38]

The principal question to be resolved in the postwar settlement concerned the long-range treatment of the vanquished. Beyond immediate disarmament and elimination of the fascist and militaristic parties, what was to be done to the aggressor nations? The view of military and civilian leaders alike was severe in 1944 and 1945. Japan, in Roosevelt's opinion, must be *transformed* so that she would no longer be a threat to the inhabitants of Asia and the Pacific. In a radio address of August, 1944, the President blamed the Japanese people for having supported the imperialistic policies of their war lords for nearly a century. "It is an unfortunate fact," he said, "that other Nations cannot trust Japan. It is an unfortunate fact that years of proof must pass by before we can trust Japan and before we can classify Japan as a member of the society of nations which seek permanent peace and whose words we can take." [39] In his last press conference, on April 5, 1945, he stated that the Japanese were the only potential aggressors in the Pacific; they must therefore be deprived of all bases outside the home islands. "They have to be policed externally and internally," he declared. The job of maintaining security in the Pacific fell to the United States—acting not for its own interest but for the world.[40]

As for Germany, which twice in his lifetime had shattered the peace of Europe, Roosevelt proposed more drastic treatment. His underlying aim was embodied in the official joint statement of the Big Three leaders at the conclusion of the Yalta Conference:

> It is our inflexible purpose to destroy German militarism and Nazism and to ensure that Germany will never again be able to disturb the peace of the world. We are determined to disarm and disband all German armed forces; break up for all time the German General Staff that has repeatedly contrived the resurgence of German militarism; remove or destroy all German military equipment; eliminate or control all German industry that could be used for military production; bring all war criminals to just and swift punishment and exact reparation in kind for the destruction wrought by the Germans. . . .

It was not the purpose of Roosevelt or the allies to destroy or enslave the people of Germany. But they must "earn their way back" into the fellowship of nations. And in their climb up that steep road, Roosevelt said, they should not be encumbered by having to carry guns. "We hope they will be relieved of that burden forever." [41] In this connection, he went so far as to favor the complete prohibition of any aviation industry in Germany. Remembering the Nazi deceptions of the thirties, he stated that the Germans might repeat the excuse that they wanted planes for "non-military" purposes only. They could not be trusted again. He wrote to Hull in October, 1944, that "Germany must be prevented from making any aircraft of any type in the future." [42]

There were, of course, many plans for the dismemberment of Germany and conversion of her people to a "safer" type of economy. The most radical plan in the West was that which Henry Morgenthau presented to Roosevelt and Churchill at the second Quebec Conference (September, 1944). This plan, which would have limited Germany's economy to agriculture, was tentatively approved in principle by both the President and the Prime Minister. Very soon afterward, however, Roosevelt (as well as Churchill) drew back from this extreme position. He stated to Hull that "no one wants to make Germany a wholly agricultural nation again"—but he wanted to be sure that German industry was effectively limited and controlled. [43]

As protection against resurgence of German nationalism, he favored the idea of dividing the country into "five or seven states." He recalled the days of his childhood visits to Darmstadt, Hesse, and Bavaria—when the provincial governments, rather than the Reich, were thought of as the real Germany. He hoped that *that* Germany might be restored—a peace-loving, industrious, and trustworthy nation. He presented this idea at Yalta, where it was concurred in by Stalin. Churchill, however, did not like it; he suggested the formation of two Germanies: one centered upon Prussia, and one embracing the southern provinces, including Austria. The Allied leaders agreed that their foreign ministers would give further study to the manner of German division. [44]

Roosevelt believed that Germany must work for long years to make up for the incalculable damage wrought by her military forces. He was shocked by the devastation which he saw in the Crimea, and he felt that the Russians, who had suffered most, were entitled to the major share of reparations. These should be in both goods and in labor; he thought it was a matter of simple justice that German prisoners, after the war, be used by the Russians to "clean up all that mess." The vandalism of the Nazis was beyond imagination, he told newsmen after his return from Yalta: "You ought to see it. I couldn't write about it without seeing it." [45] The exact figure for reparations could not be set in advance, he thought. Payments should not be so heavy that the German people would starve or become a burden upon the Western allies. At the same time, he believed that the German standard of living, in the foreseeable future, should not be higher than that of the Soviet Union.[46]

In his plans for the beaten nations, he paid little attention to the effects upon the world balance of power. In the mood of the times, he was more interested in seeing "justice" done and in removing the military forces which had so recklessly disturbed the peace. He knew that reduction of Japan and Germany would leave "power vacuums" on the Russian flanks. But the hope of the future, thought Roosevelt, required abandonment of traditional power politics. It rested upon justice and *co-operation* among the great nations.

And the question of co-operation was at heart a simple one—terrifyingly so. Could the two superpowers, the United States and Russia, work together? If they did, the peace of the world could be indefinitely guaranteed. If they did not, there would be no peace. All other issues hinged on this *one*, and the President knew it. The United Nations itself would founder in the absence of American-Russian co-operation. That organization bore the promise of ultimate world government; but at this crossroads of history, dominant power was in the hands of but two countries. For this reason he saw the UN, in 1945, primarily as an instrument for engaging Soviet co-operation.

He knew that the stakes had never been higher. Peace and prosperity, or conflict and poverty for the whole world—were in the balance. Roosevelt therefore drew upon his waning strength to establish a co-operative relationship; it was to this end that he decided to run for a fourth term.

He was aware of the gulf which yawned between the civilizations of West and East. There were formidable differences of language, religion, politics, ideology, and history. Yet he believed that co-operation between the two cultures was possible if it could once be established. He did not think that communism was a true, or in the long run, an appealing doctrine; he therefore did not fear that it would undermine the West. He did not believe, either, that differences in ideologies or economic systems prevented nations from working together. He knew that Marxism preached unrelenting struggle against capitalism, but he discounted the influence of doctrine upon human behavior. The war of ideologies, he thought, was largely a *book* argument. Historically speaking, both America and Russia were moving from opposite poles toward a middle ground.[47]

There would always be differences and disagreements, of course. And in his last days, after Yalta, the President had occasion to witness the flare-up of suspicion and bitterness on the part of the Russian leaders. But this was to be expected—especially so, because of the conditioning of conspiracy, insecurity, and violence that marked Soviet revolutionary history. He did not abandon hope that new disputes could be ironed out as they had been during the war. On the last day of his life he sent this message to Churchill: "I would minimize the general Soviet problem as much as possible, because these problems, in one form or another, seem to arise every day, and most of them straighten out. . . . We must be firm, however, and our course thus far has been correct." [48]

The essential question, in Roosevelt's mind, was whether or not the Russians were bent on military aggression. In his considered judgment, the answer was "No." After meeting with Russian leaders for the first time at Teheran, he gave his impressions in some informal remarks: "I think the Russians are perfectly friendly; they aren't trying to gobble up all the rest of Europe or the world. They didn't know us, that's the really fundamental difference. They are friendly people. They haven't got any crazy ideas of conquest; and now that they have got to know us, they are much more willing to accept us. . . . And all these fears that have been expressed by a lot of people here—with some reason—that the Russians are going to try to dominate Europe, I personally don't think there's anything in it. They have a large 'hunk of bread' right in Russia to keep them busy for a great many years to come without taking on any more headaches." [49]

One can see that Roosevelt, in his great wish for peace, was inclined to give the Soviets the benefit of any doubt. He brushed aside the harsh facts of their internal tyranny and the ruthless character of their leaders. He rested his judgment, chiefly, on what he had seen of Soviet relations with the outside world. In the wartime conferences, Stalin and his subordinates behaved like reasonable and responsible men. Whatever their violent past or ultimate ambition, Roosevelt was persuaded that they were willing to co-operate to keep the peace. Perhaps, in the end, their intention would turn sour; but he felt that the greatest effort should be made to encourage friendship. In his Fourth Inaugural, he said, "We can gain no lasting peace if we approach it with suspicion and mistrust— or with fear. We have learned the simple truth, as Emerson said, that, 'The only way to have a friend is to be one.'"

The actions of the Russians since the war may appear to Western observers as a grim mockery of Roosevelt's hopes—and (to some) as proof of his foolish delusions. But it should be kept in mind that the basis underlying East-West relations deteriorated after his death. Roosevelt proposed, and the Big Three at Yalta had agreed, that "joint action" by the Allies would henceforth govern political decisions. In place of rival alliances and mutual suspicion, there was to be a combining of strength, sharing of responsibility, and growing understanding.

But this idea withered in the summer of 1945. When the common enemy was beaten, Allied unity began to falter; and the pledge of collaboration was dishonored. It was supplanted by the old-fashioned scramble for position and national advantage. The Russians acted unilaterally to increase their security and power—they tightened their grip on what they had and reached out for more. The West, properly aroused, met these thrusts with a policy of containment and military alliances, and the Cold War fell upon us.

Roosevelt demonstrated that mutual tolerance and agreements between East and West were feasible during the long fight against the Axis. In doing this he pointed the way, perhaps, to what American and Russian leadership may one day accomplish in years of peace. The historical determinist and the cynic may brand this thought as impossible nonsense. But Roosevelt never underestimated the capacity of human beings to make their own history—and to survive as a species.

10

Roosevelt:

Radical or Conservative?

SOME SENSE—AND A DEAL OF NONSENSE—have been written in the past few years on the subject of conservatism, spelled with a small or a large "C." The swing of the pendulum in American politics has given the word "conservative" a connotation of superiority; it has become preferred semantic garb—what the "well-dressed citizen should wear." This shift is harmless enough, but it has been accompanied by a frantic search to discover what a conservative really *is* (and always has been). This investigation, which has resulted mainly in assigning new meanings to old words, has tended more to confuse than clarify.

The reason for the confusion is not far to seek: there is probably no such thing as a "conservative" or a "liberal" in a *substantive* sense. What some writers have done is to construct an "ideal" type, label it conservative, and associate with it the nobler names of history. The latter part of this process is not easy; it requires a sliding scale of exceptions to the ideal, subtle reservations, and ingenious selection of data.

This is not to say that words like "conservative" and "liberal" are without significance. Relative to a given time and place, these terms can mean something pretty definite. They have been used, they are used, and they will continue to be used. But they function poorly as "universals." Even for a given time and place, the word conservative or liberal—or radical, needs to be pinned down to a specific subject. An economic conservative may be a political radical; and even on a single question such as taxes, the same individual may wish to perpetuate one type of levy and to abolish another. The futility of sorting individuals into generic classifications of this sort is manifest. It should be equally clear that what a man thinks or does is no better (or worse), whether he be called a "conservative" or a "liberal."

Yet people are rightly concerned about the relation of important men to their times. Did they believe in and produce significant changes, or did they leave institutions about the way they found them? Applying the question in this sense to Roosevelt, was he a radical or a conservative —or something in between? It is easy to see that on particular issues he might be one or another (he was a liberal on the monetary standard but a conservative on the Bill of Rights); what we must look for is the dominant trend of his thought, the net effect of his action.

Roosevelt presented the appearance of a radical to many observers in 1933. The world, including the United States, was in a mood of anxiety and desperation. Books, articles, and speeches were filled with references to revolution. Some fainthearted citizens believed they were witnessing the demise of liberal democracy; they thought their only choice was between an authoritarianism of the Left or one of the Right.

But the new President announced that there was nothing to fear but fear itself. He did not want a revolution or to be the leader of one. He did not wish to usurp power. On the contrary, he desired, by Constitutional means, to attack the causes of revolution. In spite of his reassurances, the impression prevailed that he was, in fact, producing a revolution. No other word seemed strong enough to describe the legislative changes, "so swift and so fundamental."

Edward M. House, writing in 1933, asserted that the country was in the midst of a "social revolution none the less potential because peaceful." In his opinion, the times were such that if Congress had not delegated large authority to the President, the people would have sought a dictatorship of an "extremely radical character."[1] Ernest Lindley, who wrote *The Roosevelt Revolution* in the same year, stated that the changes wrought were more abrupt and far-reaching than any which had previously occurred in America.[2] He later apologized, however, for the title of his book. In 1936 he explained that the New Deal was not a revolution in the Marxist sense—but only in the sense that Jefferson, Jackson, and Lincoln had achieved revolutions.[3]

As time passed, the President's actions were seen increasingly in the perspective of American tradition. Charles and Mary Beard admitted in

1939 that his program had gone farther than earlier legislation in impinging upon the nation's "free enterprise" economy. But behind each measure, they wrote, was a "long series of agitations, numerous changes in the thought and economy of American society, and pertinent enactments." [4] The same idea was expressed by Henry Steele Commager in 1945: "We can see now that the 'Roosevelt Revolution' was no revolution, but rather the culmination of half a century of historical development. . . ." [5] And Clinton Rossiter, spokesman for the "new conservatism," confirmed this interpretation. Roosevelt's beliefs, he stated, were the staples of American democracy, having roots "gnarled and stubborn, deep in the American past." [6]

But if Roosevelt was not a radical, he was indeed an innovator. He believed that many of the traditional methods were no longer adequate, and he sought practical means of solving the problems which faced America in the thirties. The central task was the restoration and maintenance of economic well-being—within the framework of democracy and the Christian ethic. In a sense Roosevelt was the agent of a worldwide adjustment of institutions—adjustments required by advances in technology and human aspiration. He did not create the compulsive ideas of his time; it was his role to translate them into proper and workable forms. The truth of this interpretation is reflected in the contemporary upheavals and movements in other lands. Russian communism, German and Italian fascism, British socialism—these were various responses to the same deep-lying forces.

The general term which best fits Roosevelt is that of "moderate reformer." Here again, it is important to refer to time and place. Had he lived in Hitler's Germany, he would doubtless have been a radical; that is, he would have favored the overturn of the Nazi regime. But his theory of social action was oriented to the American scene. He believed that the way to make progress was "to build on what we have and to take from the lessons of yesterday a little more courage and wisdom to meet the tasks of the day." [7] Change, he thought, was continuous and inevitable; the only real question was what to do about it.

He recognized that there was a spectrum of opinion on how best to confront change and that the various attitudes were generally known by words like conservative and liberal. Within the framework of American issues, he thought that such terms, if defined, were a convenient means of political identification. He also knew that definitions could be drawn to satisfy or favor given points of view. One that tickled him was this: "A Reactionary is a somnambulist walking backwards. A Conservative is a man with two perfectly good legs who has never learned to walk forward. A Radical is a man with both feet firmly planted—in the air. A Liberal is a man who uses his legs, and at the same time uses his head." In these terms, of course, he smilingly considered himself a liberal.

The conservatives of his time, he observed, seldom opposed popular reforms in principle; they endeavored to block them by objecting to specific *methods*. He often tried to illustrate this tactic while talking with reporters. In 1938, after passage of the Fair Labor Standards Act (Wages and Hours), he referred to the people who gave lip-service to the principle but who had tried to stop the legislation:

> It is the attitude that says, "Oh, yes, I am in favor of decent wages, but I don't like this suggestion, this way of carrying it out." And then you say to them, "Do you like such and such a plan? and they say, "Oh, no, no, that is terrible." And then you make a third suggestion and they say, "Oh, no, no, that is awful." And then they either write or speak in favor of good wages.[8]

Since the "Yes, *but*" men offered no alternatives of their own, one could only believe that they did not want to move at all. "They like it where they are," he explained to Anne O'Hare McCormick.[9]

He took a more charitable view of the radicals. They had "some use to humanity," he felt, because they had "at least the imagination to think up many kinds of answers to problems"—even though their answers were wholly impracticable in the immediate future. And this is how he distinguished moderate reformers like himself: "Liberals are those who, unlike the radicals who want to tear everything up by the roots and plant new and untried seeds, desire to use the existing plants of civilization, to select the best of them, to water them and make them grow—not only for the present use of mankind, but also for the use of generations to come. That is why I call myself a liberal. . . ."[10] Edmund Burke, the old hero of the new conservatives, could have found no fault with this social principle.

It was Roosevelt's conviction that the nation, rather than being endangered by too much reform, usually suffered from too little. The reason for this was simple. Those who wished to keep things as they were could readily join together in a common method; straight opposition. But those who saw the need for change were almost always divided as to method. Hence, a small minority of standpatters could usually prevent the reforms desired by a much larger number. Roosevelt often recalled that it was Wilson who first brought this to his attention. The greatest problem of a progressive leader, Wilson told him, was not the criticism from reactionaries or the attacks by radicals—it was to reconcile and unite the liberals themselves.[11] Some recent writers have suggested that the lack of coherence among liberals is due to some fatal flaw in their philosophy or temperament. Roosevelt did not think so. Their disagreements resulted naturally from the fact that "most liberals are able to see beyond the end of their noses"—and are apt to want to reach the goal by different roads. Constructive building by free men is bound to provoke more differences than the simpler process of obstruction.

Conservative politicians, he stated, were likely to keep control for longer periods than liberal ones. So long as conditions remained fairly prosperous, most citizens were indifferent to underlying needs for adjustment. And when liberals did come to power, they faced mounting antagonisms—because some vested interest opposed almost every reform. The President discussed this problem in 1937 during a meeting with newspaper editors and publishers. After reviewing the accomplishments of the New Deal, they asked him if changes were coming too fast. He answered that he did not believe so, and that he had to work as fast as he could to help the nation "catch up" on needed reforms. This was true because of the limited period of control which liberals could expect. During that time, he explained, "you are constantly combating the conservative forces and they are trying to take advantage of you and you have to take every advantage of them." [12]

The cost of delaying reforms was high, he felt; the Great Depression was a particularly expensive lesson. The New Deal measures, if enacted sooner, would have cushioned the business decline precipitated in 1929. However, the consequences would have been still worse if the New Deal had been further postponed; another four years, he feared, could have led to irreparable damage. As illustration, the President pointed to the difficulties faced by Premier Léon Blum in 1936. He explained the disturbances in France in these words, during a confidential talk with reporters:

Suppose Brother Hoover had remained President until April, 1936, carrying on his policies of the previous four years; in other words, hadn't taken any steps towards social security or helping the farmer or cutting out child labor and shortening hours, and old-age pensions. Had that been the case, we would have been a country this past April very similar to the country that Blum found when he came in. The French for twenty-five or thirty years had never done a thing in the way of social legislation. Blum started in and he jumped right into the middle of a strike the first week he was in office. Well, they demanded a forty-eight hour week . . . and he put through legislation that did provide for shorter hours in industry. Then they demanded a one-week's holiday with pay and then they demanded, immediately, a commission to set up an old-age pension plan. Well, all of these Blum got through but, query, was it too late? [13]

He realized that even after reforms were enacted, they had to be continually revised. A reporter asked him in 1938 if the Wagner Act (for collective bargaining) should be amended. "Every law needs improvement and always will," he replied.[14] The New Deal itself was a means, not an end. The measures of 1933, he stated ten years afterward, were to meet the problems of 1933. "Now, in time, there will have to be a new program, whoever runs the government."[15] What Roosevelt would favor, or do, "if he were alive today," would depend upon his appraisal of the contemporary situation.

Steady and moderate reform was the best protection against drastic, unsound changes—against radicalism and revolution. In this practical sense, and in relation to his times, Roosevelt considered himself as essentially conservative. "Wise and prudent men—intelligent conservatives —have long known that in a changing world worthy institutions can be conserved only by adjusting them to the changing time. In the words of the great essayist, 'The voice of great events is proclaiming to us. Reform if you would preserve.' I am that kind of conservative because I am that kind of liberal."[16]

His preserving instinct was reflected in facets of his personality and temperament. Though he saw the need for adjustment and innovation, he had warm affection for old-fashioned things and old-fashioned ways. (The Victorian household at Hyde Park is a monument to this trait.) He treasured old friends, old landmarks, old books. Yet he was not a pietist about the past; he knew that "tradition itself involves breaks with tradition."

The final measure of a statesman's relation to his times must include not only his thought and feeling but the consequences of what he did. The impact of Roosevelt, both admirers and critics agree, was immense. As a result of that impact, what in America was weakened or lost, and what was conserved or strengthened? On the loss side, one must count greater restrictions on the freedom of owners and managers to run their business as they please. Along with these interferences have come higher taxes and a burdensome national debt (though most of this resulted from the war). Government has grown huge by previous standards, life is more bothered by regulations and red tape, and it is harder to become a millionaire.

On the other hand, our democracy stands more powerful than before; the Constitution and its guarantees remain intact. Capitalism is running on a sound basis; profits are good, and employment has been kept at a relatively high level. The Achilles' heel of the system, the cycle of boom-and-bust, has been protected by government measures. The program which once was called a threat to private enterprise has proved to be a vital preservative.

More individuals have the opportunity to secure a wholesome standard of life and security in old age. All groups and sections now feel that they are sharing in national progress, and this makes for a wider sense of satisfaction and hope. Our human resources and morale have thus been safeguarded and developed.

The balance of gains and losses point to this conclusion: we have paid a price, but the fiber of America has been strengthened, not weakened.

Against the backdrop of global revolution and war, the results of Roosevelt's leadership are seen most sharply. At the time of his death the United States stood forth as the chief surviving nation of capitalism and democracy. The entire world has been impressed by the resiliency of our system, and the most striking recognition of all lies in the revision of Marxist ideology. Prediction of impending capitalist collapse, trumpeted so brazenly in the first half of the century, has been retracted from the Communist doctrine and vocabulary.

The host of Americans who shared Roosevelt's battle against depression and tyranny have rendered their own judgment of his role. Their verdict, given over a period of twelve years, surprised many political observers. Before the election of 1936, William Allen White reviewed the accomplishments of Roosevelt's first term; he approved what had been done but predicted a negative popular reaction. The President, he wrote, may have sacrificed his career for the New Deal program: "Political leaders—especially reform leaders—often end that way. . . . Moses rarely enters the promised land." [17]

The venerable editor proved mistaken about Roosevelt and the people. They were to give him the greatest political response that any citizen has received. They sensed his warmth and desire to help; they felt their traditions were safe in his trust. There were a few individuals indifferent to Roosevelt, and some who hated him; but when he died, millions experienced the deepest sense of personal loss they had ever known. The historical record—letters, newspapers, broadcasts, and every form of communication—preserves a testimony not easily dismissed.

So Roosevelt died, but his thought and action are an enduring legacy for America and the world. They constitute more than "myth" or "legend." They are a common asset which neither liberals nor conservatives, Democrats nor Republicans, should lightly cast aside.

He was a builder. He gave strength to Western ideals and institutions. He was a positive force in history because of a rare conjuncture in human affairs: a man of high purpose, imagination, and courage was presented with great opportunity and power. That was his rendezvous with destiny.

Notes and
Bibliography

Notes

Chapter 1. Vision of the Abundant Life

1. FDR to Col. Alva J. Brasted (Chief of Chaplains, U.S.A.), Feb. 13, 1934.
2. Frank D. Ashburn, *Peabody of Groton* (New York, 1944), p. 42.
3. Address to Federated Council of Churches of Christ, Dec. 6, 1933.
4. Franklin D. Roosevelt, *Whither Bound?* (Boston, 1926), p. 14.
5. Radio address on Brotherhood Day, Feb. 23, 1936.
6. Harold Ickes, *The Secret Diary of Harold Ickes* (New York, 1954), Vol. II, p. 290.
7. Annual Message to the Congress, Jan. 4, 1939.
8. Address at Chapel Hill, N. C., Dec. 5, 1938.
9. Address to Pan-American Union, Apr. 14, 1939.
10. Acceptance address, July 2, 1932.
11. "The Age of Social Consciousness," *Harvard Graduates' Magazine*, XXXVIII, Sept., 1929, No. 149, p. 5.
12. Address, Oct. 28, 1936.
13. Undelivered address for Jefferson Day, Apr. 13, 1945.
14. Radio address to Young Democratic Club, Aug. 24, 1935.
15. Campaign address, Sioux City, Ia., Sept. 29, 1932.
16. May 4, 1941.
17. Address at White House Conference on Children in a Democracy, Apr. 23, 1939.
18. June 12, 1929.
19. Feb. 28, 1929.
20. Address at Ottawa, Canada, Aug. 25, 1943.
21. Message to legislature, Mar. 22, 1929.

22. Campaign address, San Francisco, Sept. 23, 1932.
23. Address at Vassar College, Aug. 26, 1933.
24. P. C. #488, Oct. 4, 1938.
25. Rexford G. Tugwell, "The Experimental Roosevelt," *Political Quarterly*, Vol. XXI, July, 1950, p. 247.
26. Address to White House Conference on Children in a Democracy, Apr. 23, 1939.
27. Campaign radio address, Nov. 2, 1936.
28. Address at Little Rock, Ark., June 10, 1936.
29. Address at Atlanta, Ga., Nov. 29, 1935.
30. Memorandum, Feb. 24, 1930.
31. Annual Message, Jan. 3, 1934.
32. Aug. 12, 1940.
33. Radio address, Jan. 19, 1940.
34. General Introduction, *The Public Papers and Addresses of Franklin D. Roosevelt* (New York, 1938), 1928–1932 Volume, p. ix.
35. Campaign address, Omaha, Neb., Oct. 10, 1936.
36. Address, Sept. 10, 1936.
37. F. D. Roosevelt, *Whither Bound?*, p. 27.
38. Remarks to Future Farmers of America, June 12, 1933.
39. Address at Bonneville Dam, Ore., Sept. 28, 1937.
40. Campaign address, San Francisco, Sept. 23, 1932.
41. Radio address, Jan. 19, 1940.
42. Radio dedication of Museum of Modern Art, New York City, May 10, 1939.
43. FDR to D. D. Shepard (Secretary of National Gallery), Apr. 1, 1941.
44. Dedication of National Gallery of Art, Mar. 17, 1941.
45. Dedication of Post Office at Rhinebeck, N. Y., May 1, 1939.
46. P. C. #115, Apr. 25, 1934.
47. Radio dedication of Museum of Modern Art, New York City, May 10, 1939.
48. Kindler to FDR, Feb. 18, 1936; FDR to Kindler, Feb. 20, 1936.
49. FDR to James P. Dawson, *The New York Times*, Jan. 25, 1937.
50. June 24, 1931.
51. Radio address, Aug. 24, 1935.
52. Address to United Nations Conference on Food and Agriculture, Washington, D. C., June 7, 1943.

Chapter 2. Unto Caesar What Is Caesar's

1. Aug. 28, 1931.
2. Campaign address, San Francisco, Calif., Sept. 23, 1932.
3. Campaign remarks, Joliet, Ill., Oct. 14, 1936.
4. Address, Syracuse University, N. Y., July 9, 1930.
5. Fireside Chat, Sept. 30, 1934.
6. Message to Congress, May 24, 1937.
7. Campaign address, San Francisco, Sept. 23, 1932.
8. Franklin D. Roosevelt, "The Age of Social Consciousness," *Harvard Graduates' Magazine*, Vol. XXXVIII, Sept., 1929, No. 149, pp. 6–7.
9. Address on occasion of Award for Distinguished Service to Agriculture, Chicago, Dec. 9, 1935.
10. Campaign address, New York City, Nov. 3, 1932.
11. Address at Bankers' Convention, Oct. 24, 1934.
12. Annual Message to Congress, Jan. 3, 1940.
13. P. C. #658, July 5, 1940.
14. Annual Message to Congress, Jan. 4, 1939.
15. Address, Washington, D. C., Sept. 17, 1937.

16. Memo for S. T. E. [Stephen T. Early] from FDR, Jan. 10, 1939.
17. Address on One Hundred and Fiftieth Anniversary of Congress, Mar. 4, 1939.
18. Address, University of Pennsylvania, Sept. 20, 1940.
19. P. C. #137, Aug. 24, 1934.
20. Address by radio to Jackson Day Dinners, Mar. 29, 1941.
21. Apr. 10, 1943.
22. Message to Congress, Sept. 17, 1943.
23. P. C. #962, July 29, 1944.
24. Acceptance address, July 19, 1940.
25. Third Inaugural, Jan. 20, 1941.
26. Campaign address, San Francisco, Sept. 23, 1932.
27. Address at Roanoke Island, N. C., Aug. 18, 1937.
28. Address at University of Pennsylvania, Sept. 20, 1940.
29. Campaign address, Nov. 2, 1936.
30. Special Press Conference with American Society of Newspaper Editors, Apr. 21, 1938.
31. Annual Message to Congress, Jan. 3, 1938.
32. Campaign address, Wilmington, Del., Oct. 29, 1936.
33. Address at Democratic Victory Dinner, Mar. 4, 1937.
34. Fireside Chat, Apr. 14, 1938.
35. Campaign address, Sept. 29, 1936.
36. *The New York Times*, Feb. 28, 1937, pp. 1 and 33.
37. P. C. #489, Oct. 7, 1938.
38. Dies to FDR, Aug. 27, 1940.
39. FDR to Dies, Sept. 12, 1940.
40. Oct. 6, 1936.
41. Samuel I. Rosenman, *Working with Roosevelt* (New York, 1952), p. 19.
42. Attorney General to FDR, Jan. 30, 1937, with attached report from J. Edgar Hoover.
43. P. C. #697, Nov. 26, 1940.
44. P. C. #399, Sept. 21, 1937.
45. Memo to the President from the Attorney General, Nov. 28, 1940, with attached statement as dictated by Morris Ernst, same date.

Chapter 3. Government and Economy

1. Fireside Chat, July 24, 1933.
2. July 6, 1940.
3. Raymond Moley, *After Seven Years* (New York, 1939), p. 63.
4. Gerald W. Johnson, *Roosevelt: Dictator or Democrat?* (New York, 1941), p. 164.
5. Franklin D. Roosevelt, *On Our Way* (New York, 1934), p. 35.
6. Acceptance address, July 2, 1932.
7. Kent to FDR, Dec. 10, 1937.
8. Mar. 27, 1929.
9. Address before Annual Farm Dinner of Jerome D. Barnum, Syracuse, N. Y., Sept. 9, 1931.
10. Albany, July 30, 1932.
11. *Public Papers and Addresses*, 1928–1932 Volume, p. 812.
12. Campaign address, Forbes Field, Pittsburgh, Oct. 1, 1936.
13. Address to American Retail Federation, May 22, 1939.
14. Henry Morgenthau, "The Morgenthau Diaries," *Collier's*, Oct. 4, 1947, Vol. 120, pp. 20–21.
15. Seymour Harris, *The New Economics* (New York, 1947), p. 17

16. William D. Hassett, "The President Was My Boss," *Saturday Evening Post*, Oct. 10, 1953, p. 20.
17. *The New York Times Magazine*, Aug. 15, 1937, p. 14.
18. P. C.'s for 1935.
19. Apr. 5, 1933.
20. P. C. #42, Aug. 9, 1933.
21. Jan. 15, 1941.
22. P. C. #1, Mar. 8, 1933; P. C. #10, Apr. 7, 1933.
23. Mar. 3, 1912, reported in *Poughkeepsie News-Press*, Mar. 5, 1912, p. 4.
24. Jan. 1, 1929.
25. Address to N. Y. State Press Assn., Syracuse, N. Y., Feb. 1, 1929.
26. Aug. 4, 1934.
27. P. C. #82, Dec. 29, 1933.
28. Note, Address before Code Authorities, Mar. 5, 1934, *Public Papers and Addresses*, 1934 Volume, p. 132.
29. Ross T. McIntire, *White House Physician* (New York, 1946), pp. 76–78.
30. Mar. 12, 1935.
31. P. C. #184, Feb. 15, 1935.
32. Oct. 21, 1936.
33. *The New York Times Magazine*, Oct. 16, 1938, pp. 1–3.
34. Remarks at Subsistence Homes Exposition, Apr. 24, 1934.
35. Statement on Rep. by Nat. Resources Comm. on Tech. Trends, July 12, 1937.
36. Message to Congress, Jan. 24, 1935.
37. Address at Green Pastures Rally, Charlotte, N. C., Sept. 10, 1936.
38. Message to Congress, June 3, 1937.
39. May 19, 1943.
40. Franklin D. Roosevelt, *Government—Not Politics* (New York, 1932), p. 73, quoting from *Liberty*, no date.
41. Herbert Hoover, *The Memoirs of Herbert Hoover* (New York, 1952), Vol. III, pp. 16–17.
42. Speech at Jamestown, N. Y., Oct. 19, 1928.
43. P. C. #3, Mar. 15, 1933.
44. P. C. #275-A (Spec. Conf. with Editors of Trade Papers), Feb. 14, 1936.
45. P. C. #997, Mar. 20, 1945.
46. Feb. 11, 1935.
47. Apr. 21, 1938.
48. P. C. (Spec. Conf. with Amer. Soc. of Newspaper Editors), Apr. 21, 1938.
49. P. C. #125, May 25, 1934.
50. P. C. #422, Jan. 4, 1938.
51. Note, Letter, FDR to Girdler, June 21, 1937, *Public Papers and Addresses*, 1937 Volume, pp. 272–74.
52. P. C. #360-A (Spec. Conf. with Newspaper Editors and Publishers), Apr. 15, 1937.
53. Message, Mar. 29, 1930.
54. Sept. 30, 1934.
55. Radio address on Unemployment Census, Nov. 14, 1937.
56. Acceptance speech, July 2, 1932.
57. Statement, Aug. 14, 1935.

Chapter 4. A More Perfect Union

1. Address at Little Rock, Ark., June 10, 1936.
2. Address on One Hundred and Fiftieth Anniversary of Congress, Mar. 4, 1939.
3. Address before City Club, New York, Nov. 23, 1929.

4. Memorandum, Dec. 29, 1932.
5. Roosevelt, Address before Regional Plan. Assn., New York City, Dec. 11, 1931.
6. Annual Message, Jan. 6, 1932.
7. June 10, 1929.
8. New London, Conn., July 16, 1929.
9. Mar. 2, 1930.
10. *Public Papers and Addresses,* 1928–1932 Volume, pp. 7–8.
11. Address, Little Rock, Ark., June 10, 1936.
12. Mar. 1, 1937.
13. Rosenman, *Working with Roosevelt,* p. 144.
14. Mar. 9, 1937.
15. Introduction, *Public Papers and Addresses,* 1937 Volume, p. xlvii.
16. Introduction, *Public Papers and Addresses,* 1935 Volume, p. 13.
17. June 4, 1935.
18. June 10, 1935.
19. P. C. #209, May 31, 1935.
20. P. C. #344, Feb. 12, 1937.
21. Introduction, *Public Papers and Addresses,* 1937 Volume, p. lxvi.
22. Introduction, *Public Papers and Addresses,* 1935 Volume, p. 14.
23. Introduction, *Public Papers and Addresses,* 1937 Volume, p. lxvi.
24. Edward S. Corwin, *Constitutional Revolution, Ltd.* (Claremont, Calif., 1941) p. 108.

Chapter 5. Tne People's Choice: The Presidency

1. Message to Congress, Jan. 12, 1937.
2. Moley, *After Seven Years,* pp. 128–30.
3. Marriner S. Eccles, *Beckoning Frontiers* (New York, 1951), p. 331.
4. Henry L. Stimson and McGeorge Bundy, *On Active Service in War and Peace* (New York, 1947), p. 333.
5. Donald Richberg, *My Hero* (New York, 1954), p. 166.
6. Stimson and Bundy, *On Active Service in War and Peace,* p. 495.
7. Morgenthau, "Morgenthau Diaries," *Collier's,* Oct. 11, 1947, Vol. 120, p. 21.
8. Robert E. Sherwood, *Roosevelt and Hopkins, an Intimate History* (New York, 1948), pp. 72–73.
9. Apr. 4, 1941.
10. P. C. #29, June 14, 1933.
11. Wilfred E. Binkley, *President and Congress* (New York, 1947), p. 126.
12. James Bryce, *The American Commonwealth* (New York, 3rd ed., 1897), p. 66.
13. *Ibid.,* p. 67.
14. P. C. #528, Mar. 7, 1939.
15. Sherwood, *Roosevelt and Hopkins,* pp. 931–33.
16. June 27, 1928, in Franklin D. Roosevelt's *The Happy Warrior, Alfred E. Smith* (Boston, 1928), p. 27.
17. A. Merriman Smith, *A President Is Many Men* (New York, 1948), p. 6.
18. Address before Conference of Governors, Apr. 27, 1932.
19. Campaign address, Syracuse, N. Y., Sept. 29, 1936.
20. Interview, Feb. 24, 1955.
21. Ernest K. Lindley, *The Roosevelt Revolution, First Phase* (New York, 1933), p. 21.
22. Jan. 10, 1938.
23. Jan. 13, 1938.
24. Address at Jackson Day Dinner, Jan. 8, 1940.
25. F. D. Roosevelt, *Whither Bound?,* p. 6.

26. *Public Papers of Franklin D. Roosevelt, Forty-eighth Governor of the State of New York* (Albany, 1930–1939), Vol. I, p. 7.
27. Jan. 13, 1938.
28. Rosenman, *Working with Roosevelt*, p. 16.
29. Edward J. Flynn, *You're the Boss* (New York, 1947), p. 209.
30. Radio address on Constitution Day, Sept. 17, 1938.
31. Rosenman, *Working with Roosevelt*, p. 430.
32. Radio dedication, Nov. 4, 1938.
33. Nov. 13, 1932, Sec. 8, p. 1.
34. Mar. 20, 1935.
35. May 19, 1933.
36. May 4, 1941.
37. Sherwood, *Roosevelt and Hopkins*, p. 266.
38. Roosevelt, *The Happy Warrior*, pp. 12–13.
39. Nov. 3, 1932.
40. P. C. #666, Aug. 2, 1940.
41. "Second Session of the 73rd Congress, Jan. 3, 1934, to June 18, 1934," *American Political Science Review*, Vol. 28, Oct. 1934, pp. 853–54.
42. FDR to Vandenberg, Dec. 27, 1941.
43. Feb. 19, 1935.
44. PSF Box 36 (U.S. Senate).
45. P. C. #82, Dec. 29, 1933.
46. FDR to Dies, Oct. 9, 1940.
47. P. C. #697, Nov. 26, 1940.
48. President's Conference with Dies, Nov. 29, 1940.
49. Annual Message to Legislature, Jan. 7, 1931.
50. FDR to Mrs. Ogden Mills Reid (N. Y. *Herald Tribune*), June 6, 1940.
51. Bryce, *The American Commonwealth*, pp. 6 and 270.
52. Franklin D. Roosevelt, *Government—Not Politics* (New York, 1932), p. 52.
53. June 28, 1934.
54. Sherwood, *Roosevelt and Hopkins*, p. 9.
55. Introduction, *Public Papers and Addresses*, 1928–1932 Volume, p. 8.
56. Charles A. and Mary R. Beard, *America in Midpassage* (New York, 1939), p. 948.
57. Max Kleiman (ed.), *Franklin Delano Roosevelt, the Tribute of the Synagogue* (New York, 1946), p. 41 (excerpt by Frankfurter with permission of *Harvard Law Review*).
58. May 14, 1935.
59. FDR to Walker, Feb. 13, 1936.
60. FDR to House, May 7, 1934.
61. *The New York Times Magazine*, Nov. 25, 1934, p. 17.
62. Rosenman, *Working with Roosevelt*, p. 167.

Chapter 6. The Great Game of Politics

1. Roosevelt, *Government—Not Politics*, pp. 13–16, quoting from *American Magazine*, April, 1932.
2. *Ibid.*, p. 21.
3. Address on American System of Party Government, New York City, Jan. 14, 1932.
4. Flynn, *You're the Boss*, pp. 78–79.
5. *Ibid.*, pp. 80–82.
6. Harold R. Gosnell, *Champion Campaigner: Franklin D. Roosevelt* (New York, 1952), p. 136.

7. P. C. #488, Oct. 4, 1938.
8. O'Connell to FDR, May 9, 1938; Cummings to FDR, May 18, 1938; McIntyre to O'Connell, May 20, 1938.
9. Frank Kingdon, *Architects of the Republic: George Washington, Thomas Jefferson, Abraham Lincoln, and Franklin D. Roosevelt* (New York, 1947), pp. 224–25.
10. FDR to Pittman, Aug. 25, 1934.
11. Memo, FDR to Claude A. Swanson, Oct. 25, 1934.
12. Early to R. H. Wadlow (Gen. Chair., Brotherhood of Loco. Engrs.), July 30, 1940.
13. Dec. 28, 1937.
14. Roosevelt, *Government—Not Politics*, p. 25, quoting from *American Magazine*, April, 1932.
15. P. C. #564, July 21, 1939.
16. Jan. 2, 1929.
17. Roosevelt, *The Happy Warrior*, p. 4.
18. Nov. 14, 1938.
19. FDR to Daniels, Dec. 5, 1924.
20. Address to Republicans-for-Roosevelt League, New York City, Nov. 3, 1932.
21. *Public Papers and Addresses, 1928–1932* Volume, p. 856.
22. Introduction, *Public Papers and Addresses*, 1938 Volume, pp. xxviii–xxx.
23. Lindley, *The Roosevelt Revolution, First Phase*, pp. 10–11.
24. Stanley High, *Roosevelt—and Then?* (New York, 1937).
25. Rosenman, *Working with Roosevelt*, pp. 463–64.
26. P. C. #201, May 3, 1935.
27. Address to American Youth Congress, Feb. 10, 1940.
28. P. C. #439, Mar. 4, 1938.
29. Apr. 3, 1942.
30. *Nicomachean Ethics.*
31. Quotation from *Harvard Law Review*, in Max Kleiman, ed., *Franklin Delano Roosevelt, the Tribute of the Synagogue* (New York, 1946), p. 40.
32. July 20, 1928.
33. Roosevelt, *Government—Not Politics*, p. 14, quoting from *American Magazine*, April, 1932.
34. Rosenman, *Working with Roosevelt*, pp. 29–30.
35. FDR to Daniels, June 23, 1927.
36. Jan. 28, 1929.
37. Roosevelt, *Government—Not Politics*, p. 21, quoting from *American Magazine*, April, 1932.
38. Roosevelt, *The Happy Warrior*, p. 8.
39. Roosevelt, *Government—Not Politics*, p. 20, quoting from *American Magazine*, April, 1932.
40. Eleanor Roosevelt, *This I Remember* (New York, 1949), p. 162.
41. P. C. #649-A, June 5, 1940.
42. Memo on Removal of Sheriff Thomas M. Farley, Feb. 24, 1932.
43. P. C. #89, Jan. 17, 1934.
44. P. C. #90, Jan. 19, 1934.
45. Flynn, *You're the Boss*, pp. 210–11.
46. Charles A. Beard, *President Roosevelt and the Coming of the War. A Study in Appearances and Realities* (New Haven, 1948).
47. Oct. 31, 1938.
48. Aug. 26, 1940.
49. Tugwell, "The Progressive Orthodoxy of Franklin D. Roosevelt," *Ethics*, October, 1953, Vol. LXIV, No. 1, p. 18.
50. Grace G. Tully, *F. D. R., My Boss* (New York, 1949).

51. P. C. #142, Sept. 7, 1934.
52. Memo for the Att.-Gen. from Alexander Holtzoff, April 12, 1935, and attached papers.
53. Feb. 16, 1935.
54. Commencement address, June 22, 1931.
55. Richard Hofstadter, *The American Political Tradition and the Men Who Made It* (New York, 1948), p. 347.
56. *Public Papers and Addresses*, 1928–1932 Volume, p. xiii.
57. Rexford G. Tugwell, "The Experimental Roosevelt," *Political Quarterly*, Vol. 21, July, 1950, p. 266.
58. *The New York Times Magazine*, Aug. 15, 1937, pp. 1–2 and 14.
59. Quotation from *Harvard Law Review*, in Kleiman, *Franklin Delano Roosevelt*, p. 40.
60. Frances Perkins, *The Roosevelt I Knew* (New York, 1946), pp. 163–67.

Chapter 7. Truth and Citizenship

1. FDR to Amer. Bible Society, cited in F. D. Roosevelt, *The Bible and the Nations* (New York, 1945), p. 4.
2. Address, Temple University, Feb. 22, 1936.
3. May 6, 1942, in Archibald MacLeish, *A Free Man's Books* (Mt. Vernon, N. Y., 1942), p. 3.
4. Message to the Fifth Annual Women's Conf. on Current Problems, Oct. 17, 1935.
5. Address to N.E.A., New York City, June 30, 1938.
6. P. C. #160, Nov. 23, 1934.
7. Remarks to Conf. on Rural Educ., Oct. 4, 1944.
8. P. C. #44, Aug. 16, 1933.
9. Note on Exec. Order establishing N. Y. A., *Public Papers and Addresses*, 1935 Volume, pp. 284–86.
10. Rosenman, *Working with Roosevelt*, pp. 394–95.
11. Address, University of Pennsylvania, Sept. 20, 1940.
12. Oct. 17, 1929, Albany, N. Y.
13. Radio address to Forum on Current Events, Oct. 5, 1937.
14. May 13, 1929.
15. Feb. 18, 1937.
16. Mar. 29, 1937.
17. Van Loon to FDR, Jan. 4, 1938, and FDR to Van Loon, Jan. 6, 1938.
18. Copeland to FDR, Dec. 16, 1933, and FDR to Copeland, Dec. 19, 1933.
19. Jan. 28, 1939.
20. May 29, 1931.
21. Jefferson to Prof. Pictet, Feb. 5, 1803, and Jefferson to Charles Yancey, Jan. 6, 1816.
22. FDR to Joseph V. Connolly (Pres., I.N.S.), Apr. 13, 1934.
23. P. C. #40, Aug. 5, 1933.
24. Hearst to FDR, Feb. 7, 1933.
25. Address, Albany, N. Y., Jan. 2, 1929.
26. P. C. #260-A (Spec.), Dec. 27, 1935.
27. Sept. 28, 1940.
28. FDR to Joseph Pulitzer, Nov. 2, 1938.
29. July 1, 1935.
30. Sept. 28, 1940.
31. June 29, 1935.
32. FDR to Daniels, July 30, 1942.

33. Donald Scott Carmichael, ed., *F. D. R., Columnist; the Uncollected Columns of F. D. Roosevelt* (Chicago, 1947).
34. Apr. 15, 1940.
35. June 6, 1940.

Chapter 8. The Good Neighbor

1. Pres. Statement, Nov. 23, 1933, and note, *Public Papers and Addresses*, 1933 Volume, pp. 499–501.
2. Note, Message to Pan-American Conference, Dec. 12, 1933, *Public Papers and Addresses*, 1933 Volume, pp. 521–22.
3. Pres. Statement, Dec. 16, 1936, and Note, *Public Papers and Addresses*, 1936 Volume, pp. 615–17.
4. Albany, N. Y., Feb. 2, 1932.
5. P. C. #19, May 10, 1933.
6. Oct. 10, 1933.
7. Address, Nov. 18, 1933.
8. FDR to Herbert Lehman, Oct. 13, 1938.
9. Address, Intergovernmental Comm. on Pol. Refugees, Oct. 17, 1939.
10. Statement, Apr. 13, 1940.
11. Address, White House Correspondents' Assn., Feb. 12, 1943.
12. P. C. #167, Dec. 21, 1934.
13. Aug. 3, 1944.
14. Dec. 23, 1943.
15. Mar. 25, 1944.
16. Elliott Roosevelt, *As He Saw It* (New York, 1946), pp. 115–16.
17. Jan. 24, 1944.
18. P. C. #992, Feb. 23, 1945.
19. King to FDR, Mar. 6, 1937.
20. FDR to Hitler, Sept. 26, 1938.
21. Oct. 12, 1937.
22. FDR to Hitler, Apr. 14, 1939, and Note, *Public Papers and Addresses*, 1939 Volume, pp. 201–205.
23. May 16, 1933.
24. Introduction, *Public Papers and Addresses*, 1939 Volume, p. xxv.
25. FDR to Hull, May 6, 1933, in U. S. State Dept., *Peace and War, U. S. Foreign Policy, 1931–1941* (Washington, 1943), p. 179.
26. FDR to Norman H. Davis, Aug. 30, 1933, and P. C. #47, Aug. 25, 1933.
27. Mar. 9, 1935.
28. FDR to Davis, Oct. 5, 1934 (read to the Naval Conference by Davis, Dec. 9, 1935).
29. Note to Message on Repeal of Arms Embargo, Sept. 21, 1939, in *Public Papers and Addresses*, 1939 Volume, p. 522.
30. Presidential statement, Aug. 31, 1935.
31. Sept. 19, 1935.
32. FDR to Dodd, Dec. 2, 1935.
33. Harold Ickes, *Secret Diary*, Vol. II, p. 569.
34. Note to Proclamation Forbidding Export of Arms to Spain, May 1, 1937, in *Public Papers and Addresses*, 1937 Volume, pp. 192–93.
35. Interview, Sumner Welles, Apr. 24, 1946; Rosenman, *Working with Roosevelt*, pp. 164–65; FDR to Endicott Peabody, Oct. 16, 1937; FDR to Edward M. House, Apr. 10, 1935.
36. P. C. #400, Oct. 6, 1937.
37. Sept. 15, 1938.

38. Memo by Josephus Daniels of conversation with Roosevelt, Jan. 14, 1939, in Carrol Kilpatrick, ed., *Roosevelt and Daniels, A Friendship in Politics* (Chapel Hill, 1952), pp. 181–82.
39. H. H. Arnold, *Global Mission* (New York, 1949), pp. 177–80.
40. P. C. #500, Nov. 15, 1938.
41. Conference, Jan. 31, 1939 (Extra Confidential).

Chapter 9. Stategy for Survival

1. Address, University of Virginia, Charlottesville, June 10, 1940.
2. Fireside Chat, Dec. 29, 1940.
3. Fireside Chat, Sept. 11, 1941.
4. United States-British Staff Conversations (short title, ABC-1), Mar. 27, 1941.
5. Spec. Press Conf. with Associated Church Press, Apr. 20, 1938.
6. Jan. 21, 1941.
7. Memo. for E. R. from FDR, Nov. 13, 1940.
8. Sherwood, *Roosevelt and Hopkins*, pp. 316 and 403–408.
9. Message to Congress, Dec. 15, 1941; Cordell Hull, *Memoirs* (New York, 1948), Vol. II, pp. 982–1105.
10. Annual Message, Jan. 6, 1945.
11. FDR to W. A. White, Dec. 14, 1939.
12. Nov. 30, 1939.
13. Dec. 2, 1939.
14. June 9, 1941.
15. June 26, 1941.
16. Sept. 3, 1941.
17. Annual Message, Jan. 6, 1945.
18. "Yalta Conference," Rep. of Dinner Meeting, Feb. 4, 1945 (Bohlen notes), *The New York Times*, Mar. 17, 1955.
19. Winston Churchill, *The Second World War* (New York, 1948–1953) Vol. VI, p. 402.
20. Memo for Paul Porter from FDR, July 17, 1944.
21. Rosenman, Note to Statement on Crimea Conf., Feb. 11, 1945, in *Public Papers and Addresses*, 1944–1945 Volume, pp. 537–48; Sherwood, *Roosevelt and Hopkins*, pp. 850–70.
22. Eleanor Roosevelt, *This I Remember*, pp. 23–24 and 353–64 (Appendix).
23. Memo by FDR, Jan. 19, 1944, attached to draft of plan.
24. Roosevelt, *Whither Bound?*, pp. 27–28.
25. Address to Wilson Found., Dec. 28, 1933.
26. Rosenman, Note to Declaration of the United Nations, Jan. 1, 1942, in *Public Papers and Addresses*, 1944–1945 Volume, p. 5; Rosenman, *Working with Roosevelt*, pp. 316–17.
27. Interview, Sumner Welles, Apr. 26, 1946.
28. P. C. #966, Aug. 29, 1944.
29. Statement on the Postwar Security Org., June 15, 1944.
30. Welles interview.
31. Welles interview; "Yalta Conference," Plenary Meeting, Feb. 6, 1945, 4:00 p.m. (Bohlen notes), *The New York Times*, Mar. 17, 1955.
32. P. C. #636-A (Spec.), Apr. 18, 1940.
33. Nov. 8, 1943.
34. Fireside Chat, Dec. 24, 1943.
35. P. C. #916, Sept. 7, 1943.
36. FDR to George Norris, Sept. 21, 1943.

37. "Yalta Conf." Dinner Meeting, Feb. 4, 1945 (Bohlen notes), in *The New York Times,* Mar. 17, 1955.
38. Welles interview.
39. Aug. 12, 1944.
40. P. C. #998.
41. Radio address, Foreign Policy Assn., Oct. 21, 1944.
42. Memo. for Secy. from FDR, Oct. 20, 1944, in "Yalta Conf.," State Dept. Correspondence, *The New York Times,* Mar. 18, 1955.
43. Memo. for Secy. from FDR, Sept. 29, 1944, in "Yalta Conference," State Dept. Correspondence, *The New York Times,* Mar. 18, 1955.
44. "Yalta Conference," Plenary meeting, Feb. 5, 1945, 4:00 P.M. (Bohlen notes), *The New York Times,* Mar. 17, 1955.
45. P. C. #993, Mar. 2, 1945.
46. "Yalta Conference," Plenary meeting, Feb. 5, 1945, 4:00 P.M.
47. Welles interview.
48. Rosenman, Note on Joint Statement on Crimea Conference, Feb. 11. 1945. *Public Papers and Addresses,* 1944–1945 Volume, pp. 546–47.
49. Remarks to Advertising War Council Conference, Mar. 8, 1944.

Chapter 10. Roosevelt: Radical or Conservative?

1. Introduction, Earl Looker, *The American Way: Franklin Roosevelt in Action* (New York, 1933), p. vii.
2. Lindley, *The Roosevelt Revolution,* p. 4.
3. Ernest K. Lindley, *Half Way with Roosevelt* (New York, 1936), p. 9.
4. Beard, *America in Midpassage,* pp. 247–48 and 947–48.
5. "Twelve Years of Roosevelt," *American Mercury,* Aug., 1945, Vol. 61.
6. "The Political Philosophy of Franklin D. Roosevelt," in *The Review of Politics,* Jan., 1949, Vol. II, No. 1, p. 89.
7. Address, Los Angeles, Oct. 1, 1935.
8. P. C. #494, Oct. 25, 1938.
9. *The New York Times Magazine,* Oct. 16, 1938, p. 2.
10. FDR to Pitt T. Maner (Pres., Young Demo. Clubs), Aug. 8, 1939.
11. Address, Los Angeles, Oct. 1, 1935.
12. P. C. #360-A (Spec.), Apr. 15, 1937.
13. P. C. #322, Sept. 25, 1936.
14. P. C. #497, Nov. 4, 1938.
15. P. C. #929, Dec. 28, 1943.
16. Campaign address, Syracuse, N. Y., Sept. 29, 1936.
17. Emporia *Daily Gazette,* Aug. 26, 1935.

Bibliographical Note

To the everlasting convenience of scholars, the Roosevelt Papers are concentrated in the Franklin D. Roosevelt Library at Hyde Park, New York. This is the largest collection of materials relating to one man to be found in the United States, and all but a small portion is open to examination. A few files are closed for reasons of national security; other restricted categories include reports of investigations of applicants for jobs, and materials relating to Roosevelt's personal finances. The size and range of the collection, and its availability to scholars so soon after the donor's death, are without precedent in American historiography.

The three principal file groups which were examined in the preparation of this book belong to the general section of "White House papers." The most useful one proved to be the "President's Personal File" (PPF), which is a collection of his private correspondence with individuals and organizations. It consists of more than 10,000 folders and boxes of letters. A much smaller group is the "President's Secretary's File" (PSF), containing letters of special importance which Roosevelt wished to keep separate. The largest of all the archive groups is the "Official File" (OF). These are papers which passed between the White House and the many agencies of government during his twelve years in the presidency. In all this correspondence, a high ratio of the content is routine; but only by its careful examination can the significant papers be sifted out.

The stenographic record of the President's press conferences is available at Hyde Park and constitutes one of the most voluminous sources for his thought. He held a total of 998 regular meetings with the press, plus a number of conferences with editors and other groups of visitors. The record makes a total of twenty-five thick volumes of typescript and touches upon almost every subject. The "Master Speech File," containing the drafts and final copies of Roosevelt's prepared addresses, is another valuable source for the historian.

There are, in addition to these indispensable materials at Hyde Park, important published collections of Roosevelt's speeches and papers. The primary one, of course, is *The Public Papers and Addresses of Franklin D. Roosevelt*, compiled and edited by Samuel Rosenman. These thirteen volumes, including explanatory notes and comments, give in themselves a broad picture of the President's thought, as revealed in public. For the earlier period, the most complete collection is the four-volume *Public Papers of Franklin D. Roosevelt, Forty-eighth Governor of the State of New York*, published by the State. Materials of a different sort, including some correspondence not in the Roosevelt Library (but only a fragment of what is), are included in *F.D.R., His Personal Letters*, edited by Elliott Roosevelt.

The large range of other publications, by and about Roosevelt, is indicated in the select bibliography which follows. The list is limited to works which cast important light upon his thought and interpretations of his thought.

Select Bibliography

Published Materials by Franklin D. Roosevelt

"The Age of Social Consciousness," *The Harvard Graduates' Magazine*, Vol. XXXVIII, No. 149, Sept., 1929.

Government—Not Politics. New York: Covici-Friede, 1932.

The Happy Warrior, Alfred E. Smith; a Study of a Public Servant. Boston: Houghton Mifflin Co., 1928.

Looking Forward. New York: The John Day Co., 1933.

On Our Way. New York: The John Day Co., 1934.

The Public Papers and Addresses of Franklin D. Roosevelt. New York: Random House, 1938, 5 vols.; Macmillan Co., 1941, 4 vols.; Harper & Brothers, 1950, 4 vols.

Public Papers of Franklin D. Roosevelt, Forty-eighth Governor of the State of New York. Albany: State of New York, 1930–39, 4 vols.

Whither Bound? Boston: Houghton Mifflin Co., 1926.

Memoirs Relating to Roosevelt

Barkley, Alben, *That Reminds Me.* Garden City, N. Y.: Doubleday & Co., 1954.

Bullitt, William C., *The Great Globe Itself.* New York: Charles Scribner's Sons, 1946.

Byrnes, James F., *Speaking Frankly.* New York: Harper & Brothers, 1947.

Chenery, William L., *So It Seemed.* New York: Harcourt, Brace and Co., 1952.

Churchill, Winston S., *The Second World War.* Boston: Houghton Mifflin Co., 1948–53, 6 vols.

Creel, George, *Rebel at Large.* New York: G. P. Putnam's Sons, 1947.

Eccles, Marriner S., *Beckoning Frontiers: Public and Personal Reminiscences.* New York: Alfred A. Knopf, 1951.

Eisenhower, Dwight D., *Crusade in Europe.* New York: Doubleday & Co., 1948.

Farley, James A., *Jim Farley's Story: The Roosevelt Years.* New York: McGraw-Hill Book Co., 1948.

Flynn, Edward J., *You're the Boss.* New York: Viking Press, 1947.

Grew, Joseph, *Turbulent Era; a Diplomatic Record of Forty Years, 1904–1945.* New York: Houghton Mifflin Co., 1952, 2 vols.

Hassett, William D., "The President Was My Boss," *Saturday Evening Post,* series: vol. 226, part 2, Oct. 10-Nov. 28, 1953.

Hoover, Herbert, *The Memoirs of Herbert Hoover.* New York: Macmillan Co., 1951–52, 3 vols.

Hull, Cordell, *Memoirs of Cordell Hull.* New York: Macmillan Co., 1948, 2 vols.

Ickes, Harold, *The Autobiography of a Curmudgeon.* New York: Reynal & Hitchcock, 1943.

————, *The Secret Diary of Harold L. Ickes.* New York: Simon and Schuster, 1953–54, 3 vols.

Jones, Jesse H. and Angly, Edward, *Fifty Billion Dollars. My Thirteen Years with the RFC (1932–1945).* New York: Macmillan Co., 1951.

Leahy, William D., *I Was There.* New York: McGraw-Hill, 1950.

McIntire, Ross T., *White House Physician.* New York: G. P. Putnam's Sons, 1946.

Michelson, Charles, *The Ghost Talks.* New York: G. P. Putnam's Sons, 1944.

Millis, Walter and Duffield, E. S. (eds.), *The Forrestal Diaries.* New York: Viking Press, 1951.

Moley, Raymond, *After Seven Years.* New York: Harper & Brothers, 1939.

Morgenthau, Henry, "Morgenthau Diaries," *Collier's,* Vol. 120, series: Sept. 27-Nov. 1, 1947.

Perkins, Frances, *The Roosevelt I Knew.* New York: Viking Press, 1946.

Richberg, Donald, *My Hero.* New York: G. P. Putnam's Sons, 1954.

Roosevelt, Eleanor, *This I Remember.* New York: Harper & Brothers, 1949.

————, *This Is My Story*. New York: Harper & Brothers, 1939.

Roosevelt, Elliott, *As He Saw It*. New York: Little, Brown and Co., 1946.

"Roosevelt, A First Appraisal by Those Who Knew Him," symposium, *New Republic*, Apr. 15, 1946, Part Two, Vol. 114, pp. 521–60.

Rosenman, Samuel I., *Working with Roosevelt*. New York: Harper & Brothers, 1952.

Sherwood, Robert E., *Roosevelt and Hopkins, an Intimate History*. New York: Harper & Brothers, 1948.

Stettinius, Edward R., *Roosevelt and the Russians: The Yalta Conference*. New York: Doubleday & Co., 1949.

Stilwell, Joseph W., *The Stilwell Papers*, comp. by Theodore H. White. New York: William Sloane Associates, 1948.

Stimson, Henry L. and Bundy, McGeorge, *On Active Service in War and Peace*. New York: Harper & Brothers, 1947.

Tugwell, Rexford G., "The Experimental Roosevelt," *The Political Quarterly*, Vol. XXI, July, 1950, pp. 239–70.

————, *The Democratic Roosevelt: A Biography of Franklin D. Roosevelt*. New York: Doubleday, Doran and Company, 1957.

————, "The Progressive Orthodoxy of Franklin D. Roosevelt," *Ethics*, Oct., 1953, Vol. LXIV, No. 1, pp. 1–23.

————, "The Protagonists: Roosevelt and Hoover," *Antioch Review*, Winter, 1953–54, Vol. XIII.

————, series on Roosevelt, *Western Political Quarterly:* June and Dec., 1948; Dec., 1949; Sept., 1950; June and Sept., 1951; Mar. and Sept., 1952.

Tully, Grace G., *F. D. R., My Boss*. New York: Charles Scribner's Sons, 1949.

Vandenberg, Arthur H., Jr. (ed.), *The Private Papers of Senator Vandenberg*. Boston: Houghton Mifflin Co., 1952.

Wehle, Louis, *Hidden Threads of History, Wilson through Roosevelt*. New York: Macmillan Co., 1953.

Books About Roosevelt

Bellush, Bernard, *Franklin D. Roosevelt as Governor of New York*. New York: Columbia University Press, 1955.

Burns, James M., *Roosevelt: The Lion and the Fox*. New York: Harcourt, Brace and Co., 1956.

Cameron, Turner C., *The Political Philosophy of Franklin D. Roosevelt* (Ph. D. dissertation, Princeton University, 1940). Ann Arbor: University Microfilms, no. 2926.

Dows, Olin, *Franklin Roosevelt at Hyde Park*. New York: Tudor Publishing Co., 1949.

Flynn, John T., *Country Squire in the White House*. New York: Doubleday, Doran and Co., 1940.

————, *Roosevelt Myth*. New York: Devin-Adair Co., 1948.

Freidel, Frank, *Franklin D. Roosevelt*. New York: Little, Brown and Co., 1952–1956, 3 vols.

Fusfeld, Daniel R., *The Economic Thought of Franklin D. Roosevelt and the Origins of the New Deal.* New York: Columbia University Press, 1956.

Geddes, Donald P. (ed.), *Franklin Delano Roosevelt, a Memorial.* New York: Pocket Books, 1945.

Gosnell, Harold F., *Champion Campaigner: Franklin D. Roosevelt.* New York: Macmillan Co., 1952.

Gunther, John, *Roosevelt in Retrospect.* New York: Harper & Brothers, 1950.

Hallgren, Mauritz A., *The Gay Reformer; Profits Before Plenty under Franklin D. Roosevelt.* New York: Alfred A. Knopf, 1935.

High, Stanley, *Roosevelt—And Then?* New York: Harper & Brothers, 1937.

Johnson, Gerald W., *Roosevelt: Dictator or Democrat?* New York: Harper & Brothers, 1941.

Kilpatrick, Carroll (ed.), *Roosevelt and Daniels: A Friendship in Politics.* Chapel Hill: University of North Carolina Press, 1952.

Lindley, Ernest K., *F. D. R., A Career in Progressive Democracy.* New York: Blue Ribbon Books, 1931.

————, *Half Way With Roosevelt.* New York: Viking Press, 1936.

————, *The Roosevelt Revolution, First Phase.* New York: Viking Press, 1933.

Looker, Earle, *The American Way: Franklin Roosevelt in Action.* New York: The John Day Co., 1933.

Robinson, Edgar E., *The Roosevelt Leadership, 1933–1945.* Philadelphia: J. B. Lippincott Co., 1955.

Roosevelt, Elliott (ed.), *F. D. R.: His Personal Letters.* New York: Little, Brown and Co., 1947–50, 4 vols.

Related Works

Ashburn, Frank D., *Peabody of Groton: A Portrait.* New York: Coward-McCann, 1944.

Beard, Charles A., *American Foreign Policy in the Making, 1932–40.* New Haven: Yale University Press, 1946.

————, *President Roosevelt and the Coming of the War, 1941.* New Haven: Yale University Press, 1948.

Binkley, Wilfred E., *President and Congress.* New York: Alfred A. Knopf, 1947.

Corwin, Edward S., *President: Office and Powers.* New York: New York University Press, 1940.

————, *Constitutional Revolution, Ltd.* Claremont, Calif.: Claremont Colleges, 1941.

Deane, John R., *The Strange Alliance: The Story of Our Efforts at Wartime Co-operation with Russia.* New York: Viking Press, 1947.

Feis, Herbert, *The Road to Pearl Harbor.* Princeton: Princeton University Press, 1950.

Galbraith, John K., *American Capitalism.* Boston: Houghton Mifflin Co., 1952.

Herring, Pendleton, *The Politics of Democracy: American Parties in Action*. New York: Rinehart & Co., 1940.

Hofstadter, Richard, *The American Political Tradition and the Men Who Made It*. New York: Alfred A. Knopf, 1948.

Hyman, Sidney, *The American President*. New York: Harper & Brothers, 1954.

Langer, William L., and Gleason, S. Everett, *The Challenge to Isolation: 1937–1940*. New York: Harper & Brothers, 1952.

——————, *The Undeclared War, 1940–1941*. New York: Harper & Brothers, 1953.

Laski, Harold, *The American Presidency, An Interpretation*. New York: Harper & Brothers, 1940.

Lippmann, Walter, *U. S. War Aims*. Boston: Little, Brown and Co., 1944.

Millis, Walter, *This Is Pearl! The United States and Japan—1941*. New York: William Morrow & Co., 1947.

Milton, George F., *The Use of Presidential Power, 1789–1943*. Boston: Little, Brown and Co., 1944.

Pollard, James E., *The Presidents and the Press*. New York: Macmillan Co., 1947.

Rauch, Basil, *Roosevelt: From Munich to Pearl Harbor*. New York: Farrar, Straus and Co., 1950.

Rossiter, Clinton L., *Conservatism in America*. New York: Alfred A. Knopf, 1955.

Schlesinger, Arthur M., Jr., *The Vital Center*. Boston: Houghton Mifflin Co., 1949.

——————, *The Age of Roosevelt: The Crisis of the Old Order, 1919–1933*. Boston: Houghton Mifflin Co., 1957.

Smith, A. Merriman, *A President Is Many Men*. New York: Harper & Brothers, 1948.

——————, *Thank You, Mr. President: A White House Notebook*. New York: Harper & Brothers, 1946.

Smith, Walter B., *My Three Years in Moscow*. Philadelphia: J. B. Lippincott Co., 1950.

Tansill, Charles C., *Back Door to War: Roosevelt Foreign Policy, 1933–41*. Chicago: Henry Regnery Co., 1952.

U. S. Senate, *Hearings on Military Situation in the Far East*. Washington, D. C.: U. S. Government Printing Office, 1951.

U. S. State Dept., *The Conferences at Yalta and Malta, 1945*. Washington, D. C.: U. S. Government Printing Office 1955.

U. S. State Dept., *Peace and War: U. S. Foreign Policy, 1931–1941*. Washington, D. C.: U. S. Government Printing Office, 1943.

U. S. State Dept., *Post-War Foreign Policy Preparation (1939–1945)*. Washington, D. C.: U. S. Government Printing Office, 1949.

Welles, Sumner, *Seven Decisions That Shaped History*. New York: Harper & Brothers, 1950.

——————, *The Time for Decision*. New York: Harper & Brothers, 1944.

Wilmot, Chester, *The Struggle for Europe: History, World War II*. New York: Harper & Brothers, 1952.

Index

Adams, John, 96
Administration, philosophy and practice of, 90–94
Adult education, interest in, 146–49
Advisers, Roosevelt's, 26, 83, 92, 100–101
A.F. of L., 70–71
Aged persons, views on support of, 11, 17, 73
Aggressors, blockade of, considered, 178
Agricultural Adjustment Act, 69
Agriculture, views on, 20, 60, 69
Aid to democracies, "short-of-war," by Roosevelt, 183–87
Aid to underdeveloped countries, idea of, 167–68
Aims, consistency of, 140
Air Corps, "Magna Carta" of, 179
Air power, views on, 179–80
Alaska, 166
Aldrich, Winthrop, 192
"Alice in Wonderland," quoted, 49–50
Allen, Robert S., 156
Alliance principle, rejection of, 196, 204–205
Allied unity, break-up of, 205

American Federation of Labor (A.F. of L.), 70–71
American Liberty League, 79
American-Russian co-operation, views on, 203–204
American Youth Congress, 32, 40, 42, 125, 130–31
Annual wage, Roosevelt's idea of, 70
Antitrust actions by Roosevelt, 63–65
Argentina, 181
Aristotle, and Roosevelt, 15, 17, 18, 26
Arms embargo, repeal of, favored, 175, 178–79
Arms inspection plan, support of, 173
Arnold, General Henry H., 179
Arsenal of Democracy, 65, 126, 185
Art and architecture, views on, 21–23
Asquith, Herbert, 87
Atlantic Charter, 165, 167, 184, 197
Atrocities, Nazi, 163
Austria, 163, 202
Axis powers
  aggression by, 113, 178, 181, 183
  Roosevelt's opposition to, 182, 184, 185, 187, 189
  struggle against, 191, 193, 205